MW01485661

The Art of Being Human

First Edition

Michael Wesch

Cover Design by Ashley Flowers

ISBN: 1724963678
ISBN-13: 978-1724963673

TO BABY GEORGE

For reminding me that
falling and failing
is fun and fascinating.

FIRST EDITION

The following chapters were written to accompany the free and open Introduction to Cultural Anthropology course available at ANTH101.com. This book is designed as a loose framework for more and better chapters in future editions. If you would like to share some work that you think would be appropriate for the book, please contact the author at mike.wesch@gmail.com.

Praise from students:

"Coming into this class I was not all that thrilled. Leaving this class, I almost cried because I would miss it so much. Never in my life have I taken a class that helps you grow as much as I did in this class."

"I learned more about everything and myself than in all my other courses combined."

"I was concerned this class would be off-putting but I needed the hours. It changed my views drastically and made me think from a different point of view."

"It really had opened my eyes in seeing the world and the people around me differently."

"I enjoyed participating in all 10 challenges; they were true challenges for me and I am so thankful to have gone out of my comfort zone, tried something new, and found others in this world."

"This class really pushed me outside my comfort zone and made me grow as a person."

"I expected to learn a lot about other people in this class but I ended up learning a lot about myself, too."

"I came into this class with little understanding, and came out with a massive knowledge of the world, and myself."

"This class allowed me to rethink who I am, what I am, and what I want to be by looking at 'who we are' as people."

"It changed my way of thinking about life, situations, and others around the world."

"This class is absolutely life changing."

Ten Lessons / Ten Challenges

Lesson 6: Social Structure

Lesson 7: Superstructure

Lesson 8: Globalization

Lesson 9: "The Good Life"

Lesson 10: The Art of Being Human

DEAR STUDENT,

Welcome to anthropology.

If you're like me, you have no idea what you're in for. I didn't even know what anthropology was when I first enrolled. Many people have stepped into anthropology classes expecting to fulfill a simple requirement by memorizing a few key words and regurgitating them on the exams, only to find themselves radically shaken and transformed by the experience.

One way to organize a book about anthropology – the study of all humans in all times in all places – would be to tell the entire human story, attempting to give equal space to each moment of our history.

We might start the book 12,000 years ago, a time when everybody everywhere was living in basically the same way, by foraging, hunting, and fishing for food. If the book were roughly the size of the one you're holding now, each page would cover about 50 years. The book would begin with a description of our pre-agricultural ancestors, people who lived in small bands with populations that rarely exceeded 50 people. Somewhere around page 15, somebody plants the first seeds, we start domesticating animals, and people start to settle in larger, more stable villages.

But change is slow. Halfway through the book, we're still using stone tools. Just past the middle of the book, writing emerges, along with the domestication of the horse and the invention of carts and chariots. The first empires emerge in Egypt, Mesopotamia, India, and China. And in the next chapter the Greeks, Romans, Mayans, Aztecs, and Ottomans take us to the brink of the final chapter.

With 10 pages left in the book (500 years in the past) you notice that the book is almost over, and yet almost nothing of the world that you know and take for granted exists. Most people have never ventured more than 10 miles from home. College does not exist. The United States does not exist. Most people would not be able to read this book.

A flurry of activity ensues. Packed into those final pages are the stories of European colonial empires spreading to touch nearly every corner of the globe. The Renaissance, Reformation, Enlightenment, the birth of nations, an ever more complex legalistic bureaucracy, new concepts of the family and childhood, educational reforms, and the idea of human rights emerge. With just four pages left the Industrial Revolution appears, along with the rise of science, medicine, and other new technologies.

The everyday lives of people in these last few pages are fundamentally different than all those before. And not just because of the technologies they use, but because of the questions they ask. For the first time in human history, the average person has to continually ask themselves three questions that almost no human in that long history before has had to ask:

- *Who am I?*
- *What am I going to do?*
- *Am I going to make it?*

For almost all of human history, no one asked these questions, because the answers were already known. We were who we were, we would do what our parents did, and our future was not in our own hands. Modernity brought with it a world of choices, and with choices come questions and an obligation to answer them.

And the questions go far beyond ourselves, for the second-to-last page signals an irresolvable climax. We build technologies that allow us to send messages at the speed of light. Automobiles start taking us faster and farther, dramatically changing the way we live and how we build our cities. We even learn to fly. By the end of the page, we can cross oceans in a matter of hours. But such progress is set against a backdrop of two ghastly world wars that killed nearly 100 million people. As you turn the final page, it must be apparent that this story cannot possibly resolve itself and end well.

On the last page you find that humans are more prosperous than ever, but there is a worrying and perplexing set of problems and paradoxes emerging. For while the final few pages have brought us tremendous technological advances and higher standards of living, they haven't brought us more happiness. In fact, even though we are more connected than ever, we feel *less* connected. We have more power to do and be anything we desire, yet we feel more *dis*empowered. Our lives are saturated with the artifacts of an absolute explosion of human creativity, and yet we struggle to find meaning.

The last page also describes a world of unparalleled global inequality and a precarious environmental situation. Our population is more than 20 times what it was at the start of the chapter, but the richest 225 humans on earth have more wealth than the poorest 2.5 billion people combined. Nearly one billion people make less than $1/day. Humans produce more than enough food to feed everyone in the world, yet hundreds of millions are starving, even as we collectively spend over $1 trillion per year preparing to fight one another.

The final pages describe how we created an astounding global economy running on nonrenewable fossil fuels, but on the last page, it becomes apparent that all those resources will be gone by the third page of the epilogue. Furthermore, the use of these fuels has changed the chemistry of our planet, leading to a rise in global temperature, rising sea levels, expanding deserts, and more intense storms. Perhaps most dramatic, it is in these final pages that we human beings have attained the ability to literally end the book altogether and annihilate ourselves. We might do it at the push of a button, launching a nuclear war; or we might do it slowly and painfully, through environmental collapse. Whether or not the story continues will largely be up to choices we make.

Three new questions emerge:

- *Who are we?*
- *What are we going to do?*
- *Are we going to make it?*

Anthropology is the discipline that attempts to answer these questions about humans and their place in the world. By practicing anthropology, you might just find a few answers to those other three questions (*Who am I? What am I going to do? Am I going to make it?*) and learn a little bit more about yourself and your own place in the world.

> January 14, 2015 864,646 notes
>
> tahtahtahtia:
>
> today my anthro professor said something kindof really beautiful:
>
> "you all have a little bit of 'I want to save the world' in you, that's why you're here, in college. I want you to know that it's okay if you only save one person, and it's okay if that person is you"

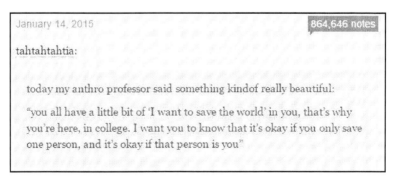

The answers to such questions might not be what you expect. In fact, the answers to these questions will only open up new questions, and you will soon find yourself on a sort of quest, question after question after question. Anthropology doesn't just seek to answer questions; it leads us to discover new questions that we have not even considered before.

You might, as I did, come to cherish these questions. Yes, they will turn you inside out and upside down. You may spend a few sleepless nights questioning your most basic ideas, ideals, values, and beliefs. But you might also come to see these questions as great gifts that reveal worlds and ideas you cannot yet imagine.

Anthropologists look for answers not just in books and data but out in the world itself, by making connections with people across vast cultural differences. This is a necessary part of understanding the entirety of the human condition. We have to understand the diversity that makes up the human experience.

It is experience itself that lies at the heart of anthropology. Anthropology opens the doors of the world to you so that you can *experience more*. In order to experience more, you will have to step outside your comfort zone and *experience difference*. And when you have experienced difference, you will be able to come back to more familiar settings and *experience differently*. Why do we want to experience more, experience difference, and experience differently? Because our experiences become an integral part of who we are. When we experience more, we can *be* more.

In sum, Anthropology is not only the science of human beings, but also the art of asking questions, making connections, and trying new things. These are the very practices that make us who we are as human beings. Anthropology is the art of being human.

This art is not easy. You will have to overcome your fears, step outside your comfort zone, and get comfortable with the uncomfortable. "Anthropology requires strength, valor, and courage," Nancy Scheper-Hughes reminds us. "Pierre Bourdieu called anthropology a combat sport, an extreme sport as well as a tough and rigorous discipline. … It teaches students not to be afraid of getting one's hands dirty, to get down in the dirt, and to commit yourself, body and mind. Susan Sontag called anthropology a 'heroic' profession."

What's the payoff for this heroic journey? If you're like me, you will discover in anthropology new questions and new ideas. You will try, as I did, to make them your own. But you can't own ideas. I did not have the ideas; the ideas had me. They carried me across rivers of doubt and uncertainty, where I found the light and life of places forgotten. I climbed mountains of fear. I felt their jagged edges, wiped their dust from my brow, and left my blood in their soil. There is a struggle to be had, for sure. You may not find the meaning of life, but you might just have the experience of being alive.

Above all, the art of being human takes practice. As such, I present this book not as a typical textbook, full of bold-faced terms for you to memorize and regurgitate on exams. There *will* be some of that, as there are always new concepts and terms to learn as you step into a new way of thinking. But above all, there will be a simple idea at work: that anthropology is not just a science. It's a way of life, and for most people, a new way of thinking that will open them up to being the best human beings they can be. So we proceed in recognition of that simple truth:

You cannot just think your way into a new way of living.
You have to live your way into a new way of thinking.

The course will proceed through ten lessons, representing the Ten Big Ideas that you can learn by studying anthropology. Laid out together in sequence, they read almost like a manifesto:

1. People are different. These differences represent the vast range of human potential and possibility. Our assumptions, beliefs, values, ideas, ideals – even our abilities – are largely a product of our culture.

2. We can respond to such differences with hate or ignorance, or we can choose to open up to them and ask questions we have never considered before.

3. When we open up to such questions, we put ourselves in touch with our higher nature. It was asking questions, making connections, and trying new things that brought us down from the trees, and took us to the moon.

4. It is not easy to see our assumptions. Our most basic assumptions are embedded in the basic elements of our everyday lives (our language, our routines and habits, our technologies).

5. "We create our tools and then our tools create us."[1]

6. Most of what we take as "reality" is a cultural construction ("real"-ized through our unseen, unexamined assumptions of what is right, true, or possible.)

7. We fail to examine our assumptions not just because they are hard to see, but also because they are safe and comfortable. They allow us to live with the flattering illusion that "I am the center of the universe, and what matters are my immediate needs and desires."

8. Our failure to move beyond such a view has led to the tragedy of our times: that we are more connected than ever, yet feel and act more disconnected.

---

[1] Quote from John Culkin, 1967

9. Memorizing these ideas is easy. Living them takes a lifetime of practice. Fortunately, the heroes of all time have walked before us. They show us the path.

10. They show us that collectively, we make the world. Understanding how we make the world – how it could be made or understood differently – is the road toward realizing our full human potential. It is the road to true freedom.

Each lesson concludes with a challenge that will allow you to "live your way" into this new way of thinking. You will talk to strangers, do fieldwork, get comfortable with the uncomfortable, try new things, break habits, reach out across great distances to discover how you are connected to other people all over the planet, encounter and come to appreciate people radically different from you, and ultimately come back home to see yourself as a new kind of person, a hero in your own way, ready to be the best human you can be.

You don't have to journey alone. Go to ANTH101.com and share your challenges and progress with others. It's the perfect place to ask questions, make connections, and try new things. It's a place to practice the art of being human.

See you there,
Professor Wesch

Lesson One
Fieldwork

People are different. These differences represent the vast range of human potential and possibility. Our assumptions, beliefs, values, ideas, ideals – even our abilities – are largely a product of our cultures.

ASKING QUESTIONS, MAKING CONNECTIONS, AND TRYING NEW THINGS

About 20 years ago, I was sitting in a university lecture hall with almost 500 other students waiting for our first lecture in anthropology class. We all had our reasons for being there, and most of them ended with the word "requirement." There was the "Social Sciences 3 of 4" requirement, the "45 hours of General Electives" requirement and the "60 hours at our university" requirement, among many others. For me, it was the "International Overlay" requirement. I had no idea what anthropology was or why it was required. All I knew was what I had learned as I looked up "anthropology" in the dictionary just before rushing off to class.

Anthropology, n. *The study of all humans in all times in all places.*

A smartly dressed, white-haired, bearded professor entered the room and showed us what appeared to be a strange ink blot test on the screen, asking us what we saw. We stared up at these apparently random splatters of ink that we were supposed to decipher like children looking for shapes in the clouds.

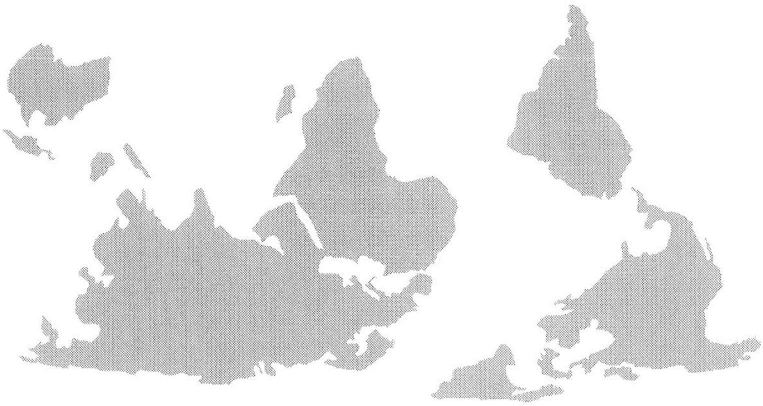

I felt proud of myself when I recognized that the splatters were the shapes of the continents and that we were looking at the world upside down, to which the professor challenged, "Is it *really* upside down? The world is a sphere. Who decided that north is up?" He then showed us a map popular in Australia (McArthur's Universal Corrective Map) with Australia standing proudly at the top and center of the world. It struck me that this map was no less true than the one I knew, which placed the United States and Europe standing proudly at the top and center.

He then proceeded to convince us that it wasn't just the world that we had upside down, it was bananas too. We had been peeling them wrong our entire lives. Monkeys and many cultures on the planet know that the best way to peel a banana is not from the stem, but rather "upside down." Even the most stubborn banana opens easily from this end, and you can then immediately throw away the fibrous and inedible black tip and use the stem as a handle.

Then he turned our whole lives upside down, challenging our most basic taken-for-granted assumptions in virtually all aspects of our lives, moving from the economic realm and on to family, society, politics, art, and religion. He challenged our views on success, love, and even happiness. Ultimately, he would challenge us to consider how even our most basic everyday activities – shopping, driving, eating – are connected to all humans everywhere, and gave us profound and unforgettable reminders of the impacts we might have on others.

He framed the course around a very simple idea: that our beliefs, values, ideas, ideals, and even our abilities are largely a product of our cultures. He introduced three seemingly simple yet tremendously powerful terms to help us explore this idea:

Ethnocentrism: holding one's own beliefs, values, ideas, ideals, and assumptions to be the only true and proper ones. This is like a prison for the mind. Until we could move past our ethnocentrism, we would be trapped, with little opportunity to change and grow.

Cultural relativism: the antidote to ethnocentrism. This is the idea that we must understand other people's ideas, ideals, assumptions and beliefs relative to their own culture. We have to suspend judgment and try to understand the world in their terms.[2] The beauty of this activity is that once we find our way into a different perspective, we can then look back on our own culture with new eyes.

Participant Observation: the hallmark method of anthropology. We do not just observe other people in our attempts to understand them. We join in. Only then can we move closer to their experience and understand them with depth and detail.

While these may seem like nothing more than bold-faced terms in a textbook, to be memorized and then forgotten, they were like fire-bombs for my mind. They were a constant reminder that my hard-set ideas about what was right, true, or possible might be wrong. It was as if a curtain had been drawn back for me to look at the world for

[2] This does not mean we withhold judgment forever and deny all judgement (which would be "moral relativism"). We simply suspend our judgment so that we can understand them. As Scott Atran, an anthropologist who studies terrorists such as ISIS notes, the key is to "empathize with people, without always sympathizing." Empathy allows anthropologists to understand others from their perspective, regardless of how reprehensible that perspective might seem.

the first time, and each of the thousands upon thousands of different beliefs and practices visible there would be a challenge to my own.

I learned about cultures that challenged my perceived limits of human potential. The Tarahumara of central Mexico can run over *400 miles* without stopping. The Moken of Thailand can intentionally control the pupils of their eyes to see more clearly underwater as they dive for clams, while also willfully decreasing their heart rate so they can hold their breath for five minutes or longer! The Inuit survive the Arctic winter by tracking and killing seals under several feet of ice. The !Kung of southern Africa find food and water in one of the seemingly most desolate deserts on the planet. The Jenna Kuruba of India start making friends with elephants from the time they are small children, training them and eventually riding on their giant backs, walking through life together as lifetime partners.

Anthropology can introduce you to cultures where fat is a mark of health and beauty, or where beauty is not a prominent mark of worth at all. Places where the body is an integrated part of who you are, useful and functional in the world, not a thing to be obsessively carving or pumped so that you can be swole, cut, ripped, or chiseled.

Some differences are cute. Others are disturbing. You might find a place where dogs or horses are considered good eating, or where pork and beef are forbidden.

It can transport you to places where people perform strange superstitious rituals, only to discover that these rituals are sophisticated ways of managing their culture and environment. For example, the complex water temples of the Balinese, which have managed water distribution across their rice terraces on the island for over 1200 years—and recently came to the rescue and saved the island from environmental collapse when new agricultural technologies were introduced.

Anthropology introduces you to worlds without clocks or calendars. Places where time is measured by the song of birds or the pangs of a hungry stomach rather than the digits of a clock. Places where there are no deadlines or jobs. No grades or schools. No laws, lawyers, or judges. No politicians or rulers. Places where smartphones, cars, and electricity are known but forbidden.

You can find differences that seem to cut to the very essence of how we perceive the world. There are cultures where the locus of thinking is believed not to be in the head, but somewhere near the heart – or where the notion of "thinking" is not separated at all from the notion of "feeling." There are cultures that believe there is not just one soul, but several.

There are places where success is measured by how much you give away, not by the size of your house or the cost of your car. Places where winning isn't everything. Places where faith is about being comfortable with the unknown, not with how firmly you believe.

When anthropology is done right, none of these things strike you as exotic oddities. Rather, they are exciting possibilities. They make you reconsider your own taken-for-granted assumptions. They can make you wonder: *If there are humans in the world who can run over 400 miles without rest, or dilate their pupils under water, or hold their breath for five minutes, or find food in an Arctic winter or desert summer … or make friends with elephants … why can't I?*

All this cultural diversity was new to me, and much of it was cracking me open to examine parts of my world and worldview I had never even seen before. The cracks reached deep into my everyday life.

My girlfriend had just broken up with me. She was the first love of my life, and at the time I was sure that she was "the one." Now here was a guy presenting me with the idea that the very notion of "the one" was nothing but a cultural construction unique to my culture, time and place. He shared stories about cultures where one man might have many wives ("polygyny") or where one woman might have many husbands ("polyandry"). He shared stories about cultures where marriage was not primarily about romance but about more practical matters of subsistence and partnership. While we all dutifully set about to memorize these new terms, I couldn't help but see that the very terms of my life were changing. A core ideal that had been the central organizing principle of my life – the idea of "the one" that I had to find to live a happy life, the idea that each one of us might have a soulmate made just for us – was clearly not an idea universally shared across cultures. It was an idea that was contingent on a vast array of cultural and historical forces. The world, it seemed, had a lot to teach me about love that I just didn't know yet.

The professor spoke softly and smoothly, as if unaware of the fact that he was lobbing intellectual fire-bombs into the audience and blowing minds. What on the one hand seemed like a bunch of simple facts to be memorized for an exam carried much deeper and more profound messages for me – that the world is not as it seems, that we know the world only through our own cultural biases, that even the little things matter, that taken together all the little things we do make the world what it is, and that if we are willing to challenge ourselves, truly understand others with empathy, and shed the comfort of our familiar but sometimes blinding, binding, and taken-for-granted assumptions, we can make the world a better place.

The idea that our most central ideas, ideals, beliefs and values are culturally constructed was liberating. It was also terrifying. I found myself struggling with questions I had never considered before. I kept going to the professor with my questions, hoping for answers. But he never offered any.

He just smiled.

Three years later I landed in Port Moresby, the capital city of Papua New Guinea. It was as far from my small-town Nebraska upbringing as I could imagine, both geographically and culturally. If I wanted the answers to my questions … if I wanted to understand just how different people could be … if I wanted to explore the vast range of human potential and possibility … this seemed like the place to be.

Port Moresby was once described by Paul Theroux as "one of the most violent and decrepit towns on the face of the planet." It frequently tops the Economic Intelligence Unit's annual survey as the world's most unlivable city. There are the normal struggles of an impoverished city: water rationing, intermittent electricity, lack of sanitation, and rampant corruption. But what really sets it apart is its crime rate. *Foreign Policy* named it one of five "murder capitals of the world." Unemployment runs from 60-90%, and opportunistic crime is a common way for people, even the most respectable people, to make ends meet.

But none of this could dampen my young spirit. I was a twenty-three-year-old small-town boy from Nebraska, eager to explore the world. Perhaps it was my small-town upbringing that had given me this sense of faith and trust in other people. I had an unwavering belief that there are good people everywhere. *Open up to people and they will open up to you*, I thought. Every place on the planet has its charm, and it can usually be found in the spirit of the people themselves. I was looking forward to diving into the life of this busy little city. I left the hotel on my first morning in the city with a full spirit and a fully-loaded backpack, ready for an all-day adventure.

It was a calm and beautiful morning in the tropical paradise. Palm trees slowly swayed above me in the morning breeze. The streets were empty, except for two teenage boys walking my way. "Hey! Moning!" they shouted.

What an exuberant and kind greeting, I thought.

They speak Tok Pisin in Papua New Guinea, a creole with words drawn from English, German, Malay, Portuguese and several local languages. Fortunately, about 80% of the words come from English, so it is fairly easy to pick up for an English speaker.

"Moning! Moning!" I called back.

"Nogat! Moni! Moni!" one of the boys responded tersely, and the two, now just 20 steps away, quickened their pace and approached me with clear determination.

I had misunderstood them, but I was clear on what they wanted from me now: They wanted my money. I glanced to my left and right and saw no hope of escape. Fences covered in razor wire crowded the street on both sides, locking me in. *Razor wire*, I thought. *Why hadn't I noticed that before?* It was an intimidating reminder of just how dangerous this place might be.

I continued to try to win them over, still hoping that I could transform this interaction into a polite inconsequential morning ritual. Perhaps if I could just be charming enough, they would let me pass; or if not charming, at least so naïve that they might take pity on me. "Morning!" I replied even more cheerfully, walking confidently toward them, and hopefully, right past them.

"*Nogat! Moni! Moni!*" he responded, slapping his pockets for emphasis.

I thought maybe I could get by them with a little humor. I pretended that I still didn't understand, and acted as if they were teaching me proper pronunciation and the proper gestures that go along with the greeting. "Moni!" I said cheerfully with my best and broadest smile while I slapped my pockets with exuberance. I hoped they might just laugh at the stupid foreigner and let me pass.

They did not think I was very funny. They blocked me, looking angrier than ever.

"*Moni!*" the boy on the left said sternly, as he pulled back his jacket to reveal a 24-inch machete.

I turned my back to them, hoping that if they struck me with the machete the first slash would hit my oversized 40-pound backpack, and I ran.

They must have paused for a moment, because I had 10 steps on them before I could hear them coming. But I was no match for two fit teenagers as my 40-pound pack bounced clumsily on my back. They were closing in fast.

I came to a street corner and veered right. A large group of young men turned to see me coming. In my moment of fear, I expected the worst from them. Blood-red betel nut juice oozed from their lips.

Everything seemed to be in slow motion for me now. One of the men spit his blood-red wad onto the pavement as the whole group turned my way and scowled. I started wondering just how bad this was going to get. I resigned myself to the attack that was to come, and recalled that a friend of mine, also an anthropologist, had been stabbed over 30 times in an attack in Port Moresby, and survived. I wondered if I would be so lucky.

"Hey!" the men shouted toward me.

With razor wire on both sides of me, and a 24-inch machete in pursuit, I had no choice but to keep running toward them. Two of the young men seemed to lunge toward me with raised arms, ready to strike.

And then it was over.

The two young men who appeared to be lunging for me were lunging for the boys, protecting me, and had chased the perpetrators into some nearby woods. The young men apologized profusely for the behavior of the boys and welcomed me to their country.

In the years to come I would find great camaraderie, conversation, and comfort hanging out with locals on street corners like that one, but at the time I was in no mood for conversation. I was shaken to my core.

I went straight to the airport.

I had no ticket, but I knew I wasn't staying in Port Moresby. I stared up at the board labeled "Departures" and contemplated my next move. Brisbane, at the top of the list, looked especially appealing. Australia's legendary Gold Coast would offer surf, sand, sun, and most importantly, *safety*. Below Brisbane was a long list of small towns in New Guinea, a few of which I had heard about in my anthropological readings.

A big part of me just wanted to go to Brisbane for a little taste of home, security, and normalcy. But the answers to my questions weren't going to be in Brisbane. They were going to be somewhere down that list.

And that's when I realized why my professor had been smiling. A basic insight dawned upon me that would forever change my life:

Great questions will take you farther than you ever thought possible.

I hopped on the next plane to somewhere down that list. But of course, the planes from a city like Port Moresby only land in slightly smaller cities, with only slightly smaller crime problems, so I immediately jumped on another plane to somewhere on a much smaller list, and then again, until I was flying into a little grass airstrip in the center of New Guinea where there was no electricity, plumbing, roads, Internet, phone service, television, or any of the other technologies that we take for granted as making up the basic infrastructure of our lives. There was no hotel to check into and no food to buy. My money would be no good. It was just what I had been looking for.

There were a few familiar sights, even in this remote outpost. A small and simple Baptist church, a two-room schoolhouse, and a small medical aid post sat at the head of the airstrip, made mostly of local materials and looking more- or-less like traditional houses but topped with corrugated steel roofing.

And there was soccer.

People of all ages crowded onto the airstrip after the plane left, whooping and hollering with joy as the ball sailed this way and that. Well over 50 people were playing in this single game, while another 100 or so looked on. A young man approached me and started talking to me in Tok Pisin. I was relieved to hear the language. I knew enough to get by in it, and I was concerned that perhaps nobody would speak it in a remote location like this. We soon found out that we were the same age, 23, and we had one very important complementary interest. He wanted to learn English, and I wanted to learn his language. We were soon fast friends. I had an Aerobie flying ring in my bag and we started tossing it around. Soon we were sailing it down the airstrip and inventing a new game that was like a cross between Soccer and Ultimate Frisbee. The Aerobie would soar overhead as a sea of pursuers rushed after it collectively chanting *"Hoot! Hoot! Hoot!"* a call that would become increasingly familiar and endearing to me over the coming years.

He took me to his home that night, and over the coming days I was quickly adopted into the family. Almost immediately they started referring to me as kin, using words like "brother" and "tambu" (which means "taboo" and is used between in-laws of similar age such as my brothers' wives).

I immersed myself in their lives, craving the full experience of what it was like to live and think as they did. I went with them to their gardens and learned how they cleared the forest and then burned it to create rich nutrients for the soil. I helped them harvest their most important staple crops, like sweet potato, taro, and bananas. I learned how to start and manage a fire, taking exquisite care to not waste too much precious firewood while maintaining a steady ember to light the next fire.

And when they offered me snake, of course I accepted. Our neighbor had found the 15-foot snake in a nearby tree. It had recently eaten a large rodent, so it was an easy catch, and came with the added bonus that the rodent could be removed and cooked up as our appetizer.

After a week of eating nothing but sweet potatoes and taro, the snake tasted like an exquisitely buttered lobster in a five-star restaurant. But as I ate, I couldn't help but notice that a snake like that could probably crawl through any one of several holes in the hut. *Surely this snake has family*, I thought, *and they will be coming for us.* I made a mental note to seal myself up especially tight that night.

I was already in the practice of sealing myself up in my sleeping bag every night, mostly to protect myself against the bugs and rodents I would see scurrying around as we sat talking around the fire every night. But it was the tropics, and we were sleeping by a fire.

Inevitably I would get too hot, slip out of my covers, wake up to something scurrying across my face, wipe it off, and cover myself up again.

After eating a 15-foot snake found just a few feet from our house, I was extra-vigilant. But it was no use. I woke up in the middle of the night to find my worst nightmare.

I was outside of my sleeping bag, completely exposed to the elements: And I could feel it, as thick as the one I had just eaten, laying across my chest. It felt cold, heavy, and about four inches thick. I couldn't see anything in the dark, but I managed to grab it with my left hand and throw it off of me. Or, at least I tried to throw it off of me. As I threw it, I went with it. *I was wrapped up with this thing somehow.* I eventually managed to wrestle it to the ground and pin it down with my left hand. I tried to free my right arm so I could pin it down with two hands, but I just could not move my right arm. I started to panic and scream.

And that's when I realized ...

I had pinned down my own right arm.

My arm had just fallen asleep and had been resting across my chest.

There was no snake.

This started an all-night cackle of laughter and richly entertaining conversation about me. My language skills were not great. I couldn't quite follow the conversation myself. The only word I could clearly make out was "whiteman," which was invariably followed by a collective laugh; gabbles of "hahahaha!" ... and then all together in unison, *"Yeeeeeeeee!!!"*

This is just one among many stories I could tell about my early days in New Guinea. While they would all seem funny, you can't help but recognize the signs of struggle. Such nightmares were just one manifestation of the fears I struggled with every day. The food and water scared me. The creatures scared me. The plants scared me. I thought that at any moment I could taste or touch something that might kill me, and the closest hospital was a seven-day trek over cold and treacherous mountains. I felt uncomfortable and disoriented most of the time.

The people were impossibly kind and welcoming, but I did not trust them yet. I did not feel worthy of the warmth they offered. I felt like a free-loader and a burden.

They organized a large dance for my enjoyment. It was an all-night affair. The men wore their longest and most decorated penis gourds, covered themselves in red ochre, painted magnificent designs on their faces and strapped bird of paradise plumes to their heads. Women wore grass skirts, carefully woven leg and arm bands, and beaded necklaces. And they danced all night. It was surreal in how magnificent it appeared—and how utterly bored and depressed I felt.

This should be a dream come true for any budding anthropologist. I should have been joyfully decoding the rich symbolism, but I just felt bored and confused. None of it made sense, and I had no idea why they thought their dance was any good. It was just a bunch of guys monotonously banging a drum as they bobbed up and down, the women doing the same, back and forth, all night long. Boring.

More than anything, I felt all alone. My language skills were not good enough to have a real conversation, even with my brothers who spoke Tok Pisin. Language was reduced to mostly practical matters.

Nobody really knew me. What we wear, how we stand, how we walk, how we laugh, when we laugh, even a simple glance made in a certain way can be expressions of our selves. But the meanings associated with all of these expressions is continually worked out within the never-ending dance we call *culture*. Step onto a new dance floor, and not only do you feel lost, you might feel like you lost yourself. My gestures, smiles, and glances were continuously misconstrued. My jokes (clumsily delivered through broken words and flailing gestures) fell flat. There seemed to be no way for me to express to them who I really was.

We learned a term for all this in our anthropology textbook: **culture shock**. Google defines it as "the feeling of disorientation experienced by someone who is suddenly subjected to an unfamiliar culture." But it can be so much more than just "disorientation." For me, it was a complete loss of self.

I fell into a deep depression. My worst moments were the moments that should have been the best. A picturesque sunset would not fill me with awe, but with a deep longing for the awe that I should be feeling. Until that moment, I had always thought of my "self" as something inside me that I had carefully shaped over the years. I worked hard to be smart, funny, and kind, characteristics that I valued. I thought of these traits as something inside me that I projected outward.

What I discovered in New Guinea was that who we are is also reflected back to us by the people around us. George Cooley called this "the looking glass self." As he says, "I am not what I think I am and I am not what you think I am; I am what I think that you think I am." When I think that the people around me don't think I am smart, funny, or kind, I start to internalize those judgments. And when I thought the people around me in New Guinea did not know who I was or what I was doing there, I found myself asking those same questions. I didn't know who I was or what I was doing there.

I may have had great questions to pursue, but I did not feel safe and comfortable enough to pursue them. I was not immersing myself in their lives. And I wasn't learning anything. I rarely spoke. I was protecting whatever was left of my fragile self. I was afraid that if I tried to speak the local language that I would be mocked and seen as the village idiot. So I stayed silent.

I was closing down and shutting out the world, counting the days until the next plane might come and take me home. I made an amendment to my earlier revelation about questions:

Questions may take you farther than you ever thought possible, but it won't matter if you can't open up and connect with people when you get there

One morning in the depths of my depression, I was walking along a mountain ridge with two of my "brothers" as the sun was rising. From the ridge where we walked we had a breathtaking view of the mountainous green landscape, the sun casting a beautiful orange glow onto the peaks. We were just above the morning clouds, and the green forested mountaintops looked like fluorescent islands in a soft white sea. A crisp blue sky framed the peaceful idyllic vision.

I saw all these things, but I couldn't really experience them. I was not well. I have always been a happy person. I've never suffered from depression or even been hampered by a mild malaise. But here I was viewing what had to be the most spectacular and wondrous vision I had ever seen, and I was literally collapsing in sadness. My inability to experience the beauty that I knew was right there in front of me destroyed my spirit. My legs grew weak. I started to stumble. My knees hit the ground. I knelt for a moment, and then simply collapsed to the ground, crying.

My brothers came to my side. They had tears in their eyes. They could not have known why I was crying, and yet there they were crying right along with me. "Brother Mike," they asked, "Why are you crying?"

All I could think about was home and my wife, so I said, "I miss my wife."

They started laughing and laughing, tears still streaming down their faces. "Oh, Mike!" they exclaimed, "we would never miss our wives! But we miss our kids," they said, starting to cry again. They shook their heads side to side while quickly tapping their tongues on the roof of their mouths, a sound I would come to know as the sound one makes when you are allowing the feelings of another to become your own.

That cry was like the sweat that breaks a fever. I felt renewed with a new joy for life. I immediately started to feel better. Something about their show of empathy made me feel understood and known for the first time in months. I felt like the word "brother" really meant something, that they would stand by me no matter what, that they would be willing to walk with me through the arduous learning process of understanding their language and culture even as I stumbled along. My joy for life was back and I was living my dream of diving into a cultural world radically different than the one in which I had been raised.

I have never learned faster than in those coming months. My fear was gone. I started playing with the local language, trying it out with my brothers and friends. I didn't care that I sounded like a two-year-old or the village idiot. Because soon I was sounding like a three-year-old, and then a four-year-old.

That's when I learned the true meaning and power of participant observation. I wasn't just learning to speak the language. As I opened myself up to this new culture, it was as if the whole ethos of the culture started to course through my veins. I could feel my whole body re-arrange itself into their postures and habits. My back loosened, my arms swung a little more freely, and my feet came alive, feeling the terrain like an extra set of hands. I learned to walk with a springy step over mountains I once had to crawl up and down. I tuned my senses to see and understand the world as they did. I learned to see the stories a plant could tell and to hear birds as clocks and harbingers of what was to come. I learned the joy of growing your own food, and of hunting, trapping, skinning, and feasting. I learned the values of humility, calm and patience required to live in a small community with people you have always known and will always know. I learned to feel the cool wind coming down over the mountain as a signal of the coming rain.

Some years later, another dance was arranged. This time, *they* did not don their best penis gourds and headdresses. *We* did. I did not feel like an imposter anymore. The dance did not feel like a performance for me. It just seemed like something fun to do together. As I started to drum and bounce along with them I immediately noticed that something wasn't quite right. My tailfeather wasn't bouncing, it just hung limply off my backside. Women were pointing and laughing at me. Apparently, this dance that I originally saw as simple and boring was more complex than I thought. My brother pulled me aside and showed me how to "pop" by backside up, making my tailfeather soar up and down. The ladies shrieked with approval. Throughout the evening women flirtatiously pulled and tugged on the bounding and bouncing tailfeathers of their favorite dancers, and soon I saw people coupling up and disappearing into the woods.

It would be easy to stand off to the side of this dance and try to decipher some deep meaning for it, the men and women both dressed as birds, moving this way and that way in an apparently timeless tribal pattern. But on this night I saw meanings that could not be deciphered from the outside. I saw meanings that could only be understood by joining in the dance yourself. It was fun. It was riddled with anticipation, excitement, and apprehension. My bachelor friends were especially nervous, hoping to catch the eye of their latest crush. Nervous laughter and teasing bounced around the open fire when we took breaks from the dance. And having rested, the boys would shake their tailfeathers ever more vigorously, hoping to win the hearts of their favorite girls.

As we danced under the full moon I reflected on the true power of those three terms at the heart of anthropology and how they had changed my life. "Ethnocentrism" challenged me to ask questions that ended up taking me halfway around the world. "Cultural relativism" challenged me to make real connections with people, to truly open up to them and understand the world from an entirely different point of view. And "participant observation" challenged me to try new things, to join the dance of this other culture, immersing myself in a different way of life.

Asking questions, making connections, and trying new things are the essence of this science of human beings. But I have found them to be much more than that. They are also the foundation for being the best human you can be.

Challenge One: Talking to Strangers

Your first challenge is to approach a stranger and engage them in "big talk" (as opposed to "small talk"). Hear their story and ask if you can share it on Instagram with #anth101challenge1

Objective: Practice the anthropological mindset of asking questions, making connections, and trying new things.

Capturing and telling the stories of humans in compelling ways is an essential component of anthropology, and these days that means mastering multiple forms of storytelling in multiple media (photography, video, audio, as well as text).

But capturing a great story is not just capturing a good picture. You will need to practice the art of anthropology – asking questions, making connections, and trying new things. Try to move past "small talk" and into "big talk." Ask big questions and offer your own answers too.

Try to get in a positive mindset as you approach strangers, and let that carry you through this challenge. Remember that people are different, and these differences represent the vast range of human potential and possibility.

Go to ANTH101.com/challenge1 for additional photo-taking tips and "big talk" inspiration.

Lesson Two
Culture

You can respond to human differences with hate or ignorance, or you can choose to open up to them and ask questions you have never considered before.

THE ART OF SEEING

There are these two young fish swimming along, and they happen to meet an older fish swimming the other way, who nods at them and says, "Morning, boys, how's the water?" And the two young fish swim on for a bit, and then eventually one of them looks over at the other and goes, "What the hell is water?" — David Foster Wallace

Culture is like water to us. We're so immersed in our own ideas and assumptions that we can't see them. It can be useful to jump out of the water now and then. This is one of the great virtues of encountering someone or some place that is radically different from what we know. We see the contrast between how we do things and how they do things, and we can then see ourselves in a new light.

The art of seeing can be broken up into four parts. First, we have to see our own seeing—that is, see how we see the world, recognizing our own taken-for-granted assumptions, and be able to set them aside. Second, we have to "see big," to see the larger cultural, social, economic, historical, and political forces that shape our everyday lives. Third, we have to "see small," paying close attention to the smallest details and understanding their significance. And finally, we have to "see it all," piecing all of this together to see how everything we can see interacts from a holistic point of view.

Learning to see in this way is the essence of learning. As Neil Postman points out, "The ability to learn turns out to be a function of the extent to which one is capable of perception change. If a student goes through four years of school and comes out 'seeing' things in the way he did when he started ... he learned nothing."

Mastering the art of seeing offers many benefits beyond just the ability to learn. The most obvious benefit is that you become better at building and maintaining relationships. Being able to see your own seeing and set aside your assumptions, see big to see where another person is coming from, and see small to truly understand them from their point of view can help you through the most challenging of relationship troubles. It can help you build better friendships, and allow you to make more friends across boundaries rarely crossed.

But mastering the art of seeing offers something even more profound. When you master the art of seeing *you will never be bored.* You will see the strange in the familiar, and the familiar in the strange. And you will have the ability to find significance in the most mundane moments. As David Foster Wallace says, "if you really learn how to pay attention ... it will be in your power to experience a crowded, hot, slow, consumer-hell type situation as not only meaningful, but sacred, on fire with the same force that made the stars: love, fellowship, the mystical oneness of all things deep down."

While his metaphor of a fish in water is useful, culture is different from water in one very important way: it is not just the environment around us. It is a part of us. It is the very thing that allows us to see and notice things at all. We see the world through our culture. Leaping out of the water doesn't just allow you to see your own culture in a new light; it allows you to see your own seeing. And sometimes, even something that looks familiar on the surface might be the source of a revealing difference.

SEEING YOUR OWN SEEING

Basketball arrived in my village just one year before me. Large groups of all ages gathered every afternoon on a dirt court that had been cleared of grass and pounded flat by nothing but bare human feet. The backboards were slats of wood carved with axes from the surrounding forest, and the rims were made of thick metal wire, salvaged from some other project. They played every day until sundown, the perfect end to a day of gardening and gathering firewood. It was a welcome and familiar sight, and I eagerly joined in.

I stepped onto the court and noticed that for the first time in my life, I was taller than everybody else. Even better, the rims had been set to about 8 feet, perfect for dunking. I rushed in for a massive dunk on my first opportunity, putting my team up 6-0. I looked to my friend Kodenim for a high five, but he looked concerned or even angry as he slapped his hand to his forearm as if to say, "Foul! Foul!"

I owned the court. I grabbed a steal and went in for another dunk, looking to Kodenim again for a fist pump or cheer. Instead, he gave me a stern look and pounded his bicep with his hand. He was trying to send me a signal, but I wasn't getting it.

Later I would find out that he was trying to send me a not-so-subtle reminder of the score. Rather than a "Base 10" counting system (cycling 1-10 then starting again 11-20 and so on), the villagers use a "Base 27" system and use their entire upper body to count it. 1-5 are on the hand, 6-10 along the arm, 11 at the neck, 12 is the ear, 13 the eye, 14 the nose, and then back down the other side. 6-0, Kodenim slaps his forearm. 8-0, he slaps his bicep.

It is a clever system that suits them well. There are no annual seasons to track in Papua New Guinea, so the most relevant natural cycle to track is not the path of the sun, but the path of the moon. A hunter can start counting from the new moon and know that as the count gets closer to his eyes (days 13, 14, and 15) he will be able to see at night using the light of the full moon. Women can use it to count the days until their next menstrual cycle.

I drifted into the background of the game as I tried to figure out what was going on. The other team started scoring, tying the game at 14. "14-14!" the score keeper announced with jubilation, pointing to his nose. Everybody cheered and walked off the court. *Where's everybody going?* I thought. *It's tied up.* "Next basket wins!" I suggested. Kodenim took me aside. "Mike, we like to end in a tie," he said, and then he smiled the way you smile at a four-year-old who is just learning the ways of the world, and gently recommended that I not do any more dunking. "People might be jealous."

The story illustrates the power of different types of cultural differences. Some differences, like the Base 27 counting system, are intellectually interesting, but they do not threaten our core beliefs, assumptions, or our moral sense of right and wrong. Such differences are fun to consider and give us an emotionally easy way to play with cultural differences and "see our own seeing."

Other differences, like the preference to end a game in a tie, are a little more challenging, because they force us to recognize that many of our core ideas and ideals are actually culturally constructed. They take what seem to be obvious and natural ideas – like the idea that sports are meant to be won or lost – and show that things need not be this way. We can then ask new questions. *Why do we value competition while they do not? What advantages are there to favoring competition vs. favoring a tie? What does this difference say about our society? What role has this obsession with winning played in my own development? Would my life be better or worse without the emphasis on winning?*

And then there are differences that shake you to your core. They are hard to see because they challenge your most foundational ideas, ideals and values. They might make you question everything about what you thought was right and wrong, real and unreal, possible and impossible.

I was about to find out that the most interesting difference I encountered on that basketball court that day was not the tie game or the interesting method of counting. It was that last thing Kodenim said to me: "*People might be jealous.*"

A few weeks later, Kodenim would fall ill and be fighting for his life. His once-strong physique would wither until his arms and legs looked like little more than a skeleton, while his stomach would enlarge and become so distended that people would describe him as "pregnant." He would put the blame for his illness on jealousy and claim that someone – probably my adoptive father – was working witchcraft on him. With lives and reputations on the line, it would not be so easy to just put aside my own beliefs, ideals, and values or "see my own seeing." I would need more tools, more ways of seeing.

SEEING BIG

A basic assumption that anthropologists make about culture is that everything is connected. Culture is a complex system made up of many different but interrelated elements. You cannot understand any one part of a culture without understanding how it is related to other parts in the cultural system. Understanding culture will ultimately require that we take a holistic perspective. We have to practice "seeing big."

Given the complexity of culture, it can be useful to have a model. Anthropologists have devised many models and metaphors for understanding culture. Many of them refer in some way to the idea that culture can be divided into three levels: infrastructure, social structure, and superstructure. Here we will use the "barrel model" developed by anthropologist Harald Prins to demonstrate what these levels refer to and how they are interrelated.

The model captures three key features of culture:

1. It is structured.
2. It is pervasive and present in all aspects of our lives, from our economy to our worldview.
3. Each element of culture is integrated with the other elements.

First, by using the word "structure," the model expands upon our common-sense notions of culture. Most people tend to think of culture as "the beliefs and practices of a group of people," but this definition hides the ways in which the vast complex of beliefs and practices in a group ultimately form into formidable structures that shape our lives, just as wood and nails can be joined into complex patterns to form the structure of a house or building. We do not define a house as "wood and nails" because it would tell us nothing about the form of those wood and nails.

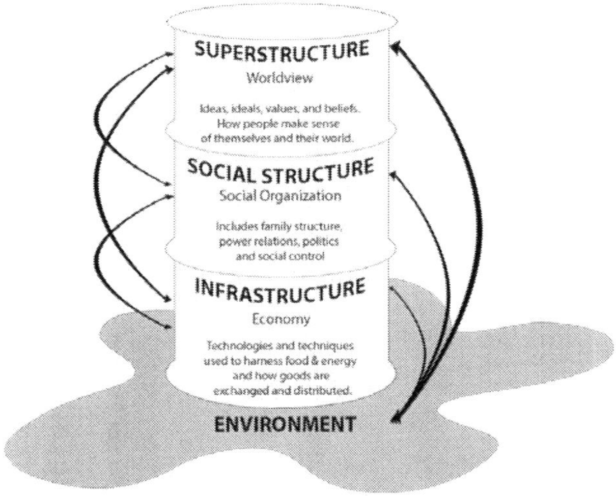

A rendition of the "barrel model of culture" developed by anthropologist Harald Prins, based on ideas first introduced by Karl Marx.

In the same way, we cannot simply describe culture as "beliefs and practices" because the long-term patterns of beliefs and practices become as real and formidable as the walls of a house. They form a structure that shapes our lives just as surely as wood and nails can form a structure that shapes a room.

Cultural structures can be difficult to see, so there is often a sense of "seeing beneath the surface of things" in order to understand why we do the things that we do. This is an especially exciting part about obtaining the ability to "see big." When we see big we are seeing big patterns and structures that are usually hidden from our everyday consciousness.

It is like pulling back the curtain on the workings of the world or cracking open the box of culture to see what really makes us tick. The model then teases apart three different levels of structure, further expanding our notion of culture beyond mere "beliefs and practices." Culture can be divided into infrastructure, social structure, and superstructure, or, in other words, our economy (technologies, techniques, exchange & distribution systems); social organization (social, political, and family structures); and our worldview (ideas, ideals, beliefs and values).

The model demonstrates that culture permeates our lives, from how we make a living (economy) to what we live for (our ideals and values).

But perhaps the most important piece of the model is the double arrows, which point to the fact that culture is integrated and dynamic. Change one thing and you change them all. A shift in the environment or a new technology can have profound effects on social structure or worldview, and vice versa.

"Seeing big" takes practice. You cannot just memorize this model and suddenly be a master of seeing big. Structure is hard to see, and seeing the complex relationships between different levels of structure can be even harder. Unlike simple math, when you try to understand a culture, there is no point at which you will know beyond doubt that you "have it right." But despite this uncertainty, it is absolutely necessary.

Let's start our practice by using the barrel model to examine American culture. We can begin by simply plugging in some simple descriptions of American infrastructure, social structure and superstructure.

Our infrastructure might be described as industrial or post-industrial with a global capitalist economy. To survive, we each must find a job, earn money, and then exchange this money for food and other goods. Our exchanges are meant to be efficient and simple exchanges of commodities.

Relationships are hidden or minimized. We usually have no idea who grew our food, who packaged it, who delivered it, or even who sold it to us. We certainly do not feel obligated to them in any way once we have paid for the goods.

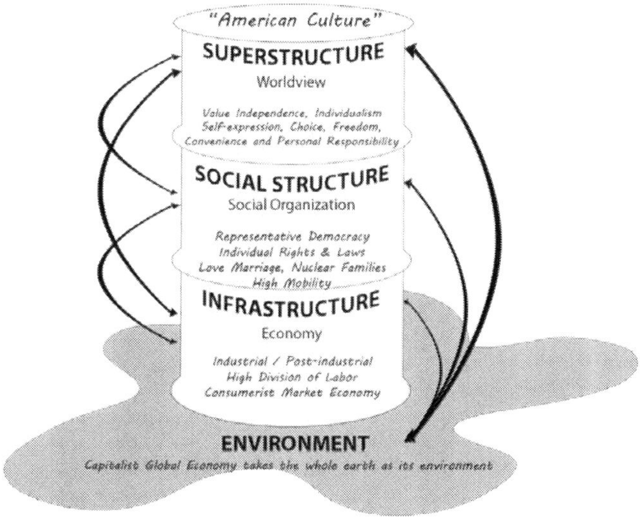

This shapes and is shaped by a worldview with a owerful sense of independence and individualism. *I earned my money. I bought these things. They are mine now.* Choices are abundant, and we can demonstrate to others who we are by the choices we make.

We not only choose what we will eat, wear, or drive. We also choose what jobs we will do, who we will marry, and where we will live (mobility). Our political system further enshrines the value of choice as we vote to choose who will represent us and make our laws.

We value and nurture individualism in our schools when we give out individual grades or champion a student's unique creativity. We celebrate and elevate sports and movie stars for their unique individual talents. We seek individual salvation or enlightenment. The values of independence, individualism, choice and freedom permeate our lives, from infrastructure, to social structure, to superstructure.We can try to tease apart the culture and find causal relationships. *Does capitalism cause individualism? Or does individualism cause capitalism? Or more broadly, does infrastructure cause superstructure or vice versa?*

But the closer we look, the more we find these elements of culture are so intimately connected that there is no way to pull them apart. Instead of saying that one element shapes another, we often say that one element "shapes and is shaped by" another.

Capitalism shapes and is shaped by individualism. Individualism shapes and is shaped by the American political system. The American labor market shapes and is shaped by individualism. This kind of relationship is called "mutual constitution." Both elements are "constituted" (made up of and made possible by) each other.

If our value on individualism waned, capitalism would change as well. If capitalism changes, so do our individualistic values.

Now let's look at Nekalimin culture. A quick sketch of the key elements of their culture plugged into the barrel model looks like this:

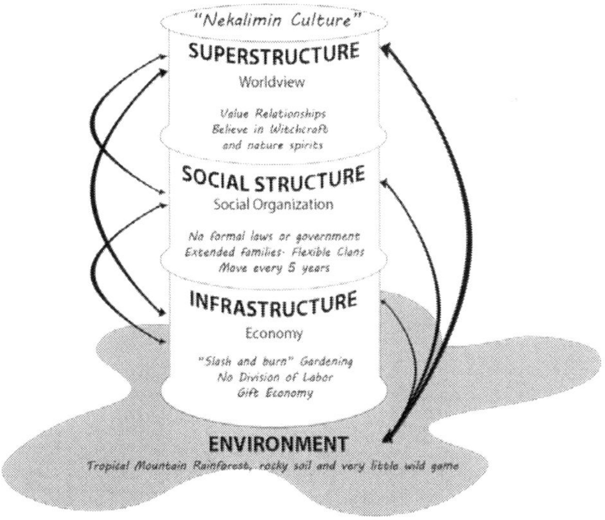

Let's do a quick tour of their land to see what this looks like in reality. They live in a tropical mountain rainforest with rocky soils and very little wild game. There is not enough game to support the culture, so they cannot survive on hunting alone. The soil is rocky, low in nutrients, and most of it is shaded by the forest canopy. However, by cutting down the forest they let the sunshine in and they can burn what they cut as a way of adding nutrients to the soil for their taro, sweet potato, and bananas.

Here is a picture of my father in his garden that has recently been cleared, burned and planted.

The nutrients from the burn will last about five years. After this, the area must be left alone so the forest can regenerate for about 30 years and then be cleared and burned again.

One immediate impact of this gardening practice is on the size and location of villages. A typical village has no more than 10 houses and a total population ranging from about 30 to 80. Anything larger requires longer and longer walks to access gardens and sources of firewood. Villages also move about every 5-10 years as the nutrients from a burned area are depleted and left to regenerate.

There are no markets or money exchanges. Food and goods are shared and exchanged as gifts rather than bought and sold as commodities. When someone gives a gift, they do not expect immediate payment. As I discovered, offering immediate cash payment can be offensive, as it suggests that you are trying to end the relationship and not have to remember them.

In this gift economy, it is the relationships that have lasting value, not goods or money. People work hard to maintain strong relationships because they know they can then call on them when they are in need. There is no incentive to hoard goods, since most of their goods (like sweet potatoes and bananas) would rot and wither away.

As the nutrients of their current gardens are depleted, people have to think about where they will make their next garden. This gives them still more incentive to maintain good relationships. They will have to make a claim on land and with no written records or deeds of ownership, those claims will depend on a general consensus that their claims are valid. These claims are made through clan membership, which is flexible enough to allow people to move from one clan area to another as long as their claims are recognized by current clan members.

With such a strong emphasis on good relations, there is no need for formal or written laws, rules or policies. There are no lawyers, rulers, or police. All people have a natural incentive to be good and to build and maintain good relationships with others because their livelihood depends on it. Since nobody has any official power over anyone else, and there is no division of labor, it is mostly an egalitarian society, with very little difference in status and wealth.

So unlike the American worldview which is dominated by the ideas and ideals of individualism and independence, the Nekalimin worldview is dominated by a focus on relationships. This focus on relationships dominates their consciousness and allows them to see and think about the world in a very different way than we do. They see and understand their connections and relationships to each other and their land much more sharply. They are keenly conscientious and aware of the complex relationships that link them to others and are able to do extraordinarily complex relationship calculus as they try to solve social problems. They believe in spirits of nature with whom they must maintain strong relationships, offering small bits of pork to the spirit of a grove or hillside in hopes that they will have good health and a good harvest. They do not see themselves as individuals separated from the world. They see themselves and their bodies as intimately connected to other people and the world around them.

And they believe in witchcraft. As Kodenim grew ever more ill, a shaman was called in to investigate. He went into a trance, the house started shaking, and a small bundle of food, smaller than a golf ball, fell in front of him, as if it had fallen from the spirit world and right into our own. He picked it up and confirmed Kodenim's worst fears. He had been bewitched.

The shaman explained that the small packet of food that came to him in a trance was a piece of sweet potato that Kodenim had eaten. It had been placed under the spiky roots of a pandanus fruit, which was now causing his stomach pain and swelling. The shaman could not identify the witch, but suggested that Kodenim try to find out who the witch might be, address the core problem between them in order to heal the relationship, and ask the witch to stop. Every night until he could solve this problem, the witches would be feasting on his body, and he would continue to wither away and die.

Despite my growing capacities to "see big" and understand these beliefs within a larger cultural context that places strong emphasis on relationships, I simply could not go along with the idea that Kodenim was being consumed by witches. I begged his family to let me take him to a hospital on the next flight out, but Kodenim himself refused. By his reckoning, his only chance of survival was to stay and fix his relationships. As a compromise I took pictures of his swollen belly and skeletal-thin limbs and attached them to a letter to a friend of mine, a doctor at the Mayo Clinic specializing in tropical diseases. Maybe he would know what was wrong and we could still save Kodenim.

Meanwhile, I knew that I was failing as an anthropologist in my efforts to truly "see" and understand my New Guinea friends. Humans are meaning-makers. We make sense of the world. The anthropologist has endless faith that no matter how odd or exotic a belief might seem, it will make sense once all the details are laid out and understood. For this, I would need yet another tool.

SEEING SMALL

Anthropologists are passionate connoisseurs of the little things. We want to understand the blooming, buzzing complexity of life in all of its nuance and detail. There are no details to small. Clifford Geertz calls it "thick description," and in the seminal article of the same name he famously spends several pages describing the many meanings one might imply or infer from something as simple and small as the wink of an eye. Our goal, as Geertz writes, is to see the "Grand Realities" of "Power, Change, Faith, Oppression, Work, Passion, Authority, Beauty, Violence, Love, and Prestige" in the give and take detail and minutia of everyday life so as to "take the capital letters off of them."

We must pay close attention not only to what is said, but also who said it, how they said it, who they said it to, when, where, and if at all possible to decipher, why. Long-term fieldwork of many months or even several years is a must for this kind of seeing. It takes time not only to learn the language but also to tune your senses and start to see what matters and what does not.

Understanding a culture in its own terms (following the foundational premise of cultural relativism) means that we must understand all the details and nuance of their worldview. Just by using the word "witchcraft" to translate their beliefs, we are already putting them into our own terms. For us, witchcraft is a backwards superstition standing against a more rational and scientific understanding of the world. We associate it with beliefs wiped out by the Enlightenment several hundred years ago.

The more I started paying attention to the little things, the more I understood that these local beliefs that I was categorizing as witchcraft were actually just one piece of a much larger, richer, and more convincing worldview. I started noticing the care and concern given to analyzing each and every gift exchange. I noticed how each gift was given along with a short and carefully delivered speech about where the materials came from, who made it, who delivered it, and who cared for it along the way. I noticed how they talked about such gifts as "building a road" or "tying a string" between the two parties so that they would always remember each other. And soon, this careful attention to relationships and the gifts that bind them was helping me understand why dunking a basketball or otherwise showboating, or looking to crush your opponent, is not valued. I started noticing a great deal of concern about jealousy and other elements that could eat away at a relationship.

What eventually emerged from these close and careful observations was an entirely different understanding of health and well-being. They understand themselves to be physically made up of their relationships. It starts from the basic recognition that the food they eat becomes who they are. This is, of course, actually true. We process the food we eat and its energy fuels our growth. For them, every piece of food they ever consume from the time they are a small child is a gift, and they are taught to know where it came from and all of the people that helped bring it into their hands and into their bodies.

The food was created through the hard work of others tending the gardens and is itself made up of the nutrients of the earth. The nutrients of the earth are in turn made up from the death and decay of plants, animals, and their own ancestors. As they take in this food it literally becomes them, and as the food itself is made up of the relationships that made it, so their bodies are made up of the relationships that made the food and brought it into their being. They understand that every last element – every atom – of their body was in one way or another given to them by their relationships. They literally *are* their relationships.

It makes perfect sense, then, that when they get sick, they would turn to an analysis of their relationships. From our Western perspective, based on a model of the body as a separate individual, we think that it is impossible that one body could magically harm another body simply by willing harm and placing their food in a bundle at the base of a pandanus tree. We call it "witchcraft." But if you see yourself as actually made up of your relationships to others and the land, it makes sense. So when Kodenim became ill, he and his closest friends started analyzing his relationships, taking inventory of all the times Kodenim had wronged another person. He had stolen a pig from my father, so my father was at the top of the list. He had also lied to Kenny, killed and eaten Ona's chicken, and had a strained relationship with his in-laws, who were especially upset with him.

My father offered to wash Kodenim as a show of his innocence. Washing is a ritual thought to "cool" the witchcraft. If my father was the witch, the soap and water would cool his witchcraft and remove it from Kodenim.

Kodenim knelt before my father as he stirred the water, and my father began to wash him. He prayed as he washed, calling on God to be his witness that he had no reason to harm Kodenim, that he loved him, and that they were really just one family. He reminisced about how Kodenim's father was like a brother to him, and that he had always looked upon Kodenim like a son of his own. I swallowed hard with emotion, knowing their history and the gravity of the situation, and noticed that Kodenim's friends and family who were standing nearby were also in a somber reflective mood, their eyes moist as they held back their tears.

Kodenim's health did not improve. So a few days later, a much larger ritual was arranged. Kenny (whom he had lied to) and Ona (he stole her chicken), as well as all of my father's extended family, attended. The event started with an open admission of the wrongs Kodenim had done, followed by heartfelt statements of forgiveness forgiveness from Kenny, Ona, and others he had wronged. Then Kodenim took a seat on a log as dozens of people lined up to wash him. This time there was no holding back the emotion of the moment. One by one, those he had wronged as well as their extended families moistened their hands and washed his head, often saying a prayer of care and forgiveness as they did this. Kodenim looked especially ill. People lingered long after the ritual, like they didn't want to let Kodenim or this special moment go.

The next day, the plane came in with news from my friend at the Mayo Clinic. He said that they would need to do blood tests to find out more, but even then he was not confident that anything could be done. He recommended staying in the village.

Kodenim died two days later.

The aftermath was difficult. Kodenim's family was hurt and angry, as we all were, and came to my father asking for compensation. They wanted a huge amount of wealth by local standards – several bushknives, two axes, clothes, bags, bows and arrows. Altogether, their request was many times the wealth of any single individual.

The request deeply offended and angered me. It challenged my most fundamental understandings of justice. Kodenim had stolen a pig from my father, causing a rift in the relationship. His family was sure it was this that had killed him. Maybe my father did not work the witchcraft himself, but he should have been looking after him more carefully, especially since Kodenim lived in the same village as my father. On my scales of justice, we were the ones who were wronged, and we were the ones who deserved payment. Kodenim had stolen from us, not the other way around.

I felt lost and confused, and tried to drift into the background and grieve Kodenim's death in my own way. I started spending more time alone, and when I was around other people, I always brought my camera and just hid behind the viewfinder. In this way, I could pretend to be doing "work" and hope to not be bothered, but my father called my bluff. "My son," he said, looking into the camera, "why don't you use that thing to show them I am not a witch!" and then gave a hearty laugh. He liked to play the "stupid old man" who didn't understand these new technologies like cameras, but he knew perfectly well that my camera could not exonerate him. He just wanted me to stop hiding. I realized something very important in that moment:

Participation is not a choice.
Only how we participate is a choice.

Sitting back and doing nothing is in itself a form of participation. You can't pretend like your actions do not matter and stand off to the side of social life.

But what to do? I did not want to contribute to the compensation as I was being asked to do. I would need to finally put it all together and practice the full art of seeing.

SEEING IT ALL

No matter how good you get at seeing your own seeing, seeing big, and seeing small, you can never really see the world as they see it. You can't "go native" and be just like them. Despite my best efforts, I could not really bring myself to believe that Kodenim had been killed by witchcraft, and that the death could have been avoided if my father had nurtured a healthier relationship with him.

"Being true to yourself" is an equally troublesome strategy. If you simply stick to your own ideas, ideals, beliefs, and values, then you are refusing to learn and grow. You fail to nurture any true empathy and understanding.

What is needed is some method that can be practiced day in and day out that slowly moves us closer and closer toward understanding. It has to be something we can remember when times get hard, something that can keep us on track even when our own feelings, emotions, fears, and biases start clouding our vision.

It was during hard times like these that I turned to the most important tools in the anthropologist's toolkit: Communication, Empathy, and Thoughtfulness. We have to keep talking to people (communication), work toward understanding them in their own terms (empathy), using and revising our knowledge and models as we go (thoughtfulness). As we improve in each one of these areas, the others improve as well. Communicating helps us understand their perspective (empathy) and revise our analytical models (thoughtfulness).

As our empathy improves, we can communicate better and improve our thoughtfulness, and as our thoughtfulness improves we are better able to imagine our way into their perspective (empathy) and communicate more clearly with them. We can summarize these relationships like this:

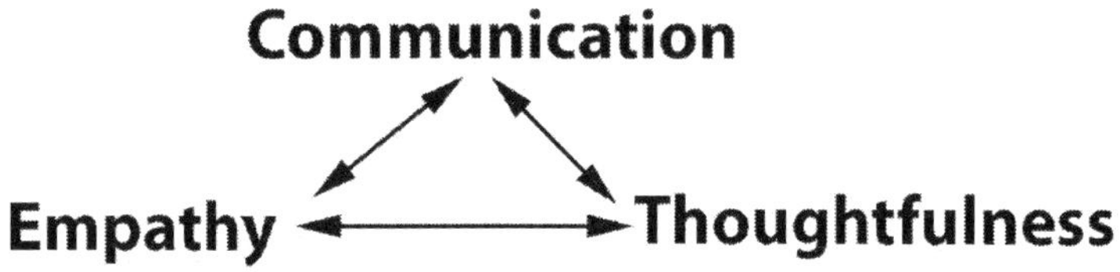

Seeing small had allowed me to understand their logic. Seeing big allowed me to see how this logic fit in with other elements of their culture. The more I communicated, empathized, and thought through the matter, the more I started to understand – not as an academic studying the matter, but as a human being deeply enmeshed in the matter myself. From that insider perspective, I now realized that witchcraft beliefs were an integral part of a much larger system that had remained hidden until then.

What was apparent as an insider was that our choice to pay or not pay the compensation would have life and death consequences for the village. We could pay the compensation, thereby reconnecting two family networks and saving the village, or we could simply choose to move out and start a new village. It turns out that witchcraft, more than the depletion of nutrients in the soil, is the engine that keeps people moving. Most villages trace their origin to a witchcraft accusation. If you stand on a high peak and look at the villages dotting the landscape, you are looking at a history of accusations, deaths, and failed compensations.

Most villages are made up of no more than a handful of families. When someone gets sick or dies, they analyze their relationships to find a strained relation. Usually one of the most strained relationships is between two families within the village. In this case, Kodenim's family blames my family. When Kodenim died, it was not just Kodenim that died. Kodenim, like anyone else in the culture, is also seen as a node in a vast network of relations. His death leaves a vast void in the network that must be repaired, or it threatens to tear apart the fabric of the society. Large compensation gifts can repair this void by reconnecting the extended families and networks that Kodenim once connected.

The entire model of culture we laid out earlier now makes sense in a whole new way. "Witchcraft" is not just this strange belief. It is an integral part of their entire culture.

"Witchcraft" makes sense at every level of culture. First, at the level of superstructure we can say that it is logical in that it makes sense within a sound and logically consistent worldview that focuses on relationships. Furthermore, witchcraft is generally called upon to explain *why* someone is sick, not *how*. Many people can offer sophisticated biomedical explanations for how someone died, but this only explains how; it does not explain why this particular person died at this particular time. Nobody has an answer for "the big Why" of death. Many in the West turn to explanations such as "it was God's will" or it was just "bad luck." These are no more scientifically verifiable than witchcraft.

Second, at the level of social structure, we can say that it is socio-logical. It makes sense socially. Witchcraft beliefs encourage people to be kind to each other and take care of their relationships in the absence of formal rules and laws. Furthermore, if a relationship does sour, there are rituals such as the washings described earlier that heal relationships.

And finally, at the level of infrastructure, we can say that witchcraft beliefs are ecological. They make sense for the environment. As villages grow to over fifty people, they tend to break up and split apart due to witchcraft accusations. This is ecologically sound, because it keeps people spread out and well within the total carrying capacity of their land. Rather than suffering massive ecological collapse and starvation during a drought, their low population density spread over many miles of land is sustained even through hard times.

Being able to truly see and understand this put me at ease. I now realized that my contribution to the compensation would heal the relationships of a village I had come to deeply love and care about. The size of the gift forced my father to call in debts of friends and friends of friends, his whole network of relations. The gift was large not only as a sign of respect and love for Kodenim and his family, it also assured us that they would never forget us and that they would one day give something in return. These gifts would make their way back through the vast network we had to call upon to bring this gift together. Still more gifts would then be given in return, and so on. We were retying the ties that once bound us together, filling the void left by Kodenim's departure.

The gifts were set out at the center of the village early one morning. Kodenim's father led his entire extended family down the path and into the village to collect the bounty. There had been much strain in these relationships ever since Kodenim first stole my father's pig. Kodenim's father examined the pile of gifts that had been brought forth. All the wealth in the world cannot replace a son, and no father wants to bury their child. But the sentiment was strong and well- received. He thanked my father and they extended hands for a handshake, tears in their eyes. The handshake soon collapsed into a hug which others joined in on, while others clapped and cried.

My own spirit was still aching from the loss of Kodenim. But as I watched the tears flow down the cheeks of my father, Kodenim's father, and the others who had gathered for that hug, I realized something that filled my soul with gratitude and peace:

This was a beautiful death.

In his final days, Kodenim was able to publicly admit his every sin. He was offered heartfelt forgiveness from those who he had wronged, all because of their beliefs in witchcraft. It may not have cleared his body of whatever it was that killed him, but it sure seemed to cleanse his soul. He died at peace.

And the hole he left in our world was filled with gifts, kindness, and good will.

GROWING UP AMONG THE NACIREMA

"We shall not cease from exploration, and the end of all our exploring will be to arrive where we started and know the place for the first time."
– T. S. Eliot

If viewing an exotic and very different culture can help us leap out of the water of our own culture to truly see it, the Nacirema need to be high on our list of cultures to examine. In 1956, cultural anthropologist Horace Miner's original article about the Nacirema provided an in-depth look at their ritual behaviors that show, in Miner's words, "the extremes to which human behavior can go." The work was so shocking and revealing that the article went on to be the most widely read article in the history of Anthropology.

As Miner explains in the article, the Nacirema are obsessed with the body, which they believe is intrinsically ugly and prone to debility and disease. Each Nacirema household has a shrine or sometimes several shrines in which private rituals are performed to mitigate what they see as ever-present and pervasive threats to their bodies. Various charms provided by medicine men are ingested, and they perform several rites of ablution throughout the day using a special purified water secured from the main Water Temple of the community.

Since Miner's time, the Nacirema have started building very large temples called "*mygs*" that contain rows and rows of various body torture devices which they use to punish their own bodies. The devices are designed to tear and damage muscles, causing them to swell. Others are designed to completely exhaust the body and use up all of its energy so that the body starts to consume itself in order to provide energy for movement.

While the Nacirema believe that these rituals make their bodies stronger and more resilient to disease, the primary purpose of these rituals seems to be to transform the shape of the body to conform to Nacirema ideals. These ideals are so extreme that they are beyond the reach of natural human capacity. To achieve these ideals, some Nacirema go so far as to have ritual specialists cut them open and inject liquids into areas of their body that they desire to be larger, or remove soft body tissues and make other parts of their body smaller.

These new temples are just one example of how cultures are always changing, and over the past 70 years, the Nacirema have changed dramatically. For the Nacirema of Miner's study in 1956, even simple black-and-white televisions were a new and exotic technology. Today the Nacirema can be found across the social media landscape on Facebook, Instagram, Snapchat and YouTube. This offers us the ability to observe this exotic culture simply by tuning in to their YouTube channels.

One of the more interesting rituals of the Nacirema is the *strecnoc*. Hundreds and sometimes thousands of people attend these rituals which take place around a large, elevated ritual platform known as an *egats*. The rituals are often at night, so he egats is lit up in spectacular fashion. Attendees gather in the dark around the egats and often consume mind-altering substances such as *lohocla* and *anaujiram* while they wait for the ritual leader to arrive. Attendees are often shaking with anticipation as they wait for the ritual to begin, and the first sighting of the ritual leader on the egats can send attendees into a frenzy of excitement, jumping up and down, screaming, with arms high in the air as if struggling to reach out and touch the ritual leader and feel their power.

In the late summer of 2013, I decided to examine one of these rituals in more detail. I did a YouTube search and watched the most-watched strecnoc of recent days. A large effigy of a bear, one of the most dangerous and feared animals among the Nacirema, was placed at the center of the egats. The bear was approximately 30 feet tall and styled to look like the small toy bears of Nacirema children.

Nacirema children, who are often required by their parents to sleep alone (a rare practice across cultures around the world), often sleep with these small toy bears, seeing them as protectors and often building up strong imaginary friendships with them.

Suddenly, a door opened up in the stomach of the large bear and the ritual leader stepped out from inside. Dancers in toy bear costumes rushed in from the sides of the egats to join her. Together they took to the center of the egats and started doing a special dance that is normally only performed in the privacy of one's own room. It is an especially wild dance, not really meant for anyone to see, in which you simply allow your body to do whatever it feels like doing. This often results in a steady but awkward thrusting or shaking motion while the arms spontaneously mimic whatever is heard in the music. If a handheld string instrument is being played, the arms might move as if to hold it (*ria ratiug*). If drums are being played, the arms move as if to play the drums (*ria smurd*), and so on. It is a very fun form of dance to do, but it is usually not meant to be seen, and some attendees were uncomfortable watching it, especially as the ritual leader moved more deeply into this private dance and let her entire body move freely but awkwardly. Even her tongue seemed to be out of control, flailing wildly about her face.

"*Make some noise!*" the ritual leader called to the attendees. They screamed into a frenzy as she started the core of the ritual, the *gnos*. The gnos is a poetry performance set to music and dance. The gnos began with a voice entering the room, projected from somewhere outside of the egats:

It's our party we can do what we want.

It's our party we can say what we want.

It's our party we can love who we want

We can kiss who we want

We can see who we want

As the voice continued to poetically espouse these core Nacirema ideals of freedom and free choice, the ritual leader continued to demonstrate these values with her body. She bent over and started shaking her backside in an attempt to isolate a contraction of her gluteus maximus muscles which then send the fatty area of the buttocks region into a wave-like motion known as *gnikrewt*. This is often interpreted as being very sexually suggestive, and the mixture of childhood toys along with such sexually suggestive dancing (tongue flailing about, buttocks shaking), was simply too much for some of the attendees.

Some were especially shocked because this ritual leader had until recently been known as Annah Anatnom, a hero among children. And she is the daughter of another famous ritual specialist, Yllib Yar Suryc, who is best known for his wholesome family-friendly performances such as "Some Gave All," (a tribute to military families) and "Achy Breaky Heart."

_nkedbang
@AntoineeG35

Follow

WTF ??? #MileyCyrus #VMA

11:05 PM - 25 Aug 2013

6 2

Karson Tager
@karsonwithak

Follow

Will Smith & his family reacting to Miley Cyrus on stage at #VMAs just won the Internet.

10:18 PM - 25 Aug 2013

2,859 1,583

Ann Elizabeth
@Ann_Eber

Follow

But seriously... WHAT HAPPENED?!! 😳 #MileyCyrus
11:01 PM - 25 Aug 2013

361 112

Ultimately, the Nacirema were deeply divided on the quality of the performance. It seemed as if there was no middle ground. You either hated it, or you loved it.

Megan Amram
@meganamram

Follow

my mom emailed me "Don't believe the press; MILEY CYRUS WAS FANTASTIC!!"
10:25 PM - 26 Aug 2013

130 365

Even as the media criticized her performance, with many saying that it was likely the end of her career, the ritual leader, Yelim, turned their words to her advantage and celebrated the event as a great success.

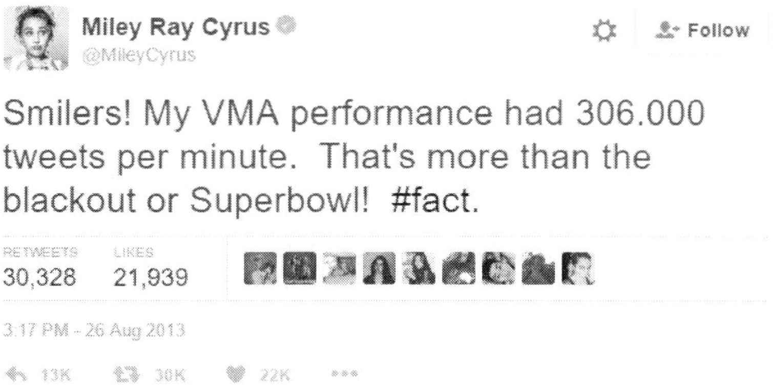

Miley Ray Cyrus
@MileyCyrus
Follow
Smilers! My VMA performance had 306.000 tweets per minute. That's more than the blackout or Superbowl! #fact.
RETWEETS
30,328
LIKES
21,939
3:17 PM - 26 Aug 2013
13K
30K
22K

As an anthropologist, I thought it was one of the most significant artistic performances I had ever seen, a telling portrait of what it is like to grow up among the Nacirema. The toy bears, the awkward "dance like nobody's watching" dancing that you do in your room as a young child, and the ritual dress that included a cartoon mouse on a little girl's tutu were clear marks of childhood, all of which were shed throughout the performance. The bears transformed into full- bodied voluptuous women. The little girl's tutu was shed to reveal a flesh-toned bikini, and the awkward and childish dancing transformed into a sexual feast of humping, grinding, and *gnikrewt*. She was shedding the skin of her childhood, initiating herself into her own adulthood right in front of our eyes, struggling to show the world that she is now a full adult, not that little girl Aannah Anatnom.

Those Nacirema who had to turn away and just couldn't stand to watch it were probably seeing a little too much of their own awkward childhood and transition to adulthood, for the Nacirema transition to adulthood is always awkward. It is, as they say, a "hot mess."

Bill Werde
@bwerde

Follow

Guys, Miley Cyrus is an all-star hot mess for a hot mess pop moment. She doesn't care what u think & that's her brand. & she just delivered.

RETWEETS 481 LIKES 204

8:46 PM - 25 Aug 2013

49 481 204

The cost of their core values of freedom and choice is that there are no limitations or guidelines on how to grow up properly. There are no clearly defined rules for what it means to be an adult. There are no clearly defined pathways for becoming independent. Instead, there are options at every turn of life. The Nacirema cherish these options. But they also make growing up very, very hard.

Children are raised with the idea that they can "be whatever they want to be." They are taught to question and distrust any message that attempts to tell them who they are or how they should behave. "Be true to yourself," is a commonly espoused Nacirema proverb. Yelim echoed these sentiments in her performance, *"We don't take nothing from nobody."* But because they "don't take nothing from nobody," like advice or values, they are left with nothing to guide them. They set off on a lifelong quest to figure out what they want to do and who they want to be. "Who am I?" is a question that dominates the Nacirema psyche.

As a result, many Nacirema make it their life goal to "find" their "self." Though most Nacirema take this goal for granted, it has not always been this way. Even in Miner's time, the 1950s, things were different. Back then people were often encouraged to conform and follow the rules of society. But by the late 1970s, books like William Glasser's "The Identity Society" and Christopher Lasch's "Culture of Narcissism" documented a shift from a culture that valued humility and "finding one's place" to one that valued self-expression and "finding one's self."

THE POWER OF CONTINGENCY AND "MAKING THINGS FRAGILE"

It is obvious at this point that the Nacirema are not some exotic culture, but are in fact American, and that "Nacirema" is just "American" spelled backwards. This was Miner's trick. He forced us to see the strange in the familiar and used the art of seeing like an anthropologist on his own culture.

This trick is one method of "seeing your own seeing" without going to an exotic culture. You can find the exotic right around you, and the more mundane, the better. Because when you reveal that even the most mundane beliefs and practices that make up your life can be viewed as strange and exotic, they also become *contingent*, which is a fancy way of saying that they need not exist or that they could have been different. Our beliefs and practices are *contingent* upon the historical and cultural conditions that led to them. And once we recognize them as contingent, we can ask new questions about them.

What is a self? Is it really a thing? Or is it something you do? Would it be better to say that we "create" ourselves rather than "find" it? And what did that other great poet, Marshall Mathers, mean when he said "You gotta lose *yourself"? Is it possible that you have to lose your self in order to find your self? If so, what is this "self" that must be lost? Am "I" the same thing as my "self"? If they are the same, how can I say "I" need to find my "self"? Can "I" really find, lose, or create my "self" or do I just need to let the "I" be my "self"?*

These are a special kind of questions. These questions do not require answers; the questions are insights in themselves. They give you new alternatives for how to think about your life. They give you a little bit of freedom from the limited perspectives offered by your taken-for-granted assumptions, ideas, and ideals.

Michel Foucault, a social theorist and historian who has had a large impact on anthropology, says that this kind of analysis is a way of "making things more fragile." It shows that "what appears obvious is not at all so obvious." In his work, Foucault he tries to show that many of the "obvious" facts of our lives that we take for granted can be "made fragile" through cultural and historical analysis. In this way, we "give them back the mobility they had and that they should always have." The ideas and ideals of our culture do not have to have total power over us. We can play with them, make them more fragile, and thereby take some of that power back.

This particular power of the anthropological perspective has been at the heart of anthropology since its founding in the late 1800s. Franz Boas, the father of American Anthropology, said that his whole outlook on life had been determined by one question:

How can we recognize the shackles that tradition has laid upon us? For when we recognize them, we are also able to break them.

LEARN MORE

- Body Ritual Among the Nacirema, by Horace Miner

Challenge Two: Fieldwork of the Familiar

Your challenge is to do fieldwork in your own culture, find the strange in the familiar, and produce a compelling photo essay of your insights.

Objective: Practice the anthropological method of seeing your own seeing – to see the strange in the familiar – and to understand how our taken-for-granted everyday life is actually contingent on specific historical and cultural conditions.

Start by thinking of things that are done in your culture that might strike an Anthropologist from Mars as strange. For example, the Nacirema keep small animals called *teps*, heal themselves through the ritual of *gnippohs*, spend lots of time obsessing over their bodies while they *ezicrixe*, spend 13 to 25 years of their lives simply training for the complexity of their lives in special places called *loohcs*, etc.

Next, go to a location where you can really observe this behavior. Try to come up with four or five interesting observations about this behavior. These observations will be the text of your essay. Then, take a photograph for each of your key points that captures what you are trying to say. This will help you construct your final photo essay that will include four or five compelling images along with the text. Submit your essay on Instagram with #anth101challenge2

Go to ANTH101.com/challenge2 for additional tips and information.

Lesson Three
Evolution

When we open up to such questions, we open ourselves up to our higher nature. It was asking questions, making connections and trying new things that brought us down from the trees, and took us to the moon.

WHO ARE WE?

The mountainous interior of New Guinea offers some of the most treacherous hiking challenges in the world. It is as rough and steep as any other mountain range, but then it is blanketed with a thick, wet rainforest teeming with painful fire ants, sharp stones, and slick mud. My colleague Dan Jorgensen, who did fieldwork just a few valleys away, calls it "vertical rainforest."

In preparation for this, I bought the best boots I could afford – stiff and strong, with mean-looking teeth promising plenty of traction. But they were no match for these mountains. My friends skittered up and down mountains with ease in their bare feet while I clobbered and hobbled along. Every step of mine seemed so heavy and clumsy compared to the graceful and light dance they did as they bounced from tone to stone. We all spent a lot of time on the ground – me crawling on all fours gazing down in terror over the mountain ledges that would surely end my life, them sitting casually up-mountain taking in the good view and enjoying a smoke.

Going down was much worse than going up. I usually took a "sit and slide" approach, seeing no plausible way to stay on two feet and get down safely. Meanwhile they bounded down the same precipice with ease, usually carrying heavy bags full of garden produce, firewood, or even babies.

One day about eight months into my time there, my wife and I were gathering bamboo for a new chicken pen. Fresh bamboo is very heavy, and the 14-foot bundles we put together were especially unwieldy. Our shoulders shrieked with pain as we lumbered along the slick trail home. After struggling for some time, an eight-year-old girl who could not have weighed more than 60 pounds swooped alongside my wife, swung her load of bamboo onto her back, and walked off as quickly as she had arrived, leaving us trailing far behind. Though my wife felt a little ashamed that she had been rescued by an eight-year-old, she was happy to be rid of the load, and walked on toward home as I continued to struggle, heaving the load 30 feet, then 20 feet, then just 10 feet at a time, then stopping to rest and rub my aching shoulder, letting the tall and imposing load stand beside me. I didn't dare let it fall, for I knew I would never be able to stand it up again.

Before long an old woman caught up, carrying a bag full of sweet potatoes on her head. Watching me struggle with the load, she offered to help. She appeared frail and weighed no more than 100 pounds. I was sure she would simply collapse under the weight, so I refused. But she was insistent. She wedged her shoulder into the standing bundle, found the balance point, let the weight sway onto her shoulder, and skittered off toward the house with that quick and light New Guinea step I had come to admire. I had to walk-run-walk like a child with his parents just trying to keep up, but she scurried further and further ahead as I struggled with the uneven terrain. By the time I arrived home, she had already dropped off the bamboo and was on her way.

My wife stood on the veranda, laughing. "Haha!" she teased, "I was feeling really bad until I saw you trailing behind that old woman carrying your bundle!" We marveled at the display of strength we had just seen. Here were two very strong, fit, young Americans shown up by a small child and a frail old grandmother.

I had always seen myself as a fit guy with great balance and athleticism, but the things that ordinary New Guineans of all ages could do simply astonished me. They crossed raging rivers of certain death on small wet logs without breaking stride. They would come to what I would consider a cliff, the end of the trail, and bound straight down it without hesitation or comment. They climbed trees I would consider unclimbable, and then walk out on a thin branch 30 feet above the ground as if it were the earth itself, and slash branches above them with a machete while not holding on to anything to secure themselves.

Yet there were some things we could do that they could not. A 20-foot steel pole, part of an old radio tower, had been abandoned in the village for some 30 years from an unfinished colonial project. It probably weighed about 150 pounds. My wife and I could both dead-lift it. Nobody else in the village, even the strongest looking men, could do so. So at least we had that on them. We could do the relatively useless task of dead-lifting a uniform, unnatural, perfectly balanced steel bar off of the ground, but we couldn't carry a bundle of heavy, unwieldy, slippery, and bumpy bamboo. We could not navigate their paths and makeshift "bridges" without sometimes reverting to crawling. We could not harvest our own tree fruit. We could not carry large bundles of firewood on our heads. In short, we might be "strong" and "fit" by American standards, but we simply could not do any of the basic tasks required for survival in New Guinea.

Watching such feats was a continuous reminder of another question that had brought me there: Who are we as human beings? What are we capable of? On a deeper level, the question is not just about physical abilities, but also about our intellectual abilities as well as our moral capacities and inclinations. What is our nature? When my friends stopped and cried with me on the mountain, were they tapping into some deep aspect of our human nature, or was that an aspect of their culture? Are we inherently good or bad? Are empathy and compassion natural inclinations, or are we more prone to be jealous and judgmental?

To explore these questions, we need to expand our view beyond humans today and look to our evolutionary past. We have to look at our closest animal relatives, as well as the fossil record, to explore what we can learn about our ancestors.

Evolution has been a touchy and controversial topic since Charles Darwin first introduced the idea in 1859. Darwin himself waited 23 years before publishing *The Origin of Species,* because he knew it would contradict the account of creation in Genesis and set off a broad public debate. Around the same time, Charles Lyell published evidence that the earth was much older than the Biblical 6,000-year-old timeline. Ever since, those of us who grow up in cultures with a Biblical tradition have had to wrestle with difficult questions about how to square scientific knowledge with our religious faith.

While evolution is still strongly debated in public, it has long been firmly accepted in science. While critics like to point out that it is "just a theory," the phrase misunderstands the definition of scientific theory. A scientific theory is not an unproven hypothesis. The National Academy of Sciences defines a theory as "a well-substantiated explanation of some aspect of the natural world." Theories are not tentative guesses or even well-reasoned hypotheses. They take in a wide range of well-established facts and laws and make sense of them. "Theories," the Academy notes, "are the end points of science."

So evolution, like any scientific theory, is not something to be simply believed or disbelieved. It is to be understood and continuously reassessed based on the evidence. As Stephen Jay Gould points out, evolution is not only a theory, it is also an established scientific fact due to the mountains of data and observations supporting it. Nothing is absolutely certain in science, so "scientific fact" does not mean "absolute certainty." Rather, a scientific fact is something that is "confirmed to such a degree that it would be perverse to withhold provisional assent."

Does this mean that God does not exist and that the Bible is wrong? This is a difficult question that each of us has to answer for ourselves. Most Americans who become college-educated end up accepting evolution (73%) and many of them see God as guiding the process or having planned the process out from the beginning of time (41%). Many professional evolutionary scientists hold this view as well, and it affords them the great joy of exploring the vastness of our world and its history. As my friend and colleague Keith Miller, who is both an evangelical Christian and an evolutionary scientist, wrote in a now-famous article on the theological implications of evolution, "Our continually developing scientific understanding of cosmic history should produce great awe at God's incalculable power and wisdom ... He instructed Job to contemplate the created universe. When we contemplate the universe today should we not, even more than Job, be overwhelmed by God's greatness?"

So one reason to study evolution is to simply stand in awe of the unfolding cosmos that has ultimately led to this moment right now. But there are other, more practical reasons as well. Studying evolution helps us understand who we are at the biological level. It helps explain how and why we get stressed, why we are prone to getting fat, and why we are prone to fall into bad habits. Most of us will die of a disease that is caused by a mismatch between the environments that we evolved to survive in, and those that we live in today. Understanding our evolutionary past can help you stay alive. It can also explain why we are prone to fall in love, feel jealous, or rage with hate or fear. Our biology is always a part of our lives. We tend to deny this fact, but the more we acknowledge it and learn about it, the better we will be able to handle the ups and downs of everyday life, stay healthy, and perhaps even do some things that we never thought possible.

As a small-town kid from Nebraska, I also had to wrestle with these questions. It was a constant source of discussion and debate in my college dorm, often taking us deep into the early hours of the morning. While my own conclusions are irrelevant to your own, I simply want to note that I am grateful that my conclusions allowed me to open up to the wealth of research and information emerging out of evolutionary science today, as they have greatly enriched my life. They have helped me understand who we are, our human potential, and most importantly, helped me regain much of the human potential I had lost through years of unhealthy habits. While this chapter cannot possibly tell the entirety of the human story or pass on all of the wisdom to be gathered from an understanding of human evolution, I hope that it can serve as an invitation for you to explore more.

20 MILLION YEARS AGO: THE MONKEY ALLIANCE

Step into the Tai Forest of Africa and you will hear a wild cacophony of calls, sounds, and melodies that would have been familiar to our ancient ancestors. Birds singing, monkeys hooting, bugs chirping, frogs croaking, and a multitude of other sounds fill the air. Listen closely enough, and you can start to tune into the conversation.

Klaus Zuberbuhler has spent years studying the calls of the primates in this forest. In one study, he started by playing leopard sounds and then listened for the response. Diana monkeys sitting in the forest canopy always responded with the same recognizable alarm call. He played the shrieks of an eagle and heard what he thought was the same call. But back in his lab he created a spectrogram of the calls and discovered that they were actually different calls. The Diana monkeys were distinguishing threats from above, like eagles, from threats from below, like leopards, with subtle variations in pitch. They were singing, and using their songs for survival.

One day, Klaus was walking through this forest when, suddenly, his ability to tune into this conversation became a matter of life or death. Diana monkeys were sounding an alarm from high in the trees above him. A leopard was in the area. As he moved through the forest, the calls moved closer and seem to follow his every move. The leopard was stalking him! He kept his ears tuned into the Diana monkeys overhead and quickened his pace, walking with anxious deliberation toward the safety of his camp. He dared not run.

Inside Klaus's body, an ancient stress response kicked in. He was filled with a rush of adrenaline. Without making any conscious decisions, he cashed in on the fat he had stored up for just such an occasion. It was transformed into glycogen, which raced through his bloodstream, powered by his racing heart. His awareness heightened. Meanwhile, all of his body's long-term projects ceased. The body shut down repair, growth, and reproduction. His body was fully primed and in the moment. No time for long-term goals now.

This basic biological stress response is one that he shares with the monkeys, as well as the leopard and all other creatures of the animal kingdom. Everyone in that life or death drama is completely in the moment as their fight or flight response kicks in.

The monkeys above swarmed the leopard. They did not run away. Their calls could be heard across monkey species, allowing monkeys of different types to form a sort of monkey alliance, constantly calling out and staring down at the leopard from multiple angles to let the leopard know they had him in their sights. Leopards like to attack by ambush. As the monkeys swarmed overhead, the leopard knew its cover was blown, and it gave up the hunt. Klaus made it safely back to camp, saved by his distant brothers and sisters, exhilarated by the experience of hearing, and actually understanding, the language of these distant relatives, separated by over 20 million years of evolution. For a moment, he remembered that he too was part of that great monkey alliance.

Though the Diana monkeys of today are not the Diana monkeys of 20 million years ago, fossil evidence shows that creatures that looked very much like Diana monkeys existed 20 million years ago, and are likely the common ancestor of ourselves *and* those monkeys who were sounding the alarm from those trees.

How did we split and become separate species? In order for new species to occur, there has to be some form of reproductive isolation. This usually happens as populations become geographically isolated from one another and end up occupying different environments. Slowly, generation after generation, some genes are passed on while others are not, and given the different environments, the two populations eventually become so different they can no longer reproduce with one another. They are now permanently isolated reproductively, and have become separate species.

The past 25 million years in East Africa have been an especially prime period for speciation among primates. Climate changes, along with high levels of volcanic activity, dramatically reshaped the Earth. creating numerous environmental niches within a fairly small geographic region. Populations that found themselves in lush jungle rainforests adapted very differently from those who found themselves in more sparsely vegetated woodlands or open savannahs. By 13 million years ago, our ancestors split from orangutans, and by eight million years ago, from gorillas. We split from chimpanzees and bonobos (a.k.a. pygmy chimpanzees) by about six million years ago.

WHY WE SING

The ability to sing is shared widely among birds and mammals. And while our closest relatives are quite good at communicating through singing, the most complex use of a "singing" language among mammals might not belong to them, but to prairie dogs. While they may not share much DNA with us, they do share a similar challenge. Much like the early hominids who first came down from the trees, prairie dogs are easily spotted in the wide-open grasslands by a vast range of predators. Singing is a survival strategy.

Prairie dogs have created different calls for coyotes, badgers, and hawks, all of which require different defense responses. In experimental situations, biologist Con Slobodchikoff has demonstrated that prairie dogs can sing different chirps to indicate the shape, color, speed, size, and mode of travel of a potential incoming threat.

While not as sophisticated as the songs of prairie dogs, most birds and mammals have at least some rudimentary singing abilities that allow them to communicate. The simplest singing systems in the animal kingdom involve two sounds, a low-pitched growl often used as a threat, and a higher pitched melody used to indicate friendliness, submission, or vulnerability. A dog growls deeply as a threat, and yelps or squeals meekly when threatened. A dog might also use a high-pitched whimper as he cuddles into a human, a clear request for a pet or cuddle. Weaver birds, crows, guinea pigs, rats, Tasmanian devils, elephants, and monkeys use low and high tones in similar fashion. "Simply stated," noted Eugene Morton of the National Zoo after a review of over 70 species, "birds and mammals use harsh, relatively low-frequency sounds when hostile and higher-frequency, more pure tonelike sounds when frightened, appeasing, or approaching in a friendly manner." Linguist John Ohala notes that these pitch variations are part of a universal "frequency code" that extends across species, in which low, deep, full sounds indicate dominance and aggression, while high thin sounds indicate harmlessness, submission, or a plea for connection. You tap into it every time you lower your voice to admonish your dog or raise your voice to ask for a snuggle.

There is significant evidence that our ancestors were using a much more complex singing system to connect and collaborate. Thousands of miles from the cacophony of the Tai forest or the chirping of prairie dogs on the North American Plains, Ann Fernald was sitting in an obstetrics unit in Germany listening to some interesting songs as well, those coming from the mothers of newborn humans. The hospital attracted mothers from all over the world;

many languages, and many cultures. But when they spoke to their babies it was as if they were all tapping into that same evolutionary heritage that Klaus was trying to uncover in the Tai Forest. They raised their pitch, exaggerated their emotional tone, slowed down, shortened their sentences, and often repeated themselves. They were using that ancient singing language, and though they were coming from many different cultures and speaking many different languages, Ann knew the tunes. It was there that she discovered four universal songs of baby-talk:

1. The approval song with its rising and then falling pitch (GOOD girl!);
2. The warning and prohibition song with its short, sharp staccato (No! Stop!);
3. The lingering and smooth, low frequency comfort song ("oh .... poor little baby ..."); and
4. The song she calls "The Attention Bid," a high, rising melody, often used for asking questions and calling attention to objects ("Where's the BALL?").

To explore just how universal these songs might be, Greg Bryant and Clark Barrett of UCLA recorded English-speaking mothers talking to their babies and went into the Amazon rainforest to see if the Shuar, a group of remote hunter- horticulturalists, also knew the tunes. They did.

The universality of the songs indicates that they are very old. Our first ancestors probably knew similar tunes. We hear similar tunes among our closest relatives, gorillas and chimpanzees. When lowland gorillas hear strange sounds or spot obscured observers, they sound a mild alert that Dian Fossey called the "question bark." The bark, with a rising intonation that falls at the end, was described by Fossey as sounding like "Who are you?"

Jane Goodall describes "inquiring pant-hoots" that rise in pitch, like human questions used by chimpanzees. After the pant-hoot a chimp will listen quietly for a response from another chimp, and in getting one, learns the whereabouts and identities of other chimps nearby. Long before full human languages developed 100,000 years ago, we were probably sending messages through simple songs like these. And the songs we sang said a great deal about who we were. We asked questions. We showed compassion for one another. We helped each other avoid dangers, and we offered each other encouragement. Taken together, they represent four key capacities: teaching, learning, cooperation and compassion. All would have been great assets as we walked off into the dangerous open grasslands.

SIX MILLION YEARS AGO: WE WALKED

As you think about just how vulnerable Klaus was as he walked through a forest full of dangerous predators like that leopard, consider just how astounding it is that we ever evolved to come down from the trees at all. Yet we did. About six or seven million years ago, we start to see the tell-tale signs of bipedalism (walking on two legs) emerging. Hominid bones found from that time show a pelvis starting to tilt sideways, an S-shaped spine, and a stiffened foot with upward curving toes, all of which would help us walk without waddling but reduced our capacities to climb trees.

But why? Why would we come down from the safety of the trees where fruit was plentiful and predators were not? How could we even begin to escape or compete with the big cats who could run up to 60 mph and had powerful jaws and ferocious fangs and claws? We had no weapons – natural or man-made – and weren't even as tall or large as we are today. We were just 4 feet tall and weighed about 110 pounds, the size of a husky third-grader.

How did we do it? Why did we do it?

We probably had no choice. The Earth was cooling and forests were shrinking, especially in East Africa, where our ancestors lived. Dense rain forests were giving way to woodlands and open grasslands. Fruit dwindled along with the dwindling forests. What fruit was left was being eaten up by monkeys who had developed abilities to eat unripened fruit, picking over the trees before we could even get to them.

As fruit sources dwindled, one strategy for survival was to simply get better at obtaining fruit. The ancestors of chimpanzees did this, using their remarkable agility to swing through trees in order to get at hard-to-reach fruit, and to occasionally pick off unsuspecting prey. Another strategy was to adapt to a fruitless diet where there was less competition. The ancestors of gorillas did this, moving to a diet of leaves and growing to large sizes that slowed their metabolism, requiring fewer calories.

But while these strategies could work in dense forested environments, they would not work in lightly forested woodlands and grasslands where our ancestors lived. Leaves and fruit were not as plentiful. Instead of focusing on just one food source, we developed abilities eat many kinds of food, including meat, and to move more efficiently on land so that we could cover more ground and thereby gather more food. We also retained some of our climbing abilities so could exploit a wide range of foods in the trees, on the ground, and under the ground (roots and tubers).

In other words, we didn't give up on tree-climbing and become bipedal overnight. One of the best-preserved skeletons from four million years ago, nicknamed 'Ardi,' shows that our ancestors at this time retained grasping toes and other features that would still allow them to climb remarkably well by modern human standards, but they were also not as efficient at walking as we are.

Many people assume we became bipedal so we could use tools, but we wouldn't start using tools for at least a million years after we first started walking. The original advantage of walking on two legs was efficiency. While chimps only walk about 1.5 miles a day, a modern human can walk about six miles a day using the same amount of energy. Our earliest ancestors were probably not as efficient at walking as we are today, but even a slight increase in efficiency would have allowed them to travel and gather foods over a wider range and still maintain the calorie balance they needed to survive and reproduce.

Over time, the more efficient walkers were more likely to reproduce, and so generation after generation we became more and more adapted to walking, able to cover more and more territory.

While standing up made us more visible to predators, it also allowed us to spot them and take away the element of surprise, just as those Diana monkeys did for Klaus. This is where our ancient ability to sing would be so important.

Singing, collaborating, and walking on two legs would set off a cascade of changes that would make us who we are today. With our hands free, we could carry food back to our young and elderly, broadening our abilities to share, and eventually develop more sophisticated tools and technologies. Each technology not only improved our abilities to acquire food, but would also change how we worked and lived together. The hominid brain grew as we were able to obtain more calories to fuel its growth, and it needed to grow in order to deal with the increasing demands of cooperation and navigating increasingly complex social relationships.

By 2.5 million years ago, we were fully committed to life on the land. Our capacities to climb and live in the trees had dwindled along with the size of our arms, fingers, and toes. We could no longer grab a branch with our feet or swing effortlessly from tree to tree. But our legs were now long, straight, and efficient. We were no longer just walking. We were running, but before we could run efficiently, we would have to develop yet another key adaptation.

2.5 MILLION YEARS AGO: WE GOT FAT AND SWEATY

Our growing brains required a constant source of energy, which would have been difficult to maintain if it also required a constant source of food in sometimes unpredictable and sparse environments. Fortunately, we got fat. Fat is rich in energy, storing nine calories in each gram (vs. just 4 calories per gram of carbohydrate or protein). When food was scarce, we could call upon the fat reserves we stored on our bodies to sustain us. Those who could survive through the leanest of times would be those who would reproduce to create the next generation. And generation after generation, we got fatter.

The average monkey is born with about 3 percent body fat, while we humans are born with fifteen percent. A healthy human child will blossom to an energy-potent 25 percent body fat before settling back down into the teens in adulthood. A typical female hunter-gatherer has a body fat of about 15 percent, while a male weighs in at about 10 percent – thin by American standards, yet still much fatter than chimpanzees.

Getting fat was essential to our survival, and to this day we maintain a remarkable ability to pack it on when the feeding is good. Our tastes evolved to help us gorge on high calorie foods whenever they were available, so we have natural cravings for fatty or sweet foods, both of which are especially high in calories.

As we gained the capacity to store fat, we also lost our fur and covered our skin with sweat glands, allowing us to stay cool even in the heat of the African equatorial sun. While other animals have to rely on circulating air through their bodies as quickly as possible by panting, we can simply let the air move around us as we sweat, making us the most efficient air-cooled bio-engine on the planet.

TWO MILLION YEARS AGO: WE RAN.

By two million years ago, our ancestors started to look very different from chimpanzees. Our bodies became more adapted for life on the ground, not in the trees. Our legs grew longer and thinner near the ends, giving us a longer and lighter step. Our toes got shorter, our butts got bigger, and our arms grew shorter, allowing us to be more stable and efficient while running. Our heads became more separated from the shoulders, creating the need for the nuchal ligament, used to stabilize the head. Our joint surfaces expanded to reduce the shock of each footfall. The plantar arch and Achilles tendon gave us more elastic energy. Our legs became biological springs. The springy arch of our foot increases our running efficiency by 17%.

The combination of running adaptations makes running only 30-50 percent less efficient than walking. By 2004, the research team of Daniel Lieberman, Dennis Bramble, and David Carrier had identified 26 adaptations in the human body that were necessary for running that are not required for walking. As Chris MacDougal famously summarized, we were "Born to Run."

Despite all these remarkable adaptations for running, we're not very fast compared to other animals. The fastest land animals have four legs, allowing them to thrust themselves to speeds well over 40 mph and sometimes, as in the case of the cheetah, to over 60 mph. The fastest humans can only run about 27 mph.

But despite being slow, we had several key advantages. Our ability to sweat would allow us to move around in the heat of the day, while the most dangerous predators and scavengers rested in the shade. Though we did not yet have spear-tipped projectiles for hunting, we would have been able to gather plant foods and scavenge for meat across great distances in the heat of the day. Walking on two legs also freed our hands and allowed us to enter potentially dangerous situations to find or scavenge whatever we could, grab it, and then quickly carry it back to safer ground.

These abilities might also help explain a peculiar mystery in the archaeological record. By 1.9 million years ago, there is evidence that we were successfully hunting wild game such as kudu and wildebeest. But stone spear heads do not appear until 300,000 years ago, and it is nearly impossible to kill a large animal with a wooden tipped spear unless you're very close to the animal, which is impossible if the animal is not in some kind of distress. So if we were successfully hunting large game 1.9 million years ago, long before the invention of adequate weapons – how did we do it?

It turned out that being fat, sweaty, and able to cooperate is a deadly weapon. Lieberman's research team found that our running abilities, combined with our ability to burn fat reserves and cool ourselves with sweat, allowed us to jog faster and farther than most quadrupeds can sustain, especially in the hot midday sun. All we had to do was flush an animal like a kudu or wildebeest out of the herd and scare it into a gallop. It would need to pant to cool down, but it cannot pant while running. If we could keep it on the run over a long period of time, it would collapse of heat exhaustion. We could literally run our prey to death. They called it "persistence hunting."

Lieberman and his team had the biological markers and the mathematical evidence to support their claim. But while there were several stories of persistence hunting in cultures around the world, there had not been a confirmed observation that such a feat was possible.

The evidence they needed would come from a college dropout driven by a very big question. In the early 1980s, Louis Liebenberg was taking a philosophy of science class at the University of Cape Town when he started asking the big question of how humans ever came to contemplate big questions in the first place. He had a hunch that the first complicated thinking might have come from the challenge of tracking wild game, which would have forced early humans to use a great deal of imagination and reasoning to decode the path and whereabouts of an animal based on a few tracks in the earth. Like all great questions, the question took him farther than he ever thought possible, and before long he was trekking out into the desert to find one of the last bands of the Kalahari Bushmen still living a more or less traditional way of life. After finally finding them, he settled in and lived with them for four years.

One day they invited him on a hunt. They walked for nearly twenty miles before finally coming upon a herd of kudu. They started running. The herd scattered, allowing them to separate one from the herd. Each time the kudu ran under a tree to rest. they would flush it out into the sun while corralling it away from the herd, keeping it isolated. After a few hours of being chased, the kudu started to falter, and then fell to the ground. The Bushmen had their prey, and Louis had unequivocal evidence that persistence hunting is not only possible, but still happening today.

This means that for the past two million years, our ancestors have been routinely walking and running 20 miles to chase down wild animals. The traits that allowed them to do this are the same traits we have today. Yet today, few of us can run even a few miles at a time, let alone 20.

The Raramuri of the Copper Canyons of Mexico also engage in persistence hunting, running deer and wild turkeys to death. By frightening large turkeys into a series of take-offs, they eventually tire and lack the strength to get away from the hunters.

The Raramuri give us an enticing glimpse into the full potential of our endurance running bodies. Reports of their astounding running abilities reached bestselling author and sports journalist Chris MacDougal, who eventually found his way to their homeland to see them in action and write the bestselling book *Born to Run*. He reports that the Raramuri (also known as the Tarahumara) regularly run over 100 miles at a single go.

Most remarkably, Raramuri of all ages can run like this. In fact, it is often the elders – those over 50 years old – who are the fastest. In 1992, a few Raramuri came to the U.S. to race in the Leadville 100, an ultra-marathon of 100 miles over the Colorado Rockies. They wanted to bring their best, so they brought Victoriano Churro, a 55-year-old Raramuri grandfather.

Historian Francisco Almada reports that a Raramuri man once ran 435 miles without stopping, and reports of others running over 300 miles are not uncommon.

What allows the Raramuri to run so far, over such tough terrain, and for so long (well into old age), is that they run with that same gentle skitter step I had come to admire among my friends in New Guinea. Like our ancestors, they are running barefoot or with very thin homemade sandals. This forces them to stay light on their feet, taking short quick strides and landing on the ball of their forefoot in order to absorb the impact, rather than striding out and striking their heel, the style preferred by most runners shod in thick-soled running shoes.

Noting the low injury rate among barefoot runners around the world, Dan Lieberman did a study of the Harvard track team, comparing athletes who were forefoot strikers (barefoot style) versus those who were heel strikers. The injury rate for heel strikers was 2.6 times that of forefoot strikers.

But perhaps the most striking feature of the running style that Chris MacDougal and others found among the Raramuri, and that I witnessed among my friends in New Guinea, is the pure joy they take in running. It is not a penance for indulging in too much food. It is not "exercise" or "working out." It is fun. "Such a sense of joy!" legendary track coach Joe Vigil exclaimed as he watched the Raramuri laugh as they scrambled up a steep mountainside 50 miles into the Leadville 100.

When Ken Choubler, the race's founder, saw the Raramuri running after over 50 miles on his grueling mountain course, he would tell MacDougal that they looked normal—"freakishly ... normal." They didn't have their heads down, face grimacing with pain, just trying to tough it out. They were enjoying themselves. "That old guy?" MacDougal writes, "Victoriano? Totally cool. Like he just woke up from a nap, scratched his belly, and decided to show the kids how the big boys play the game."

Victoriano, age 55, won the race that day, edging out a younger Raramuri runner for the win. The top non-Raramuri competitor was six miles back.

MODERN HUMANS AND THE CREATIVE EXPLOSION

Taken all together, the evidence suggests that starting approximately two million years ago, we were still relying on the gathering of fruits, nuts, and tubers over a wide area as our primary means of subsistence. We scavenged and hunted when opportunities arose, and we were starting to develop some basic stone tools to cut and process our food.

A positive feedback loop started to emerge. The better we got at obtaining food, the more calories we had to grow our brains. As our brains grew, we got better at obtaining food. By about 500,000 years ago, we had enough intelligence to invent a stone-tipped spear capable of penetrating thick animal hides at great distances, and our upright running bodies were adapted to throw them with a force and accuracy unmatched among all other animals. A chimpanzee can be trained to throw, but they can only throw at about 20 mph. A human can wind their upright body up like a rubber band and let the rotational force of their full body, along with the rotation of their shoulder, combined to generate speeds of up to 9,000 degrees of rotation per second. Even a mediocre human athlete can throw up to 70 mph with remarkable accuracy. Most impressively, we could not only throw accurately enough to hit a rabbit, we could hit a *moving* rabbit. Our ability to hit a moving rabbit requires yet another key human skill: imagination.

Neil Roach, anthropologist at George Washington University, told MacDougal that "this ability to produce powerful throws is crucial to the intensification of hunting." Once we could obtain a steadier high-quality source of meat, "this dietary change led to seismic shifts in our ancestors' biology, allowing them to grow larger bodies, larger brains, and to have more children."

The positive feedback loop would continue as we domesticated fire approximately 400,000 years ago, allowing us to obtain more and more high-quality calories from our foods by cooking them. We could also stay warm in colder climates, expanding into new territories, and share stories and information as we sat around the fire well into the night, having artificially extended the day for the first time.

By 200,000 years ago the first modern humans, *Homo sapiens*, had arrived. Genetically, they were us. If you could transport a newborn from 200,000 years ago into the present, they would learn our language, go to school, and fit right in. Every human on the planet today can trace their roots back to these African ancestors, 200,000 years ago. We had dark skin to protect us from harsh ultraviolet rays of the sun. Compared to the animals we evolved from, we were fat and sweaty. But we could run long distances, throw, make tools, use our imaginations, and perhaps most importantly, communicate and collaborate better than any other creatures in the world.

Communication and collaboration allowed us to develop even more sophisticated technologies, including clothing, that would allow us to spread out of Africa and settle all over the world. Our trade networks expanded, allowing innovations to be shared over greater and greater distances. The archaeological record shows an explosion of creativity starting around 50,000 years ago, sometimes called *the Creative Explosion.* A technique for the mass manufacture of thin stone blades was discovered. Tools became more sophisticated and versatile. Atlatls, notched sticks into which we placed the butts of our spears, increased the amount of force we could use to hurl those spears, achieving faster speeds and more power. Nets and fishhooks allowed us to expand our diets to more seafood, while new methods of food preparation such as grinding and boiling allowed us to use and process more and more of the calories available to us. We told stories, painted pictures, made jewelry, and developed a rich, symbolic world that would tie us together into larger, more complex groups.

In short, we invented *culture.* We asked questions, made connections, and tried new things. From that moment forward, the pace of our cultural innovation would far outstrip the human body's ability to adapt to the new environments we created.

LEARN MORE

- The Story of the Human Body by Daniel Lieberman
- Born to Run by Chris McDougall
- RadioLab Podcast: Wild Talk
- RadioLab Podcast: Musical Language

THE (UN)MAKING OF THE MODERN BODY: RE-CLAIMING OUR HUMAN POTENTIAL

Our adaptations developed over millions of years in woodlands and open grasslands, where food was often low in calories and sometimes hard to find, not calorie-dense, plentiful and sitting on supermarket shelves; a place where cats were large and a constant threat to your life, not domesticated house pets; a place where you had to walk or run to get your food, not drive your car or submit an order on Amazon. Most importantly, it was a place where a strong desire for calorie-rich foods and an ability to store them as fat were useful strategies for surviving and passing on your genes, a place where a stress reaction that sends adrenaline rushing through your body could save your life, and a place where you wouldn't have to think about how to sneak in your exercise for the day. As such, we now struggle against our most basic instincts and impulses to maintain our minds and bodies in good health.

MISMATCH DISEASES

The ailments that come about from the mismatch between how we have evolved and the environments we now inhabit are called *mismatch diseases.* Mismatch diseases result from one of three conditions: (1) too much of something, (2) too little of something, or (3) new things or behaviors we have not yet adapted to. For example, compared to the environments of our ancestors, we have (1) too much fat and sugar, (2) too little movement and exercise, and (3) we aren't biologically adapted to the complexities of modern life, such as complex social networks, economic pressures, media, social media, and many others.

As a result, we suffer from several mismatch diseases related to overeating, lack of exercise, and high stress. Obesity, Type 2 diabetes, cavities, anxiety, depression, high blood pressure and other stress-related ailments that lead to strokes, heart attacks and other illnesses are just a few of the mismatch diseases that might result.

Remember Klaus's stress reaction as he fled from the leopard? The problem is that modern life can potentially induce a series of similar reactions, but while Klaus's situation was brief (a few minutes) with simple decisions and actions (evade the leopard) and a clear ending point (safety back at camp), many of our modern stressors are long-lasting (What am I going to do with my life?, 30-year mortgages), involve complex decisions, may not require any action (and therefore no outlet for all that extra energy and adrenaline), and have no clear ending point. Many people today live with a constant feeling of stress, and the health implications are tremendous. Long-term stress wreaks havoc on our cardiovascular system, which can lead to adult-onset diabetes. Our amygdala, which controls our fear response, grows and becomes hyper-reactive, leading to anxiety disorders. Our dopamine, which controls emotion, is depleted, leading to depression. And our frontal cortex, the place where we make decisions, atrophies, leading to poor judgment. Ultimately, Robert Sapolsky notes, "Most of us will have the profound

Westernized luxury of dropping dead someday of a stress-related disease."

A large number of addictions might also be considered mismatch diseases. We evolved to crave calories, sex, love, friendship, security, comfort, and novelty. Modern technology provides what are known as "supernormal stimuli" in all these areas. A supernormal stimulus takes key features from the natural objects we have evolved to crave and magnifies those aspects that are most stimulating, while offering very little or none of the actual reward we need.

In the 1950s, birds were tricked into preferring fake eggs with more vibrant colors over their own. In the human domain, a glazed donut is a cheap calorie-bomb loaded with a perfect ratio of fat and sugar stimuli encased in a soft form that's as easy to digest as it is to hold in your hand. It gives us all of the pleasure of eating a rich meal with none of the nourishment. We evolved to crave fat and high-calorie foods, and to gorge on them when we could; but the abilities to pack on the fat did not evolve in the context of cheap, plentiful donuts, greasy cheeseburgers, and sugary, high-calorie drinks. Our tastes and ability to store fat are a mismatch for today's environment of abundance, so we now face health risks from being too fat.

But we have "junk food" in other domains as well. Pornography offers supernormal sexual stimuli while providing none of the love, connection, and offspring that may result from real sex. Movies, TV shows, and video games provide a constant onslaught of novelty, excitement, and drama without any need to get out of our chairs. These supernormal stimuli not only exaggerate the things we have evolved to crave (sex, love, novelty, excitement), but do so without us having to put ourselves at any risk, socially or physically.

In short, there is a "junk food diet" available in virtually every domain of our needs and desires. When we feel stressed, lonely, hungry, or any of the other evolutionary triggers that would normally spring us into action to go out into the world to find food or a mate, we can instead gorge on pizza, donuts, porn, and movies. While none of these things will make us "sick" or addicted in moderation, they are dangerous in excess, and it's worth considering how we might experience life differently without them.

Junk food, porn and Netflix have become so common in our culture as to become the norm. About 74% of American men and 64% of American women are overweight. On average, we watch over five hours of TV every day. And while few people admit to watching porn, a recent study by the Max Planck Institute estimated that 50% of all Internet traffic is sex-related.

Most people would probably not even consider the idea that we can be "addicted" to something as mundane and normalized as junk food, porn, or Netflix. We tend to reserve the word "addiction" for hard drugs and alcohol. But recent studies in the science of addiction are demonstrating that there are deep and important changes inside the brain of those who have behavioral addictions that are similar to those with drug addictions.

At a biological level, our cravings are driven by dopamine, a neurotransmitter in the reward circuitry of the brain that plays a key role in elevating our motivation to take action. Dopamine levels rise in anticipation of a reward or when under high stress, encouraging us to act. Supernormal stimuli make dopamine levels spike, which is why they are so difficult to resist. However, when we indulge in these supernormal stimuli too often, we become desensitized to dopamine. Everyday pleasures seem bland and unsatisfying. We lack motivation, and when normal stimuli are no longer enough, we're forced to seek out supernormal stimuli to give us that rush of dopamine, and key brain changes emerge that are similar to those we see in substance addicts. There is reduced activity in the areas of the brain that control willpower and reduced abilities to handle everyday stresses, which often trigger more relapses into the addictive behavior. This can lead to a vicious cycle in which we feel very little pleasure and lack the willpower to avoid our "junk food diet" when we face even a minor stress. We take the edge off with a little indulgence, which only makes us want more while reducing our willpower and stress-resistance.

Most importantly, we become more and more numb to the pleasures of everyday life.

DISEASES OF CAPTIVITY

The dorsal fin of a killer whale in the wild stands strong and straight, an awe-inspiring symbol of their power as it crests over the water. But if you've ever seen a killer whale at SeaWorld, you'll notice that their fins curl lazily over to one side, a condition sometimes called "floppy fin syndrome." Scientists hypothesize that lack of movement, constant turning in tight spaces, dietary changes, and other aspects of captivity cause the condition. Though it's not life-threatening, it *is* a powerful symbol of how artificial environments can shape a biological body.

Our bodies are no different. We have crafted an artificial environment with soft chairs, beds, and pillows where the ground is always firm and perfectly flat, complete with transport devices that allow us to sit in comfort as we transport ourselves from one artificial comfort pod to the next, and the temperature is always about 72 degrees. We prepare food on counters, not squatting on the ground. We sit on toilets rather than squatting in the woods. We walk on sidewalks while wearing padded shoes with raised heels.

As a result, our bodies are like the floppy fins of SeaWorld. Katy Bowman, an expert in biomechanics and author of several bestselling books on natural human movement, refers to the floppy fin as a "disease of captivity," and claims that so are our "bum knees, collapsed arches, eroded hips, tight hamstrings, leaky pelvic floors, collapsed ankles" and many more modern ailments. These diseases of captivity are a special subclass of mismatch diseases that affect the alignment and function of our bodies.

As a quick test of just how much of your own basic ability to move like our ancestors has been lost, try to sit in a deep squat with your feet flat on the ground. This is a natural rest position for humans. You see children playing in this position for long periods without experiencing any discomfort. People all over the world who live in environments with few chairs can rest in this position well into old age. Most Americans have lost the ability to get into this position by age 20, and only a very small percentage find the position comfortable and restful. In a survey of resting positions worldwide, anthropologist Gordon Hewes found that deep squatting "has a very wide distribution except for European and European-derived cultures."

While this may seem like an unimportant skill, it's a quick demonstration of our lost potential and has serious implications for our health, abilities, and longevity. An inability to squat may indicate weak glutes or a weak core, which are essential to balance and basic human movements like running, walking, and jumping. Your hips might lack the flexibility and mobility they once had. Hip mobility is essential for stability and balance, so tight hips put you at risk for serious injury. And the movements we make to adjust for tight hips often lead to back pain and other ailments. As you age, these conditions become a matter of life and death. As Katy Bowman points out, "the more you need to use your hands and knees to get up from the floor, the greater your risk of dying from all causes." Perhaps it's a telling sign of just how damaging our comforts might be that Katy Bowman chooses to live in a house with almost no furniture.

Another test: try walking or running barefoot – but go easy on this one. Don't try to go out and run 100 miles like a Raramuri, or even one mile if it's your first try in a while. The muscles and tendons that hold up your arch and give you the spring you need to run barefoot are probably weak with underuse. You might seriously injure yourself because of your dependence on shoes. You probably won't get very far anyway because of the pain on your skin. Without the natural callouses of barefoot humans, every little pebble and stick will deliver piercing pain, and you may find many surfaces either too hot or too cold. Your feet are like prisoners trapped in the dark, sensory-deprived caves of comfortable shoes, coming out into the light for the first time. It will take a while to adjust to the light.

It's worth it, though. Over time your feet will adapt and regain much of their lost potential. Your skin contacting the Earth will deliver key signals to your brain to make you more sure-footed and balanced. Your posture and flexibility will improve as you stand flat-footed without an artificially raised heel or supported arch, and over 100 muscles and 33 joints that have weakened in their captive state will be set free to strengthen and unleash their full potential, helping you become stronger, faster, injury-resistant, and more agile. Harvard anthropologist Dan Lieberman notes that in the Kenyan villages where he works, most people grow up barefoot and he has yet to encounter a fallen arch or many of the other foot ailments that plague many Americans.

"We aren't really sick," says Katy Bowman, "we are just starved." We are missing key nutrients, "movement nutrients." Our bodies are made up of cells. When cells get activated, they get fed with oxygen, which flushes out cellular waste and revitalizes them. We feed our cells by using them, by putting them under load. Those muscles and tissues we put under more load grow and stay healthy, while those we don't use wither and die. When it comes to body tissues, you either use it or lose it. Your body changes shape as some parts grow stronger and others wither. The alignment of your body parts shifts as some muscles pull more strongly on your joints than others. Ultimately, the shape and alignment of your body is the result of how you move.

Instead of "exercise," Katy Bowman suggests that we need a steadier and balanced diet of movement. Someone who exercises regularly works out for about 300 minutes per week. But our ancestors were moving *3,000* minutes per week; and their movements fed all their body tissues, not just a few select spots. Bowman suggests moving away from modern comforts that restrict movement and reduce muscle load, such as shoes, chairs, desks and sidewalks. She recommends incorporating as much natural movement into your everyday life as possible. Replace that short drive with a nice walk or run. Even better, run it barefoot. Even better than that, get off the sidewalk and let your feet and legs receive the rich movement nutrients of balancing along uneven surfaces with small surprises at every step.

Recent headlines point out that "sitting is the new smoking," with consequences for your health that are *worse* than smoking. The problem is that many people are replacing sitting with standing by using standing desks, but this is only slightly better than sitting. "Standing is the new sitting," Bowman says. We need to move.

A steady diet of rich and varied movements will strengthen your full body and bring it into alignment. When your body is in alignment, your muscles can work together with your joints and the elastic power of your tendons to get the most out of every movement. Tom Myers, an expert in human anatomy, suggests it might be worth considering the entire human body not as a collection of 600 muscles, but just one, held together by a stretchy rubbery tissue connected throughout your body known as the fascia. The fascia is "a crisscross of fibers and cables, an endless circulatory system of strength," he told Chris MacDougal. "Your body is rigged like a compound archery bow ... left foot to the right hip, right hip to the left shoulder, and it's tougher than any muscle." Such power is the result of millions of years of evolution. Our bodies are exquisitely crafted for complex, precise, and powerful movements such as running long distances, throwing with great precision, and fine tool making. Yet few humans ever utilize even a fraction of this potential, and the potential withers before it can be materialized.

RECLAIMING OUR HUMAN POTENTIAL

French Naval Officer Georges Hebert traveled the world and noticed that he found the fittest and most capable people in the most remote French colonies. Of the indigenous people of Africa and the mountain tribes of Vietnam, he famously noted that "Their bodies were splendid, flexible, nimble, skillful, enduring, resistant, and yet they had no other tutor in Gymnastics but their lives in Nature." He found strong, fit women in such places that assured him that gendered differences in strength were largely cultural.

In 1902, he was stationed at Martinique when a violent volcano eruption turned the normally idyllic island retreat into a living hell. A black cloud moved out from the volcano at 420 mph, and superheated steam of over 1,000 degrees shot into the nearby city of Saint-Pierre, killing 30,000, the entire population of the city, in a matter of minutes. There were only two survivors in the main city. Thousands continued to fight for their lives where the initial blast had spared them. It was a horror of hot steam, scorched earth, and fiery rain, with pit vipers slithering violently about as they were chased off the mountain by the coming heat.

Hebert's job was to go into that hell and rescue as many people as possible. He coordinated the rescue of over 700. Afterwards, he would reflect on what allowed some people to survive while others perished. He learned that those who survived had a remarkable capacity to move spontaneously and creatively to avoid danger, while those who perished simply froze in fear and hopelessness.

Driven by a desire to train people for future calamities, he dedicated himself to understanding human movement. He watched children play and identified "10 natural utilities" (walking, running, crawling, climbing, balancing, jumping, swimming, throwing, lifting, and fighting), and created outdoor training facilities where people could practice these basic skills. They looked like playgrounds for adults. He had one firm rule: No competing. He felt that competition would encourage people away from true fitness. Once people start competing, they start focusing on specializing some movements over others, and end up out of balance and unable to perform with the spontaneity and creativity of our full human potential.

He called his method "methode naturelle," the natural method, and it was based on one simple mantra: "be fit to be useful." Hebert saw no use in appearing physically fit, with large biceps and large chest muscles. He simply wanted his navy recruits and anyone else who used the method to be able to perform when it mattered. Though he was averse to competition, he wanted to prove the worth of his methods, so he put a bunch of ordinary navy recruits through the program and soon had them performing as well as world class decathletes.

He also released a short film demonstrating his own talents. In the film, he leaps out of his dining room chair, runs outside, and scales a 30-foot tree in seconds, leaps down from branch to branch, and then proceeds to climb up the sides of buildings with equal speed, first by himself and then with a child on his back. He then races to catch a moving train and leaps off of the moving train from a towering bridge into the water below.

Unfortunately, all of his recruits died, along with his method, in the grim and deadly days of World War One. By the end of the Second World War, the methods were all but forgotten.

As Europe and America rebuilt into increasingly post- industrial economies with more and more jobs that required sitting for long hours, people sought the most efficient ways possible to exercise, trying to squeeze their daily dose of movement into smaller time frames and smaller spaces. Specialized weight machines, treadmills, and stationary bikes transformed gyms into big business where steroid-injected hard-bodied men and impossibly skinny women were the icons of good health. (Think back to the "Nacirema.")

The machines are not designed to make us useful. They are designed to shape our bodies toward cultural ideals that are displays of superficial fitness rather than true health and wellbeing. Women are encouraged to lose weight, so they tend to focus on fat-burning aerobic exercises rather than strength and agility. Men are encouraged to build broad shoulders and large chests, so they focus on lifting heavy weights with their upper bodies, often losing mobility in their shoulders and making them more prone to injury and less able to do basic human movements.

Many of our gym exercises pull our bodies more and more out of alignment, like the floppy fins of SeaWorld. Overwork your chest, and your shoulders shift forward. Artificially isolate your quads, and you create imbalances in your legs that can lead to knee problems. A healthy, functional body is a body that is aligned through a healthy mix of diverse movements.

The worst effect of this focus on appearances is that the body itself becomes alienated from our being. It becomes an object to be manipulated and shaped to fit this ideal, rather than an integral part of our being. We focus on how we look rather than the simple joy of moving.

Recently, Hebert's methods are being rediscovered and reinvented in a number of different movements. Free-running parkour groups are spreading all over the world and look to Hebert as one of their founding fathers, taking his mantra of "be fit to be useful" as a core gospel. Erwan Le Corre, founder of movant, is perhaps the most dedicated student of the method. He tried to track down any remaining ancestors of Hebert's method, and then set about immersing himself in studying those who had inspired Hebert.

Ido Portal, who studies movement practices all over the world – from Afro-Brazilian Copoeira to the many martial arts of Asia – incorporates a vast range of movements into his everyday life to explore the boundaries of human movement potential. Portal sees this as a deeply human pursuit, tied to our evolution. "Movement complexity is by far the reason why we became human," he says, "The reason for our brain development is related to movement complexity."

Today there is a new emergence of natural training methods around the world often going under the name "functional fitness." Cross Fit, the world's most successful and fastest-growing fitness movement, encourages their trainers to eliminate mirrors and focus on helping people be more functional rather than just looking good. Others, like the BarStarrz and other "body weight warriors" are finding ways to use nothing but their own body weight and the objects in their environment for their training.

By 2015, America's fastest growing sport was obstacle racing. *American Ninja Warrior* became one of America's most popular TV shows, and hundreds of thousands tested themselves in Tough Mudders, Warrior Dashes, and Spartan Races, intense obstacle races that require a diverse array of human movements and endurance. Though there is a competition element to many of these events, most people are simply there to see if they can complete the course, and cooperation is often essential. Many of the obstacles cannot be overcome without the aid of others. Once someone receives aid, they usually pay it forward. And as they do, they seek to find that same joy in moving through the world that Hebert witnessed around in remote African villages, that Coach Vigil saw as the Raramuri ran, and that I saw among my friends in New Guinea.

THE POWER TO CHANGE OUR HABITS

By my mid-30s, I was well on my way to falling victim to any one of the many mismatch diseases that plague our time, and I had already developed several diseases of captivity. I could not sit in a squat. I could not even run. At 29, I tore my meniscus and developed a mysterious hip pain that no doctor could explain. Every time I tried to go for a run, I would wake up the next day with a swollen knee and an immovable leg. So I gave it up. I became mostly sedentary, dedicating myself to my work. By 35, my body had adapted to life in a chair. My weight was creeping upward. I couldn't touch my toes. A couple of flights of stairs started to feel like a chore. I also started developing a number of other health issues, such as high cholesterol and high blood pressure. Our bodies not only evolved to run, throw, and squat, we had to conserve energy every chance we could, so we evolved to rest and seek comfort. I found comfort in abundance and gorged on it.

Fortunately, we not only developed adaptations to seek comfort, store fat, and feel stress, we also developed the power to intentionally reflect on our activities and change them. The core of our humanity, the ability to ask questions, make connections, and try new things offers a way out.

These abilities are reflected in the evolution of the brain. The oldest part of the brain lies at the core of the brain at the stem: the basal ganglia. Named the "reptilian complex" by neuroscientist Paul MacLean, it evolved hundreds of millions of years ago. It guides our basic autonomic body processes and is responsible for instinctual cravings and behaviors. On top of this is what MacLean calls the "paleomammalian complex," sometimes simplified as the "mammal" brain. It evolved along with the first mammals and is responsible for emotions, long-term memory, and more complex behaviors. Surrounding all of this is the newest part of the brain, the neocortex. It is responsible for higher order cognition, complex behavior, language, and spatial reasoning. In humans, the neocortex has grown to become 76% of the brain.

As our neocortex expanded, we became less and less controlled by nature and more by culture, less by impulse and more by reason, less by instinct and more by habit.

Habit is the compromise between being completely controlled by our instinct and being completely free to make intentional decisions about whatever we want to do. It is the trade-off we have made between instinct and reason in order to maintain speed and efficiency. Though we have become more and more adept at making complex decisions, it would be too slow and inefficient to have to make decisions about every single thing we ever did on a day-to-day basis. To improve speed and efficiency, our brains developed the ability to do our most repetitive routines without making any decisions at all. We could do them by habit.

Habit formation works by passing control over the most routine behaviors to the more primitive basal ganglia. As we do a routine over and over again our brain can determine what prompts the routine to begin ("the cue") and what prompts it to end ("the reward") and creates a "chunk" of automatic behavior. Brushing your teeth is a "chunk." You get the cue (time for bed) and without wrestling with any complex decisions simply go through the motions of putting the toothpaste on the brush, brushing your teeth, and rinsing the brush. "Chunking" allows complex activities to be controlled by the super-efficient "lizard brain" of the basil ganglia.

Habits were essential to our evolutionary success, but as we know, not all habits are good. Because habits are controlled by the same region of the brain as our instincts and impulses, some habits can feel like unchangeable urges that are out of our control, but we *can* change them.

In *The Power of Habit*, Charles Duhigg tells the story of a woman named Lisa, an overweight smoker who struggled to hold a job and pay off her debts. When her husband left her for another woman, she hit rock-bottom. Alone, depressed and without any feeling of self-worth, she decided she needed some kind of goal to straighten out her life. She set the goal of trekking across the deserts of Egypt. She had no idea if such a trip were even possible, but she did know that the only way to make such an arduous journey would be to quit smoking. She gave herself one year to prepare.

The only significant intentional decision she made was to quit smoking, and she did so by going for a jog each time she felt the urge to light up. As Duhigg points out though, this one simple change changed everything. It "changed how she ate, worked, slept, saved money, scheduled her workdays, planned for the future, and so on." She made that trip to Egypt, and within four years she was a happily engaged home-owner and marathon runner with a steady job as a graphic designer.

The key to changing our habits is understanding how they work. A habit is made up of three parts, which together make up what Duhigg calls "the habit loop." First, there is a cue – a trigger that tells your brain to follow a chunk of automatic routine behavior. The second piece is the routine itself. The final piece is the reward. If the reward is strong, the habit is reinforced and becomes more and more engrained and automatic.

What allowed Lisa to change is that she did not attempt to change the cue (the urge to light up). Cues come from outside of our control. They are in our environment or deeply embedded in our brain. After years of smoking she could not remove the urge or sit idle and simply resist it. Her brain was telling her that she had to act, so she did. But she changed *how* she acted. She replaced the "chunk" or routine of smoking with running. Importantly, running offered her brain a sufficient reward – a runner's high, a feeling of good health, and a sense of accomplishment – so the new routine received additional reinforcement each time she did it. Eventually, it became a habit and she no longer needed to make a conscious decision to go running. It became automatic.

To change a habit, you have to study the cues that trigger the habit and understand the true reward that you seek. For example, if you have a habit of eating ice cream every night with your friends, it might not just be the satiating taste of ice cream that you crave. The true reward might be that it's a break from the stress of studying, or time out with friends. Carefully note the time and circumstances of your next ice cream craving. Are you stressed or overwhelmed by your work? Are you feeling lonely? Are you hungry? Do an experiment to see if just a walk down the hall and a chat with friends fulfills your needs, or if you are just hungry, grab a healthy snack and see if that gets you past the urge. Whatever creates a sufficient reward can become your new habit.

Sometimes you have to do more and actually change the environment around you. Make it easy for yourself to engage in good habits and more difficult to engage in bad habits.

For example, as I adapted to my inactive life of chairs and cars that was leading to the demise of my health, my bike ended up stored away on a hard-to-reach hook in the garage overhanging my car. In this environment, the bike was simply too far out of reach to seem like a reasonable possibility. Removing the bike would require backing the car out, getting out a ladder, and then trying to keep my weak and stiff body balanced on the ladder while lifting the bike off the hook and down onto the ground. It would have never happened had my neighbor not given me a new bike seat for my two-year-old old son that I felt obligated to try out to show that I appreciated the gift.

After trying out the bike seat, I was too lazy to put the bike back on the hook, and just stuffed the bike back into the garage behind the car. Suddenly there was a shift in my environment. When I walked out to my car to drive to work the next morning, the bike was behind the car. As I was moving the bike out of the way, I remembered the fun I'd had on it with my son the day before, and the next thing I knew, I was riding the bike to work.

I parked the bike behind the car again that day and every day. Every morning for several weeks I would struggle with the decision of whether or not to bike or take the car. Taking the car involved moving the bike out of the way, driving the car out of the garage, and then re-parking the bike in the garage before leaving for work. It was complicated, so the bike kept winning. Within a few weeks, I wasn't even asking myself whether I should take the bike or the car. It was a habit. And it stuck. No amount of snow or cold weather could break it. The next year I didn't even bother buying a parking pass. Two years later I sold the car.

I started looking at my other habits. At work, I often found myself checking Facebook and cruising the Internet. I found that the cue was stress. Each time I felt stressed and overwhelmed, I sought relief on the Internet. I decided to replace the routine of Internet surfing with push-ups. So each time I started feeling stressed, I did push-ups. It cleared my head, gave me a quick rush of endorphins, and I could get back to work.

I started making a habit of breaking habits and trying new things. My body started to transform. Before long, I looked and felt as good as I had when I was twenty years old. But soon I surpassed even that and started feeling stronger, lighter, and more agile than I ever thought possible. I started thinking back to my friends in New Guinea and the remarkable things they could do. *Could I do those things?* I wondered.

I learned to do handstands, then some basic gymnastics, and then turned to people like Erwan Le Corre and Ido Portal, who were exploring the limits and potential of human movement.

As I was writing this chapter, I started another new habit: running. I made a simple rule for myself: *If I'm taking the kids, take the bike. If not, run.* I strapped on a backpack and started running everywhere. I ran slow, easy, and smooth, using the light barefoot step of our ancestors that I had seen in New Guinea and that MacDougal saw among the Raramuri. My body immediately began to adapt. My muscles ached for a few days, but quickly grew stronger to adjust to the new loads. Within just a few weeks it was a habit. I didn't even bother to go to the garage anymore to grab the bike. I just stepped out into the cold morning air and let it rip.

I was most concerned about how the experiment would affect my bad hip and knee. As I expected, they ached through the first two weeks, and I was sure that I would be giving up on running for good after 28 days. But by week three, the pain seemed to be subsiding.

By Day 28 I felt so good I couldn't stop. I kept running. I had come to enjoy the freedom of moving through the world without a car or bike to worry about. Everything I needed was always right with me. I felt free, fast, light, and agile. And I enjoyed the steady stream of endorphins that came with the ongoing "runner's high" I received in little bits throughout a day of running here and there.

One day, while listening to a good book on my headphones, I ran for 90 minutes – only stopping because I had to run to a meeting. I was sure that after a long run like that, I would soon be feeling the familiar hip and knee pain that would leave me immobile for a day or so. But I woke up the next day with no pain. I started running longer and longer distances, blissfully absorbing audiobooks as I ran. Using the light, elastic gate of our ancestors, I skittered along trails just as my friends in New Guinea do. Even after a 20-mile day, I didn't feel tired or winded. Instead I felt a blissful calmness. I started wondering where my limit might be.

So one ordinary Wednesday, I set off running into a brisk 36-degree morning. My feet skittered across the earth with ease, and I felt as if I were being carried gently along by the continuous whirl of my feet doing what they were meant to do. My breath was steady and easy. I lost myself in the deep thought of a good book. Three hours later, I noticed that my friend's class was getting out, so I stopped in to visit with him. I had already run 18 miles and I wanted to know, *Could I run a marathon?*

After a brief chat with my friend, I hit the trail again. The next 8 miles were as blissful as the first 18. It was a strange experience. I have been enculturated to believe that running 26.2 miles is almost superhuman, and most certainly extreme and dangerous. I have been led to believe that you have to be crazy to do it, that you only do it when you really have "something to prove." I would never have thought that it could be fun, enjoyable, or relaxing.

Relaxing? Strange as it may seem, that is what I felt above all other feelings as I finished. I felt deeply relaxed. My friends were amazed, and said they couldn't believe that I was able to train for a marathon. I felt confused by the word "train." At no point did I ever feel like I was "training" for anything. I realized that instead of "training," I had simply slowly been changing my habits over the past six years. I went from a lifestyle that involved a lot of sitting in cars, at desks, and on sofas to a lifestyle of constant movement. By the time I ran the marathon, I was habitually moving a minimum of 8 to 10 miles per day.

The best way I can describe it is that I just got into the habit of moving, and one day I just happened to run 26 miles.

LEARN MORE

- Natural Born Heroes by Chris McDougall
- Move Your DNA by Katy Bowman
- The Power of Habit by Charles Duhigg

Challenge Three: The 28 Day Challenge

Your challenge is to try something new or change a habit by dedicating yourself to doing it every day for 28 days.

Objective: Practice trying new things, experience more, and to reflect more deeply on how humans learn and create new habits, as well as how you, specifically, can better identify what conditions or techniques work best for you when you are trying to learn something new or change your habits.

Step 1: Choose something you would like to do (or stop doing) over the next 28 days. Take a picture of yourself doing this thing and post it to Instagram #anth101challenge3

Ideas: Slow Media Diet, Slow Carb Diet, running, a new instrument, movement, exercise, gratitude, writing, or stop doing something (smoking, sugar, alcohol, video games, Netflix, porn)

Step 2: Post regular updates of your progress. Post videos of your progress if possible. It is always fun to really see how much you have learned.

Step 3: At the end of 28 days, reflect on the following:

- How successful were you?
- Under what conditions were you most successful?
- What were your barriers to success
- How can you get past them?
- What did you learn about how you learn?

For details and inspiration go to anth101.com/challenge3

Lesson Four
Language

Our most basic assumptions are embedded in the basic elements of our everyday lives.

THE POWER OF LANGUAGE

On her first day as a sign-language interpreter for a local community college, Susan Schaller spotted a deaf man sitting alone and intensively studying the people around him in a Reading Skills class. She introduced herself with a greeting gesture and her name sign, as if to say, "Hi, my name is Susan." He copied her, as if to say back, "Hi, my name is Susan."

What's your name?" she asked. "What's your name?" he responded. He studied her carefully, copying her every move, and asking for her approval with his eyes. She soon realized that this 27-year-old man, named Ildefonso, had no concept of language. "We were only inches apart, but we might as well have been from different planets; it seemed impossible to meet."

She could not help but recognize his desire to learn, and felt called to teach him. It was long, arduous, and frustrating work. Nothing she did seemed to break through.

Eventually, she settled on the idea of doing an "imaginary Ildefonso skit" in which she would talk to an empty chair as if

Ildefonso was sitting there, then pop over to the other chair to respond, thereby modeling a conversation between herself and an imaginary Ildefonso. It was a bizarre scene and felt strange. Week after week she had these imaginary conversations. "I began to worry about my sanity," she writes.

After a grueling, mind-numbing, and apparently hopeless session, Ildefonso suddenly perked up. "The whites of his eyes expanded as if in terror," Schaller writes. He was having a breakthrough. He sat still, as if pondering the revelation, and then excitedly started looking around the room, "slowly at first, then hungrily, he took in everything as though he had never seen anything before." He started slapping his hands down on objects and looking for Susan to respond. "Table," she signed as he slapped his hand on the table. "Book," she signed as he touched a book, and then "door," "clock," and "chair" in rapid succession has he pointed around the room. Then he stopped, collapsed his head into his arms folded on the table, and wept.

"He had entered the universe of humanity, discovered the communion of minds. He now knew that he and a cat and the table all had names ... and he could see the prison where he had existed alone, shut out of the human race for twenty- seven years."

LANGUAGE LEARNING IN NEW GUINEA

When I first arrived in the rainforests of New Guinea, I saw three things: trees, bushes, and grass. Of course, there was a wide range of different types of trees, bushes, and grasses, but having no language for them, they disappeared into a large mass of stimuli that I simply knew as "the forest." I had no language to make sense of what I was seeing – no web of meanings to create the background upon which what I saw could take on some significant definition. I could not tell food from foul, or medicine from poison, and I was completely mystified by the meanings my friends could glean from the forest as we walked. With their eyes always scanning their surroundings, they were constantly reacting to the messages they could see and hear, variously lighting up with delight and sighing with disappointment, laughing, groaning, shaking their head this way and that as they went.

Anxious to explore their world of meanings, I set about learning the language. The first phrase I could identify seemed to be a common greeting, as I heard it over and over again every morning as we watched people stroll by the house on their way down the mountain toward their gardens. "*Neliyongbipkatopbani!*" they would sing out as they passed. I wrote it down and repeated it to my brother Lazarus, asking him what it means.

"It means, *I am going to the garden.*" he said. "Great!" I thought to myself, a subject, verb, and an object. I could use this to start unlocking the language using a technique we call frame substitution. With frame substitution, the researcher uses a known phrase as a "frame" and just tweaks ("substitutes") one part of it to see what changes.

"How do you say, *He is going to the garden*?" I asked. "Eliyongbipkatopbana." The words were too fast for me to decipher where one word stopped and another began, so I ran them all together in my notebook.

A pattern was emerging. The change in subject from "he" to "I" had changed the beginning and end of the phrase (**Ne**liyongbipkatopban**i** vs. **E**liyongbipkatopban**a**).

I sat still and pondered the revelation for a moment and then excitedly started asking for more words. I felt like Ildefonso awakening to a new world. I was having a breakthrough. I excitedly started scribbling notes into my notebook. Other bits of language I had recorded suddenly made sense. It was as if had broken a code and a world of mystery was revealing itself to me. Like Ildefonso pointing in rapid succession to tables, books, doors, clocks, and chairs, I also started gathering new terms using the framework of this sentence as a starting point. I asked how one would say "she is going to the garden" and found the beginning and end changed again. I started rattling off different subjects, from he and she and on to they and we.

Then I was ready to discover the pronoun and verb ending for "you."

"How would you say, '*You are going to the garden*?'" I asked.

"Neliyongbipkatopbani," he answered, which was already established as "*I* am going to the garden."

"No, no." I corrected, "*You* are going to the garden." "Neliyongbipkatopbani," he responded again.

"No, no!" I responded in frustration. "*You! You* are going to the garden."

"No, no," he said. "I'm staying right here. You are still very confused."

WHAT IS A WORD?

One of the biggest challenges of learning a language among people who do not read and write is that they do not necessarily think about their language as a collection of discrete words in the same way that we do.

Likewise, one of the biggest challenges of learning a language among people who *do* read and write is that they don't not always talk like they write. Learning the written form may be entirely different from learning how to speak. One of comedian George Carlin's favorite English words was "ommina," as in "Ommina go catch the bus and head home." Humans can make about 4,000 different sounds. About 400 of these are used in languages around the world, with most languages using about 40 different sounds. The sounds a language uses are called *phonemes*. These sounds include consonants and vowels, and in some languages there are also clicks and tones.

If you do not learn a phoneme when you are young, it can be difficult to speak and understand later in life. English speakers struggle to understand the tones in a tonal language. Japanese speakers often struggle to pronounce the "r" sound used in many languages. And the plethora of unique "clicks" used in Khoisan languages of southern Africa are difficult for everyone except the

Khoisan. English-speakers learning Korean often struggle not only to say certain words but also to distinguish words like pul and phul, which both simply sound like "pull" to an English speaker, but phul uses an aspirated 'p' thereby distinguishing the word as "grass" rather than "fire."

Sometimes these phonemic differences create unique abilities in the cultures and speakers that use them. The Piraha of the Amazon use just 11 sounds, including three tones. The heavy use of these tones allow the Piraha to whistle messages to one another through the rainforest across great distances. In West Africa, speakers of tonal languages can use "talking drums" that allow the drummer to vary the pitch to mimic speech and send messages up to five miles. Tonal languages might also have an effect on human abilities. In one study, Diana Deutsch found that Mandarin speakers were nine times more likely than English speakers to have perfect pitch, the remarkable ability to precisely name any pitch, whether it comes from a piano or the hum of an air conditioner.

Though the local language contained a few new phonemes that made it difficult for me to learn, I was fortunate that many of the people in the village spoke Tok Pisin, a creole that had developed over the past few centuries of contact with Europeans. The language is a mix made up of mostly English-derived words along with some German and local words. I had no trouble saying "You are going to the garden" in Tok Pisin (you simply say "*yu go long gaden.*") Tok Pisin has become a national lingua franca, facilitating communication for speakers of over 800 different languages in Papua New Guinea. With a relatively small vocabulary made up of many familiar words, I was able to converse in the language in a month and became fluent soon after that.

But it was the local language that enchanted me. As psychologist Lera Boroditsky notes, "If people learn another language, they inadvertently also learn a new way of looking at the world." I sensed that I was on the verge of a new way of seeing the world.

I changed tactics and returned to the foundations of frame substitution to build on what I already knew. "How would you say, '*he is going to the house*'" I asked. "Emi**am**katopbani." Now the code was breaking again. I noticed that the only change between that phrase and the phrase for going to the garden was *am* vs. *yongbip*, and could conclude that these were the words for house and garden, respectively. I excitedly asked for more and started filling my notebook. I reveled in my new language abilities. Mastering a common greeting like this gave me something to hold onto in what was otherwise a sea of unfamiliar sounds. But then a new mystery emerged the next morning. A man walked by my house as I was sitting on the veranda and said, "Neli yongbip ka*met*bani." By the time I unraveled what he meant by the statement, I was forced to realize that they were not just speaking differently. They were thinking differently too.

TRANSCENDING SPACE AND TIME

Vivian: Have you ever transcended space and time?
Edward: Yes. ... No. Uh, time not space. ... No, I don't know what you're talking about.

- I Heart Huckabees

The man was passing from the other direction, heading uphill, and that turned out to be the key difference. Ka**met**bani indicated that he was going uphill, while ka**top**bani indicated going downhill. Using frame substitution I found a vast collection of words indicating specific directions. This does not seem particularly different from English, in which we might say "I'm heading down there / up there / over there / etc." The key difference is not that we *can* say these things. It is that they *have* to. The direction indicator is built right into their grammar, so they have to say which direction they are facing or going every time they say hello. In this way, it is similar to Pormpuraaw, spoken by Australian Aborigines on the northern tip of

Queensland, Australia. As Lera Boroditsky says, "If you don't know which way is which, you literally can't get past hello."

In some languages these directional orientations take the place of left and right, so a speaker might say, "your north shoe is untied" or even "your north-northwest shoe is untied." As a result, people who speak languages like this exhibit the uncanny capacity for dead reckoning. They know exactly which direction is which at every moment of the day. Even small children know exactly what direction they are facing, even in unfamiliar territory after long travels. Stephen Levinson recounts that a speaker of Tzeltal (a Mayan language in the Mexican state of Chiapas) was blindfolded and spun around over 20 times in a dark house, yet he still knew which way was which.

I knew very little about all this at the time. I only knew that my friends in New Guinea were experiencing the world differently than I was. I felt much like Wilhelm von Humboldt must have felt when, in the early 1800s, he started to realize that American Indian languages had radically different grammatical structures from European languages. "The difference between languages is not only in sounds and signs but in worldview," he proclaimed. While he recognized that any thought could be expressed in any language, he became keenly aware of the fact that a language shapes thought by "what it encourages and stimulates its speakers to do from its own inner force." In other words, if you have to figure out what direction you are facing every time you greet someone, you get pretty good at telling direction.

Enchanted by the possibilities of new ways of thinking, linguists and anthropologists set about documenting undocumented grammars in earnest. By the early 1900s, Edward Sapir emerged as one of their most prominent leaders. "What fetters the mind and benumbs the spirit is ever the dogged acceptance of absolutes," Sapir wrote in his *Introduction to the Study of Speech.* Like Humboldt, Sapir saw a path toward new ways of seeing and thinking about the world through the documentation of languages. Sapir championed the idea as the "principle of linguistic relativity." Much as Einstein's Theory of

Relativity has done, Sapir thought linguistic relativity could disrupt our ways of seeing and understanding the world.

Sapir's most famous student and colleague was Benjamin Whorf, a genius fire inspector with a degree in chemical engineering who was fascinated by languages. While working as a fire inspector, he noticed that several tragic fires were caused by people carelessly smoking next to "empty" gas barrels. Of course, the "empty" barrels were actually full of highly flammable gas vapor.

Most famously, Whorf became interested in Hopi concepts of time. He noted that in English we talk about time as a "thing" and objectify it as seconds, minutes, hours, days, etc. It was a brilliant analysis starting from the insight that time is not really a "thing" but is simply the experience of duration, of a "getting later." The Hopi, he argued, have "no words, grammatical forms, constructions or expressions that refer directly to what we call 'time.'" He tied this into a broader observation of how our grammar shapes how we talk and think. For example, our grammar obliges us to provide a subject for every verb, so we say "it rains" or "the light flashes" when in fact neither the rain nor the light even exist without the action itself. When a light flashes the Hopi simply say *rehpi*. Whorf would go on to claim that our grammar made it difficult for us to understand Einstein's Theory of Relativity, which merges time and space, matter and energy, but make it easy to understand Newton, in which objects do specific actions. He suggested that if science had emerged within an Amerindian language, the Theory of Relativity might have been discovered much sooner.

Unfortunately, his claims about Hopi time may have gone too far. The idea that the Hopi have no concepts of time was discounted in the opening quote of Ekkehart Malotki's comprehensive book on Hopi Time, in which Malotki quotes a Hopi man using several concepts of time that Whorf assumed did not exist:

Then indeed, the following day, quite early in the morning at the hour when people pray to the sun, around that time then, he woke up the girl again.

Whorf fell into disrepute among many linguists after this, but nobody expressed the core insight that language can shape thought more eloquently or forcefully. His works revealed what Stephen Levinson called a "seductive, revolutionary set of ideas." Levinson goes on to note that "many eminent researchers in the language sciences will confess that they were first drawn into the study of language through the ideas associated with Benjamin Lee Whorf."

As linguists have turned away from Whorf, what was once known as the "Sapir-Whorf Hypothesis" or as Sapir dubbed it, "the Principle of Linguistic Relativity," is being re-shaped as what Guy Deutscher has called the Boas-Jakobsen principle. Deutscher points out that unlike Whorf, who pushed the notion that language shapes thought too far, Boas and Jakobsen championed a more tempered approach that, as Jakobsen summarized, "languages differ essentially in what they *must* convey and not in what they *may* convey." In this way, language shapes how we think by forcing us to think about certain things over and over again – like direction for my friends in New Guinea.

Over the past 30 years, careful controlled experiments have shown that language does indeed shape how we think. For example, in one task researchers asked participants to look at three different toy animals in a row setting on a table. The animals might be placed from left to right, facing "downhill" for example. Participants have to memorize the order of the animals and then turn around and place the animals in the same order on another table behind them. This forces the participant to make a decision about which answer is "right." One right answer would be to place the animals from left to right, but now left to right is not "downhill," it is "uphill." In such experiments, almost all speakers of Tzeltal (a language that requires speakers to know which direction they are facing) chose to orient the animals from right to left in a "downhill" orientation, while almost all Dutch speakers did the opposite.

Though this may seem like a minor difference, Lera Boroditsky points out that how we think about space can affect how we think about other things as well. "People rely on their spatial knowledge to build other, more complex, more abstract representations," she notes, "such as time, number, musical pitch, kinship relations, and emotions." For example, the Kuuk Thaayore of northern Queensland in Australia arrange time from east to west rather than left to right. When they were asked to arrange cards that indicated a clear temporal sequence such as a man aging or a banana being eaten, they arranged the cards from east to west, regardless of which direction they were facing. Mandarin speakers think of time as moving downward so next month is the "down month" and last month is the "up month."

Beyond time and space there are other interesting grammatical differences across languages that may shape how we think, but these domains have not been investigated thoroughly. For example, the Matses of the Amazon rainforest have the most complex system of verb forms that linguists call "evidentials." They operate much like tenses but require speakers to indicate precisely how they know what they know. In Matses, if you want to say, "he is going to the garden" you have to indicate whether you know this by direct experience, you are inferring it from clear evidence, you are conjecturing based on previous patterns, or you know it from hearsay. In the West we have a vast complicated philosophical field called Epistemology to explore how we know what we know. The Matses may be master epistemologists just by virtue of how they are required to speak.

WHERE THE SKY IS NOT BLUE

That our grammar affects how we think is now well- established, but what about our words? In one famous example, often mistakenly attributed to Whorf, the Eskimo are said to have hundreds of words for snow. This is not exactly true on a number of counts. First, there is no single Eskimo language, and many languages spoken in the region use polysynthetic word structures that allow them to make an infinite number of words from any root. For example, a complex phrase like "Would you like to go window shopping with me" can be expressed in just one word. In such a system, there are endless possibilities building from the root words for snow (of which there are only two). However, linguist David Harrison notes that the Yupik identify at least 99 distinct sea ice formations including several that are essential to life and death on the ice, such as *Nuyileq*, which indicates crushed ice that is beginning to spread out and is dangerous to walk on. It should not be surprising that the Yupik would have so many words for sea ice formations. Of course, an avid skier also has several words for snow and ice that are unknown to most English speakers, such as chunder, powder, moguls, zipper bumps, and sastrugi. Just as we learned in the previous section, our language does not limit us from perceiving new things and inventing words for them, but once we have a word for something and start habitually using that word, it is much easier to see it.

I experienced this myself in New Guinea. As I learned the language, the forest came alive for me in the same way that the whole world came alive for Ildefonso as he discovered language. The more words I learned, the more I came to see and understand the significance of the world around me. The monotonous diet, which had consisted of little more than taro, sweet potato, and bananas, was greatly enhanced as I came to recognize over thirty types of taro and sweet potato, and over fifty types of banana, each with its own distinct texture and flavor.

Sometimes, the words people use to describe the world clearly reflect and support the social structure and core values of their culture. One particularly well-documented example is in the domain of kinship terms. For example, Hawaiians use same word (*makuahine*) for mother as they do for aunt, a reflection of the importance they place on family and their tendency to live in extended families. If you were born into a culture where wealth is passed through the father's line (patrilineal systems) you might refer to your father's sister as "mother-in-law," indicating that her children (your "cousins" in our system) are suitable marriage partners. This form of cousin marriage can be advantageous because it keeps the wealth within the patrilineage. If you marry outside the patrilineage, the family wealth would need to be divided. Our own system, which distinguishes one's closest blood relatives (mother, father, brother, sister) from more distant relatives (aunts, uncles and cousins), reflects and supports a social structure and core values emphasizing independent nuclear families.

The core idea here is that we use our words to divide and categorize the world in certain ways which then influence how we see and act in the world. But how far does this go? For example, if we imagined a culture that had no word for blue, would the people of that culture experience "blueness"? Could they see it? Would they see it just as you or I see it?

This is the question that struck William Gladstone in 1858 when he noticed something peculiar about Homer's epic classics, *The Iliad* and *The Odyssey*. There were very few color terms throughout both texts, and the few times that colors were mentioned, they seemed a little off. Honey is described as green, the daytime sky is black, and the sea is described as the color of wine. There seemed to be no word for what we would normally call "blue." After careful study, Gladstone came to the conclusion that the Greeks might have seen the world very differently from us, perhaps mostly in black and white with the occasional shade of red.

Nine years later, Lazarus Geiger found that the color blue was also missing from the texts of ancient India, and from biblical Hebrew. He attempted to unveil the deep history of numerous languages and found that the word for blue was a relatively recent invention in each one. Furthermore, he noticed that the order in which colors were added to a language seemed to follow a universal pattern. First a language would have words for black and white, then red, then yellow or green, then yellow and green, and finally blue. Over the next twenty years, anthropologists and missionaries gathered color terms from all over the world and the universal pattern was confirmed.

Geiger wondered whether or not people without words for such colors could see the colors or not. "Can the difference between them and us be only in the naming," he wondered, "or in the perception itself?" Do they really not see the color blue? Thus opened up to science one of our favorite old philosophical nuts. *Is the "blue" you see the same "blue" that I see?* Is it possible to know?

Ten years later the question was one of the hottest topics of the age. Anatomist Frithiof Holmgren suspected that a deadly train crash in 1875 was caused when the conductor failed to see and obey a red stop light. He set about testing other conductors for color-blindness and promoted the importance of color perception for international safety. In this environment, Hugo Magnus suggested that color-blindness was a vestige of relatively recent human abilities. The ability of our retina to see colors had been evolving, he argued, and it would continue to evolve. Red was the first color we saw because it was the most intense, followed by yellow and green. He proposed that the ability to see blue was a relatively recent human ability, and suggested that so-called "primitive" tribes saw the world of color much as we see it at twilight, with muted gradations and only the most intense colors easily distinguished.

But color tests around the world failed to confirm that people of different cultures varied in their ability to perceive color differences. Nubians, Namibians, and Pacific Islanders had no trouble sorting and matching color samples.

But there was still the mystery of why Homer would describe the sea as "wine-dark" or honey as green, and why the word for blue would be so late in coming in the evolution of languages.

Sometimes we have some basic assumptions built into our questions that lead us astray. If you ask, "how did humankind's sense of color evolve over the past 3,000 years since Homer?" then you are already assuming that our sense of color has evolved. It is easy enough to discard that assumption, but harder to see and discard a much deeper assumption about the nature of color itself. We think of colors in terms of hue, which is dependent on the color's wavelength and is independent of its intensity or lightness. What is apparent now is that many languages, including that of Homer's, were not describing "color" as we think of it at all, but were instead describing intensity. The Greeks did not classify colors by hue, but by darkness and lightness. Kyaneos referred to darker colors such as dark blue, dark green, violet, brown, and black while glaukos referred to lighter colors such as light blue, light green, grey or yellow.

So why does "red" come first in the history of languages, followed by yellow, green, and finally blue? We do not know for sure, but there may be a mix of reasons both natural and cultural. Our closest primate relatives show increased excitement around the color red, which may signal danger (blood) or sex, and experiments with humans also show physiological effects. Red is of great importance symbolically in most cultures, and red dyes are the easiest to find and manufacture, with most cultures having some source for red dye that is often used in art and skin decoration. Yellow and green are important in identifying the health and ripeness of many plants, and yellow dyes are also fairly easy to find and manufacture. Blue is not especially important or easy to find and manufacture. Indeed, blue dyes do not appear until about three thousand years ago, and its rarity conferred it a special status in early civilizations.

More importantly, some color words in other languages carry other important meanings that can change how they are used. For example, anthropologist Harold Conklin notes that the Hanunoo of the Philippines say that the brown-colored section of freshly cut bamboo is "green" since green is not exclusively a color term but a label of freshness.

While it is now well-established that people of different cultures can see all the same colors, there is some evidence that our color words shape how we see them. For example, neuropsychologist Jules Davidoff worked with the Hemba in Africa, who do not have a word for blue. When he showed them 12 color samples, 11 that we would call "green" and 1 that we would call "blue," they could not determine that the "blue" one was the odd one out. But, they have many words for different shades of green, and when shown a pallet of 12 green squares with one slightly different they immediately saw the difference. English speakers cannot do this. (You can try at http://languagelog.ldc.upenn.edu/nll/?p=17970). His work suggests that once we name a color, it is easier to notice it, and we often collapse color differences toward our modal version of a color, making it difficult to distinguish between different shades that match the same category. In other words, when people who have no word for blue look out at a sky that they categorize in the same color category as black, the sky probably appears a bit darker than it does to us.

METAPHORS BE WITH YOU

Though grammar and words can be shown to shape how we see and think about the world, linguists George Lakoff and Mark Johnson have proposed that the most profound influence on our thought is at the level of metaphor. They point out that metaphors are pervasive throughout our language and often unnoticed. For example, we often unconsciously use the metaphor ARGUMENT IS WAR to describe an argument. We say that claims are *defended* or *indefensible*. We *attack* and *demolish* our *opponents*, *shooting down* their points, hoping that we can *win*. To drive home the significance of this metaphor, they ask us to consider what it would be like if we lived in a culture that instead used an ARGUMENT IS A DANCE metaphor in which the participants try to dance together, find the beauty in each other's moves, and ultimately create something beautiful together.

The key point of Lakoff and Johnson is not just that we use metaphors in how we talk. It is that "human thought processes are largely metaphorical." As Neil Postman notes, "A metaphor is not an ornament. It is an organ of perception ... *Is light a wave or a particle? Are molecules like billiard balls or force fields? Is history unfolding according to some instructions of nature or a divine plan?*" In virtually every domain of our lives and worldview, metaphors are operating, shaping our perception.

Most of the metaphors we use in our thought are what they call "dead" metaphors; that is, that we do not see them as metaphors at all. Take for example the metaphorical concept that Michael Reddy has called the "conduit metaphor," in which we think of ideas as objects and words as containers for those ideas. We put ideas into the containers (words) and send them (along a conduit) to other people. After careful analysis, Reddy notes that about 70% of all expressions we use about language are based on this metaphor. We say that we *have* ideas, that sometimes they are *hard to capture* in words, and that sometimes it is hard to *get an idea across.*

This metaphor lies at the heart of many "common sense" notions of education, which, as it turns out, are incomplete and misguided. The common-sense notion is that a teacher's job is to put ideas into words and send them to the students, who then will have the ideas. Massive lecture halls on college campuses have these assumptions built right into them, with fixed stadium seating facing the front of the room where the professor takes control of over a million points of light on giant screens, all specifically designed to help the professor "convey" the ideas into the heads of the students.

But this is not a complete picture of how learning works. Ideas do not just flow into people's heads and fill them up. When a new idea enters the mind of another, it enters a complex system with its own structure of interests, biases, and assumptions. The learner does not just absorb ideas whole. But precisely what is going on when learning happens is difficult to describe, and so we must rely on other metaphors.

There are a wide range of possibilities beyond the "Mind is a container" metaphor that can open us up to new possibilities. For example, Reddy suggests that we might think of the mind as a toolmaker. When new ideas come to us that we think might be useful, we use the idea to make a tool. But because my experience, interests, problems, and biases are different than yours, I make a different tool.

This, like the "mind is a container" metaphor, strikes us as partially true, though also incomplete. But by expanding our metaphor vocabulary. we constantly open ourselves up to new possibilities for how we think about the most important aspects of our lives.

Consider some of those really big questions that are constantly on our minds in the modern world: *Who am I? What am I going to do? Am I going to make it?* All of them are propped up on unexamined dead metaphors. Understanding what these metaphors are and how they shape our thoughts and actions might help us find answers to these questions, or perhaps lead us to new questions.

For example, when asking the question "Who am I?", we will often say that we are trying to "find ourselves." This is a metaphor, and it can shape your thoughts and actions. The attempt to find the self assumes that there is a solid core self to be found. To find it, we might try different career paths, bounce between relationships, or travel from place to place looking for it. And each time we fail to find it, we feel a little more "lost." The experiences seem wasted. But if we change the metaphor and instead see our task as one of "creating ourselves," those same experiences can be seen as part of the creative process, each one becoming a part of who we are as we go about creating the self. Of course, neither of these is precisely right. They are both incomplete, but each fills in gaps the other missed. The notion of creating yourself overlooks the fact that we are all inherently different—that we all have different tendencies, capacities, and limits; while the notion of finding yourself can overlook our capacities to change and create new tendencies, develop new capacities, and overcome limits.

And then there's the possibility that both of these metaphors put too much emphasis on the self altogether, and perhaps we should be considering a different metaphor. As the great poet Marshall Mathers once noted, "You better *lose* yourself, in the moment, you own it, you better never let it go." Of course, losing yourself may mean moving beyond language altogether. This is what happened to neuroscientist Jill Bolte Taylor during a stroke: the language center of her brain shut down. She says, "I lost all definition of myself in relation to the external world... Language is the constant reminder 'I am.'" And how did she feel in this state? "I had joy. I just had joy," she told Radiolab in an interview.

I found a peace inside of myself that I had not known before ... pure silence ... you know that little voice that says, "Ah, man, the sun is shining"? Imagine you don't hear that little voice ... you just experience the sun and the shining. ... It was all of the present moment.

Though we are not likely to be willing to give up our language, we can try to take control of it, and doing so requires that we recognize that even simple verbs such as *is* or *does* are, in the words of Neil Postman, "powerful metaphors that express some our most fundamental conceptions of the way things are." We *are* hungry. The Spanish "*have* hunger." This distinction is perhaps not very interesting or meaningful until we put it into other domains. We might *have* the flu but we do not *have* criminality. People *do* crimes and we have large systems in place to find out exactly who did a crime and why. Of course, these ideas can change. Not long ago one could *be* angry but could not *have* anger. Now, new ideas about how anger works allow people to recognize how anger can be seen as a treatable condition for which people can receive much-needed help.

The key idea is that metaphors permeate our thoughts and deeply shape how we make sense of the world. They do not necessarily reflect the unchanging and absolute nature of reality. Metaphors are the primary lens through which we make meaning of the world. As long as our metaphors are dead and unexamined, they control us and our thought patterns. When we examine the metaphors that guide us, we gain the freedom to create new ones and become meaning-makers. As Neil Postman once famously noted, "word weavers are world-makers."

WORD-WEAVERS ARE WORLD-MAKERS

Ellen Langer, professor of psychology at Harvard University, ran a simple experiment in which she gave two groups of students an object. One group was told, "This is a dog chew toy" while the other group was told, "This might be a dog chew toy." Later, when an eraser was needed, only the group that was told that the object "might be" a dog chew toy thought that it might also be used as an eraser.

The key difference is in how our minds pay attention to things and ideas we consider pliable and conditional vs. those we consider fixed and absolute. When we think of things and ideas as pliable and conditional we play with them, and by playing with them, we become more likely to find new, creative uses for them as well as remember them later on.

If I knocked on your door and offered you $10,000 for a 3' x 7' slab of wood, what would you do? Most people become frustrated that they do not have a pile of wood nearby, but they are holding a 3' x 7' slab of wood in their hand, the door itself! When we name something ("door"), it tends to become fixed and absolute as that thing in our mind, and disappears as all the other things it might become. We fall into the trap of categories. As Nobel Prize-winning physicist Niels Bohr says, "Our thoughts have us, rather than us having them."

To pay attention to these alternatives and to be aware of the pliable and conditional aspects of our world is to be mindful. The power of mindfulness is wonderfully summarized by Ken Bain, who notes that "all of us possess enormous power to change the world and ourselves by shifting the language and categories we employ. *Maybe I'm thinking about this wrong. Is there a different way of seeing my problem? Are there different words I might use?* The brain becomes more creative. Life becomes more exciting and fun."

This power to change the self by changing our words is well-documented. In one experiment, Langer and her team ran a short seminar for maids at large hotels designed to inform them that their jobs were good exercise. "Although actual behavior did not change," Langer reports, they "perceived themselves to be getting significantly more exercise then before." Remarkably, their bodies actually reflected this change. Over the next month they lost an average of two pounds over the control group. They lost ½% body fat and their blood pressure dropped 10 points.

Langer points out that such results are largely the result of the placebo effect. And what is the placebo effect? It is the power of your mind to actually change your body and heal itself. When you change your beliefs in a way that is thoroughly convincing to your mind, your brain chemistry actually changes. In fact, every drug in the world is actually already present in the brain. That's why they work. Our brain has receptors for them. "Every pharmacological agent or drug that there is," Tor Wager told Radiolab's Jad Abumrod, "there is a chemical produced by your brain that does that thing" (http://www.radiolab.org/story/91539-placebo/). But the power to change the self by changing your language does not stop with the physical self. It runs deep into the very essence of how you understand yourself as well.

FINDING YOUR "STRENGTHNESS"

Most of us have deep unconscious understandings of ourselves that are not always flattering. We tend to push away these dark parts of ourselves and rarely examine them. In doing so, we might also be pushing away the parts of ourselves that make us who we are.

When we adopt a mindful approach to the world, we see ourselves as pliable and conditional rather than fixed and absolute. We can see our capacity for growth and change. This helps us see those darker parts of ourselves because we recognize that they might not always be so dark. In fact, we might even see these dark aspects of ourselves as the source of our greatest gifts.

When Gillian Lynne was a little girl, her teacher was often frustrated with her. She would not sit still in the classroom, constantly dancing around the room. The teacher asked her mother to have her examined. After looking her over, the doctor turned on the radio and left the room to retrieve her mother. The doctor brought her mom to the door and asked her to look inside. Gillian was being Gillian, dancing around the room to the music. "Your daughter is not sick," the doctor said. "She's a dancer."

Gillian's mom promptly removed her from school and enrolled her in dance school. She went on to be one of the greatest dancers and choreographers of modern times, best known for her work in *Cats* and *Phantom of the Opera.*

What appeared to be a weakness in one context (dancing around the classroom) has become a great strength and widely celebrated in another (dancing across the stage). In this way, our weaknesses may in fact be strengths. Perhaps we are mistaken in separating them. As word weavers making new meanings, perhaps a new word can help us see parts of ourselves that otherwise remain hidden: *strengthness.*

A strengthness can be any apparent weakness that is a strength in another context or generates strength over time. For example, one former student struggled greatly with anxiety and panic attacks. Over her years of struggle with this weakness, she developed a remarkable capacity to calm herself in times of stress. Years later, when her boyfriend was struggling with the stress of graduate school, she was able to pass on some of her wisdom to help him calm himself. He went on to finish his Ph.D. thanks to her remarkable abilities, and so did she. Now a practicing Ph.D. in Clinical Psychology, she has helped hundreds of patients overcome the same debilitating anxiety and panic attacks that once plagued her.

New words like "strengthness" can help us see ourselves and the world in new ways. They shape how we see. We act based on what we "see." As Neil Postman sums it up:

If we "see things" one way, we act accordingly. If we see them in another, we act differently. The ability to learn turns out to be a function of the extent to which one is capable of perception change. If a student goes through four years of school and comes out "seeing" things in the way he did when he started, he will act the same.

Which means he learned nothing.

LEARN MORE

- A Man Without Words by Susan Schaller
- My Stroke of Insight: A Brain Scientist's Personal Journey, by Jill Bolte Taylor
- Through the Language Glass by Guy Deutscher
- Metaphors We Live By by George Lakoff & Mark Johnson
- Teaching as a Subversive Activity, by Neil Postman

Challenge Four: Word Weaving

Your challenge is to invent a word, phrase, or metaphor that you think would make the world a better place and then try to spread it among your friends.

Objective: See your own seeing by reflecting on the language and metaphors you use and how you might choose different language or metaphors to change the way you think and act. New perspectives open up new questions, so this might also help you ask new questions and make new connections to new ideas.

Step One: Invent a word, phrase, or new metaphor. Examples in this lesson included "strengthness" and new metaphors about arguments, education, and the self. What about love? Maybe we could use a different word to describe our complex feelings. Or maybe we could re-imagine metaphors like "falling in love." Anything goes.

Step Two: Introduce the word, phrase or metaphor in basic conversation as if the word has always existed and see if your friends catch on and start using it themselves.

Step Three: If they ask about it, give them a strong pitch as to why it should exist.

Step Four: Show us or tell us about your adventure. Post a video or share your story with #anth101challenge4

Lesson Five
Infrastructure

"We shape our tools and then our tools shape us."

TOOLS AND THEIR HUMANS

In the late 1960s, anthropologist Edmund Carpenter was hired as a communications consultant for what was then the Territory of Papua and New Guinea. Colonial administrators were seeking advice on how they might use radio, film, and television to reach, educate, unite, and "rationalize" remote areas of the territory as they moved toward independence. It gave Carpenter what he called "an unparalleled opportunity to step in and out of 10,000 years of media history." He recorded and created some of the most remarkable events in local media history throughout the territory, such as the first times people actually saw their own photographs in Polaroids.

When I arrived in New Guinea 35 years later, I stepped off a plane onto a remote landing strip and walked one hour down a road made for cars that no cars travel, that goes nowhere, built as part of a government development project. It ends a few hundred meters from Telefolip, what was once the sacred spiritual center of the Telefomin people. I did not know that Edmund Carpenter had been there, but upon my first glimpse of the village, I immediately recognized it from a picture in Carpenter's book. The picture, taken 35 years ago, features a movie camera sitting on a tripod in the center of the village. A Telefol man leans over hesitantly as if trying to steal a peek through the viewfinder. A young boy scurries out of the view of the lens.

I reached out to Carpenter to find out more about his time in Telefolip, and he generously sent me copies of over 30 hours of film footage he took during his time in New Guinea. In one haunting sequence, he snaps Polaroids of two men standing outside their house and hands them the photos. Carpenter recounts that when he

first gave people pictured of themselves, they could not read them. To them, the pictures were flat, static, and lifeless—meaningless. He had to point to features on the images and features of their own faces. Finally, "recognition gradually came *into the subject's face. And fear."

You can see it in the film footage. The man with the hat suddenly seems self-conscious about the hat. He hesitantly takes it off, hesitantly puts it back on, and finally just stands awkwardly with his hat off, staring at the image and then back to the camera that took the image.

The other man retreats to a house to be alone, staring at his image for over 20 minutes.

Carpenter describes their reactions as the "terror of self-awareness," evidenced by "uncontrolled stomach trembling." He describes the depths of the effect as one of "instant alienation," suggesting that it "created a new identity: the private individual." He argued that the Polaroid and other recording media created a situation in which, "for the first time, each man saw himself and his environment clearly and he saw them as separable."

As an anthropologist, he understands that such a change is not likely to come from just one small event, but it participated in a whole host of other changes that were currently underway in New Guinea, such as the arrival of schools and missions, and the preparations to move toward national independence and self-government. Nonetheless, he could not shake the sense that these media forms were having dramatic effects on their consciousness.

He describes one village where he handed out Polaroids with great regret. He says that when he returned to the village months later, he didn't recognize the place. "Houses had been rebuilt in a new style. . . . They carried themselves differently. They acted differently. . . . In one brutal movement they had been torn out of a tribal existence and transformed into detached individuals, lonely, frustrated, no longer at home— anywhere."

Such experiences left Carpenter disillusioned about the effects of technology, especially communication technologies, on indigenous peoples, and concerned about the effects of media everywhere. "I felt like an environmentalist hired to discover more effective uses of DDT," he lamented.

When I stepped into the village thirty-five years later, the once-thriving spiritual center of Telefol life had been reduced to a ghostly shell of what it once was. The once magnificent men's house had recently collapsed. There were no plans to rebuild.

The other houses have all been abandoned. The residents have moved into Western style pre-fab houses lined perfectly along that government road that doesn't go anywhere. Powerlines power up

radios, televisions, refrigerators, and lights. Traditional houses have been made into "kitchens" reserved for cooking.

While powerlines had not yet reached the region of New Guinea where I ultimately settled in to do my research, many of my friends were eager for photographs of themselves and their families. I set up a simple solar panel system that gave me about two hours of power each day to write notes on my laptop, and a simple printer that I could use to print pictures. I took a picture with my brothers along with a middle-aged man, and then printed it to give to them. The older man looked at the picture and excitedly pointed to my brothers, naming them as he pointed. Then he pointed to the man in the middle, himself, and said, "*Who is that?*" He saw himself so rarely that he did not even recognize himself. I would see this happen over and over again. It rarely happened with younger people, who often had small mirrors they used for shaving or decorating their faces. But many older villagers did not grow up with mirrors, and have never sought to own one.

Contrast this with our own everyday practices. How many times per day do we engage in the practice of objectifying the self into an image? Or study the self in image form? How many glances into the mirror? How many Snapchats? How many scrolls through the photo gallery on our phones, Facebook, or Instagram? It's so often that we need not even be looking at a mirror or image. Most of us have a pretty good sense of how we look in our mind's eye. We adjust this or that button, untuck our shirt just so, tuck our hair back behind our ear, or adjust our hat ever so slightly as we imagine how others might be seeing us at any given moment. We are constantly aware of ourselves as objects that are constantly under the scrutiny and judgment of others.

We take mirrors and photographs for granted, yet clearly they have a profound effect on those who have never encountered them. Is it possible that they also have a profound effect on us that has since gone unnoticed? What if you gave up mirrors and all images for a week, a month, or a year? Would your consciousness change?

Carpenter braved the possibility of career suicide to publish his studies on these matters. He was severely criticized by some leading anthropologists for his media experiments. He had anticipated the criticism in the book itself, admitting, "It will immediately be asked if anyone has the right to do this to another human being, no matter what the reason."

His defense, although framed within the context of a generation ago and half a world away, should still resound with us today. "If this question is painful to answer when the situation is seen in microcosm," he asked, how is it to be answered as millions of people are allowing new media to permeate their lives, "the whole process unexamined, undertaken blindly?"

His point is that we live a life completely immersed in technologies. But do we really understand how they shape us? We usually look at them as great comforts, wonderful conveniences, important necessities, or the source of fantastic experiences. But how do they change us? And how might we be different if we gave them up or if these technologies never existed?

"WE SHAPE OUR TOOLS, AND THEN OUR TOOLS SHAPE US."

This quote from media scholar John Culkin is sometimes literally true. Over long periods of time, the interaction between humans and their tools can even reshape our DNA. Over the millions of years that we have been using hand tools, there has been an evolutionary advantage to having nimble and dexterous fingers. Over time, our hands evolved an ability to manipulate objects with increasing precision, allowing us to create more precise objects which in turn create an ever- increasing advantage on more precise hand control. Our hands and our hand-tools co-evolved in their complexity. Fire is another example of a tool that changed our DNA. Fire allowed us to cook our food so that we no longer had to spend hours of our day chewing fibrous meats and tubers. Over time, we can see in the skeletal record that our jaws have become weaker and less robust since the invention of fire.

The power of technologies to literally shape our bodies is beautifully demonstrated by this famous photo published by Phil Hoffman in The American Journal of Orthopedic Surgery in 1905.

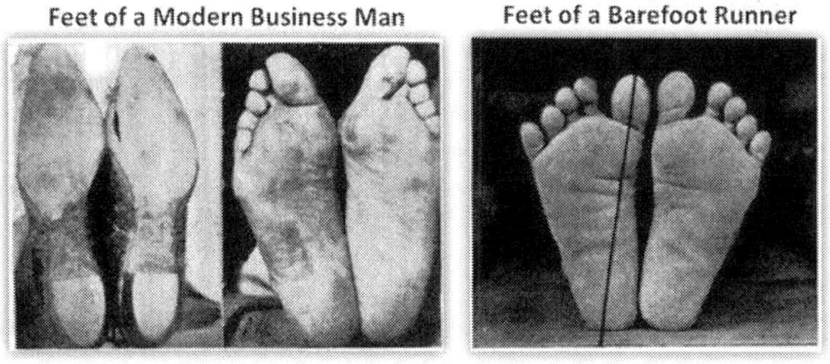

Shoes have not yet been around long enough to actually change our DNA. If you go barefoot long enough, or from a young enough age, you can also attain the amazing ability to spread your toes, engage all of your nature-given talents for balance and agility, and handle the roughest of surfaces without the aid of shoes. Similarly, coats and sophisticated climate controls like air conditioning and heating have reduced our ability to withstand cold and heat. Our comforts make us weaker.

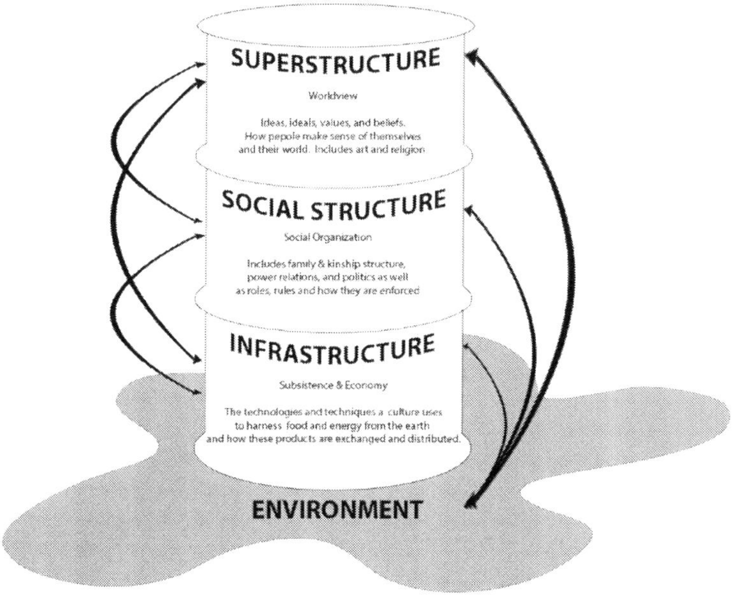

The idea that "we shape our tools and then our tools shape us" is sometimes mistaken as a claim for technological determinism, the idea that technology determines how we live, think, and act. But it would be wrong to only point out how our tools shape us. As noted in Lesson Two, cultures are complex and interrelated in such a way that no one element completely determines the other elements of the system. Instead, each element "shapes and is shaped by" another.

As we noted then, modern capitalism shapes and is shaped by modern individualism. American individualism shapes and is shaped by the American political system. The American labor market shapes and is shaped by individualism. And so on. In other words, culture is made up of a complex web of relationships of "mutual constitution" and it is this idea that we point to with the phrase, "we shape our tools and then our tools shape us."

We can now use the "barrel model" introduced in Lesson 2 as a guide to a profound set of questions about technologies and how they might affect us. At the level of infrastructure, how does a new technology shape our subsistence and economy? What other technologies will it make more important or necessary? What technologies might it displace and make obsolete?

When one technology requires or strongly influences the adoption of another technology, we call it **entanglement**, and when you follow the lines of entanglement far enough, you arrive at the realization that a new technology can have far-reaching effects far beyond what was originally intended.

Take the example of clothing. In the late 1970s, the first clothes started to arrive in the New Guinea village through trade networks with neighboring clans where they had government aid posts and missions. Then, in the early 1980s, missionaries started bringing in clothes and giving them to the locals. Many people immediately converted to Christianity in hopes of receiving the luxurious goods, and missionaries worried that they might be creating "clothes Christians" – people whose faith was only worn on the skin and did not penetrate to the soul.

Though the clothes offered comfort and protection from the elements that the natives had never experienced before, they presented a host of new problems. First, they had to be washed, so they needed soap. They could not be dried effectively in their huts due to the smoke and the thatch roofs infested with insects hungry for cloth, so they needed new houses with tin rooftops. The tin rooftops required nails to hold them in place. The nails required hammers to nail them in. The tin was square and standardized, so they needed some basic geometry and trigonometry to design their new houses. Geometry and trigonometry required that they go to school. School required paper, pens, and backpacks to carry it all. And all of this required money. As it turns out, clothes are deeply entangled with a vast range of other technologies that would ultimately encourage remote New Guinea villagers to join the global economy.

There are examples of entanglement all around us. For example, if you take a walk starting from the center of my hometown of Manhattan, Kansas, you will notice that the homes near the center of town built prior to 1930 usually have large front porches and no garages. If they do have a garage it is almost always separated from the house and was built much later than the original house. The reason for the absence of the garage is obvious. The garage is a technology entangled with cars, of which there were very few prior to 1930. But what about the front porch? As we walk away from the town center and enter the neighborhoods built after 1950, suddenly the front porch is gone.

What happened? Air-conditioning. Large front porches allowed people to stay cool in the summer, and had the pleasant side-effect of creating "front porch culture" where people would sit and greet their neighbors, creating strong social bonds. The air-conditioner eliminated the need for these porches, and they disappeared, along with that sense of community. Now the most prominent feature on the front of most suburban homes is a large double-wide garage door.

This example makes it clear that technological change is not limited to technology. Technologies shape how we make a living (infrastructure), how we connect, collaborate, and interact with one another (social structure), and can even participate in a wide range of cultural changes that lead to new core values and beliefs (superstructure). To see how this can happen, let's take a brief look at the last 12,000 years of human history.

"THE WORLD UNTIL YESTERDAY"

Humans have been hunting and gathering their food for over two million years. Viewed on that time-scale, it really is only yesterday that we were still living without most of the technologies we take for granted today. As Jared Diamond calls it, the world of hunters and gatherers is best understood as "the world until yesterday." Up until just 12,000 years ago, all humans everywhere lived basically the same way. In the popular imagination we were hunters, and indeed we were. But the evidence suggests that we acquired the vast majority of our calories from foraging: gathering fruits, nuts, tubers, and other foods.

Our simple manner of making a living had significant effects on how we lived and what we lived for. Using simple tools such as baskets and string bags for carrying the foods they find, and bows, arrows, spears, and blowguns for hunting, a typical forager can produce only enough food for themselves and a small family. So we lived in small bands of no more than about one hundred people.

When an area was picked over, we needed to move to where the picking was better. When a herd moved on, we needed to move with them. So we lived with few possessions that might weigh us down.

This basic pattern of life was the foundation of all human life for over two million years. There were a few key inventions that changed human life over the course of these two million years; fire about 400,000 years ago, language about 200,000 years ago, and the "Creative Explosion" about 50,000 years ago that brought about the first clothing, fish nets, art, and more sophisticated stone blades. But the foundation of our survival, the way we harnessed energy from the Earth, remained foraging and hunting.

There are very few foraging cultures in existence today, but we can learn something from the few that we do observe. Most remarkable is their vast knowledge and awareness of the natural world. Wade Davis tells of a Waorani hunter in the Ecuadorian Amazon who could smell and identify the urine of an animal from up to 40 paces away. Foragers manage to find food in even the most extreme environments. The San Bushmen of the Kalahari desert in southern Africa notice small things that you and I would not notice in their desert landscape that allow them to track wild game for miles or that tell them where to dig to retrieve roots and tubers. Some tubers can be squeezed to retrieve water in a landscape otherwise devoid of this basic human necessity. At the other extreme, Inuit of the Arctic look for subtle signs on the barren white ice that indicate where a seal might be coming up to breathe. They make a small hole in the ice and wait, spearing the seal as it comes up for a breath. To you and me, it looks like these people are pulling something out of nothing.

Since their mode of subsistence can only support a small, sparse population, the social structures of these societies are simple and informal compared to the complex bureaucracies and government systems of modern states. The average person in a remote band will almost never encounter a stranger. Disputes can be settled without the need for formal laws, lawyers or judges. Social order can be maintained simply by the mutual desire to maintain good relationships with one another and to support one another as needed. With no need for formal social institutions, there are no formal leaders, no offices to hold, no authority to lord over others.

There is no need for money or marketplaces. People simply gather food and share it with others in a gift-based economy. In a gift-based economy, you benefit by giving to others when you have more than you need because you know they will give back when they have more than they need. In this way, giving a gift provides insurance against hard times. As such, people in gift economies place a high value on their relationships, which can feed them when the going gets rough, rather than material goods that are simply burdensome to carry around and may mark you as wealthy and burden you with requests for gifts from others.

This value on relationships extends to the natural and animal world as well. Hunting cultures revere the animals they hunt. They are deeply thankful for them, and offer thanks to the animals they kill for giving themselves to them. Their myths and rituals celebrate the animals and often speak of a covenant made between the hunters and their prey. For example, the Niitsipai of North America (often referred to as the Blackfoot) tell the story of a young girl who offers to marry a bison if the herd would just sacrifice themselves so her people could survive. The bison agree to this and teach her their song and dance of life, the famous "buffalo dance," which they perform so the bison will continue to give themselves to the people in exchange for renewed life through the dance.

In this way, the tools they use take a role in shaping all aspects of their lives, from the way their societies are ordered and maintained, to their core values, religious beliefs, rituals, and knowledge.

Though they lack the technologies and material goods that we associate with wealth and affluence, Marshall Sahlins once described them as "the original affluent society." Studies of their work habits show that foragers only work to gather food for about 15 to 20 hours per week, and this "work" includes hunting and berry-picking, activities that we consider high-quality leisure activities. Indeed, most of them do not distinguish between "work" and "leisure" at all. Their affluence is not based on how much they have, but in how little they need.

A popular story illustrates the point nicely. A rich businessman retired to a fishing village in Mexico. Every morning, he went for a walk and saw the same man packing up his fishing gear after a morning of fishing. He asked the man what he was doing. "I caught some fish to take home to my family. I'll take a siesta while they cook this up, wake up to a nice dinner, and then pull out my guitar and sing and dance into the night. Then I'll wake up and do it again."

"I'll tell you what," the businessman said. "I have been very successful in my life, and I want to pass on all my knowledge to you. Here's what you need to do. Fish all day, and have your wife sell the surplus at the market. Save your money and buy a boat so you can catch more fish. Save that surplus and buy a whole fleet of ships.

Eventually you can invest in a packaging and supply company and make millions."

"That sounds good," the fisherman said. "Then what?"

"That's the best part. You sell your business and all of your assets, buy yourself a nice little cottage on a beach in Mexico, go fishing every morning, take siestas, wake up to a nice meal and then pull out your guitar and sing and dance into the night."

THE LUXURY TRAP

Starting about 12,000 years ago, humans domesticated plants and animals and started farming and raising livestock. Wheat, barley, pigs, goats, sheep, and cattle were domesticated in the Middle East. Maize, manioc, squash, gourds and llamas in the Americas. Taro in New Guinea. Rice, beans, and pigs in China. All over the world, simultaneously and independently, foragers shifted from their nomadic way of life and settled into growing villages to cultivate crops.

Given the apparently idyllic life of leisure, hunting, and gathering berries, why did humans start farming, build massive cities, complex technologies and burgeoning bureaucracies that ultimately sentence our youth to 13 to 26 years of schooling just to understand how to live and operate in this complex world?

Of course, the apparently idyllic life of foragers that provided ample leisure time was also riddled with the dangers of infectious disease, dangerous animals, deadly accidents, intertribal violence and unpredictable weather patterns that could reduce food and water supply. Infant mortality rates were high, and it was difficult to provide adequate care for elders if they were lucky enough to live that long.

But the life of an agricultural peasant a few thousand years later was probably worse. We know that the turn toward agriculture eventually led to the tremendous wealth of our current times, but agriculture did not produce this wealth overnight. The first farmers would have faced the same dangers of infectious diseases, animals, accidents, violence and weather of their foraging ancestors, but instead of walking around picking berries and hunting, they made a living by toiling in the fields under the brutal sun. They became dependent on a diet with fewer foods and nutrients. So we're back to the original question. Why did we do it?

The answer proposed by Yuvaal Hurari, author of the recent best-seller *Sapiens: A Brief History of Humankind*, is that humans fell into what he calls "The Luxury Trap." One generation reasons that it will make their life easier if they domesticate and plant a few seeds so they can establish more permanent villages. Life is good and food is plentiful for several generations. But as the carrying capacity rises, the people have more children. After a few generations, what started out as a luxury has become a necessity. Eventually the land can barely support the burgeoning population, and people have to work harder than ever to make a living.

Once humans started planting crops, the same piece of land that could support a few dozen people could support a few hundred. And once humans started irrigating that land and using animal-pulled plows, that same piece of land could support a few thousand. As Harari notes, the same area that could support about a hundred "relatively healthy and well- nourished people" hunting and foraging could now support "a large but cramped village of about 1,000 people, who suffered far more from disease and malnourishment."

It didn't matter that life was harder, less enjoyable, and more precarious for the agricultural peasant than it was for the nomadic forager. There was no going back. "The trap snapped shut," as Harari says.

The broad sweep of changes that came along with the domestication of plants and animals were so revolutionary that they are often referred to as the Neolithic Revolution. Growing societies required increasingly complex institutions to manage them. Government, law, taxes, markets and bureaucracy were all formed in the wake of the Neolithic Revolution. Over time, the clear trend was toward greater production and wealth, a greater diversity of products to consume with this wealth, and a greater diversity of jobs to produce the goods, manage the wealth, and provide services to an ever-growing population. But there were negative effects as well. These farming societies were less efficient than our foraging ancestors, burning far more energy per human. Social and economic inequality rose, and we worked longer and harder than ever before. For better or worse, human society and culture was forever changed.

The changes of the Neolithic Revolution set the stage for another revolution nearly 12,000 years later: the Industrial Revolution. As revolutionary as the domestication of plants and animals might have been, most of what we take for granted today was still not in existence just 250 years ago at the dawn of the Industrial Revolution. At that time, over 90% of humans were working in agriculture. Today, less than 40% of humans are farming, and the number is as low as 2% in industrialized nations like America. The Industrial Revolution ushered in an age in which more work would be done by machines than by muscle. Before the Industrial Revolution there were no cars, planes, phones, TVs, or radios. No suburbs, parking lots, or drive-thrus. No Coke, Pepsi, or Starbucks. No grades or compulsory schools. No Prozac, Zantac, or Zoloft. No Tweets, Snaps, or Finstas. No texting or emojis.

But by far the most dramatic change that occurred in the wake of the Industrial Revolution was what Harari calls "the most momentous social revolution that ever befell humankind: the collapse of the family and the local community and their replacement by the state and the market." Prior to the Industrial Revolution, Harari estimates that less than 10 percent of the products people commonly used were purchased at the market. People were still mostly reliant on their families and communities for food, shelter, education, and employment. When they had trouble, they turned to their families. As Harari summarizes, the family was "the welfare system, the health system, the education system, the construction industry, the trade union, the pension fund, the insurance company, the radio, the television, the newspapers, the bank and even the police."

New communication and transportation technologies enabled markets and governments to provide these services in ways that enticed people out of the security of their families and into the marketplace as individuals. People became more mobile – physically, socially, and morally. But, as Harari notes, "the liberation of the individual comes at a cost." Our strong ties to family and community started to wither, a trend that has continued to the present day.

We are enculturated to think of technological change as good, but all of these technologies and changes have some negative side effects, and many of them can be understood in terms of Harari's notion of the luxury trap. For example, cars were invented to make it quicker and easier to get from one place to another. In response, Americans spread out into the countryside, creating suburbs, and now spend nearly a full hour getting to and from work on average. In some cities, the average is nearly two hours, more than eliminating the supposed advantage of the car. Our communities transformed to accommodate the car. By far the largest public spaces sponsored by tax dollars are highways and parking lots. In order to accommodate cars, our communities had to spread out into the familiar suburban sprawl. In many suburbs, basic services and necessities are no longer reachable on foot, and the car, which was once a luxury, has become necessity. People rarely walk anywhere, reducing our physical health while also making it less likely for us to know and interact with our neighbors. That trap has snapped shut too.

But perhaps even more harrowing is to examine the cost of our technologies on the environment. Since the Neolithic Revolution there are now just 40,000 lions but over 600 million house cats. There are 1.6 billion wild birds on the planet but over ten times as many chickens. In total, humans and their domesticated pets and livestock make up nearly 90% of all large animals on the planet. If current trends continue, 75% of species will be extinct within the next few centuries.

Humans also produce over 300 million metric tons of plastic every year, some of which is drawn by ocean currents into the Great Pacific garbage patch, an island of trash bigger than the state of Texas.

Carbon dioxide levels continue to rise due in part to the burning of fossil fuels, raising global temperatures and leading to more extreme weather events. Sea levels have risen seven inches over the past 100 years, and in the next 100 will rise high enough to threaten major cities such as New York, Mumbai, and Shanghai.

Overall, our impact is so great that we will leave a lasting imprint on the earth. The International Commission on Stratigraphy is debating whether or not to formally declare that we have entered a new epoch in the history of the earth, the Anthropocene.

We know that we simply cannot go on living as we do without burning through our resources and disrupting climate patterns to a point that the earth may not be hospitable to human life. For these reasons, Jared Diamond once suggested that what appeared to be our greatest technological triumph, the domestication of plants and animals that set all of these forces in motion, might actually have been our greatest mistake.

A POST-HUMAN FUTURE?

We now sit at the brink of what many think is yet another revolution in human affairs. One harbinger of what might be to come is the supercomputer Watson. Developed by IBM, in 2011 they set it up to compete against the greatest Jeopardy players of all time. As the 74-time Jeopardy champion Ken Jennings fell further and further behind, he conceded the match in the final round by writing on his final answer, "I for one welcome our new computer overlords."

Computers are becoming more powerful every moment. They drive cars, do taxes, trade stocks, manage complex budgets, play chess, write music, and even write articles we read in newspapers and online. They are even addressing problems and challenges that we struggle to comprehend. Scientists at Cornell University created a computer program, Eureqa, which can analyze large data sets to find patterns and create formulas that match the data. Eureqa has been able to discover formulas that scientists could not, and sometimes even finds a formula that works, but scientists don't understand *why* it works.

The stock market is now dominated by computer algorithms, with over 75% of all trades being made by computers. Computers read headlines and make trades based on incoming news in milliseconds, before a human even has time to finish reading the headline.

As CGP Grey notes in his video, "Humans Need Not Apply," humans have spent years creating "mechanical muscles" (large machines) to augment and replace manual labor. Now "mechanical minds" are making human brain labor less in demand. Some robots have already taken jobs. ATMs are so ubiquitous they have become invisible, but they replaced many human bank tellers. Similarly, self-checkout machines at supermarkets are reducing the demand for cashiers.

Uber already has self-driving cars picking up passengers in cities around the United States. This may be disruptive to our culture in ways that we cannot yet comprehend. Without labor costs, Uber may be able to offer luxurious and convenient rides for anybody anywhere for a cost so low that fewer people will decide to purchase a car. Just as the Internet has started to provide meta-data and signals meant only for robots, so our cities might soon be redesigned to accommodate robot drivers. But even this is too limited a vision. Self-driving cars are really part of an automated transportation and delivery system that will be able to ship everything everywhere – by land, air, and sea, a system which currently employs more people than any other major economic sector in the United States. Within the next ten years, the demand for labor in this sector could collapse.

Meanwhile, software algorithms are reducing the demand for tax professionals, lawyers, journalists and many other fields. And Watson is not only great at Jeopardy. Watson works in the medical field, and some see it as the predecessor of a future "Dr. Bot" that will provide sophisticated personal diagnoses.

Some bots are even producing creative works like art and music. David Cope, a professor of music at UC Santa Cruz, has developed a computer program that can analyze scores of music from a particular composer and then create new music that sounds like it was written by that composer. The music is good enough that it has fooled top music critics and professionals into thinking it was produced by a talented human.

In short, it appears that if you are not in the process of creating an algorithm, you might be replaced by one. And of course, even your job as a software engineer creating algorithms might not be safe. Already, many engineers create learning algorithms that are designed to write new algorithms on their own.

Some see this as the beginning of what is called "the Singularity." The Singularity is a state of runaway technology growth, a point beyond which human thought can no longer make sense of what is happening. Futurists like Ray Kurzweil think this moment is coming soon – within our lifetimes - and it will arrive when a machine is created that is smart enough and capable enough to design and create its own replacement. At that point, the replacement will design and create *its* own replacement, and that replacement will create its replacement, and so on, with each one better than the last, so that within a very short period of time there will be a computer so intelligent and capable that humans will be baffled by its power. We will likely have no way of comprehending it other than in divine terms. We will probably think of it as a god.

Kurzweil also predicts that as computers continue to become smaller and faster at an exponential rate, we will soon have molecular-sized nanobots operating in our bloodstreams to battle disease. He believes that advancements such as these will allow people alive today to live well into their 100s, and he predicts that by then we will have non-biological alternatives for living matter that will replace our bodies and allow us to live forever.

He also predicts that nanobots and other technologies will enhance our cognitive capacities and allow us to enter fully immersive and realistic virtual realities. We will be able to act and move in these worlds just as we do in the real world, but these worlds could be populated by artificial intelligent beings, or other humans who have entered the world with us – much like an MMORPG – but it will feel entirely real. Noting that millions of ordinary people are already spending more time in virtual worlds than they do in the real world, Edward Castranova predicts that we may see a mass exodus to the virtual world.

All these changes bring up fundamental questions about what it is to be human. Kurzweil and his colleagues are transhumanist. They are on a quest to enhance human capabilities and overcome disability, disease, and death. It may sound crazy, but we are all transhumanist in a sense. We all support and believe in the fight against cancer and other diseases. We support and believe in treatments that allow people with disabilities to live with them or overcome them. And we do everything in our power to avoid death for ourselves and loved ones, assuming our health is good. As science and technology progress, will we eventually draw a line and say: beyond this, we let people die? Beyond this, we let people suffer with their disability or disease?

And what if we do overcome death? Will life still have the same meaning? If you were going to live forever, would you be in school right now? And what are you in school for, if all the jobs are done by robots? It could create an existential crisis in which we lose our sense of meaning and significance. Others think that this future may create a *literal* existential crisis, in which hyper-smart and logical robots realize that humans are a drain on the planet and reason that there is no reason for our existence at all.

Perhaps we should be grateful for our limits. Our limits may bring us pain, struggle, and suffering, but they also bring meaning to our lives.

LEARN MORE

- Oh, What a Blow That Phantom Gave Me!
  by Edmund Carpenter

- The World Until Yesterday
  by Jared Diamond

- Sapiens: A Brief History of Humankind
  by Yuval Noah Harari

- The Second Machine Age
  by Eric Brynjolfsson and Andrew McAfee

MEDIATED CULTURE

Four years after I first arrived in New Guinea, new media arrived in the village. It wasn't cell phones, the Internet, or even television. It was writing, which came in the form of census and law books, sponsored by the state. Of the 2,000 people who lived in the region, only 10 could read and write effectively, and they were the ones who would try to carry out the state mandate to census the population and bring them under the rule of law.

Doing a census sounds easy. All you have to do is list people's names in a book. The problem with doing this in these remote villages was that many people did not have formal names. They already knew everybody they encountered and usually used a relationship term to refer to them, like mother, father, sister, brother, friend, trading partner, etc. Eventually they settled on creating "census names" for which they adopted the English term "census name" into their language.

As anthropologist Roger Rouse has pointed out, the emergence of individualism as we know it today emerged from the micro-rituals and routines of what he calls the "taxonomic state," such as censusing and mapping, which allow the state to see its citizens. As people in the village took on fixed, static names, they could start to build more stable individual identities which might one day be objectified in the form of an identity card such as a passport or driver's license.

Inspired by the clean, straight lines of their books, the census officials dreamed of eliminating the haphazardly built traditional villages in favor of houses built along clean, straight lines, with each house numbered to match the census book. The villages would have the additional advantage of having high populations, making it easier to govern the people from a central location while also increasing their population numbers so that they would receive more funding from the state. Their lives were quite literally being made over "by the book."

At the same time as the census came in, so did the rule of law. Until then, all disputes had been settled out in the open as affairs of the local community. The goal was not to establish guilt but to heal the relationship. When law came to the village, individuals were taken into the courthouse and measured against the letter of the law. The court is not necessarily interested in healing relationships but in determining motives, intentions, and guilt, all of which are intimately tied into the logic of individualism.

Several people resisted these changes. They did not want to move into new houses and villages. They liked how they lived and settled disputes. So the government leaders held a meeting. First, it was decided that the only people who could vote were those who could read and write. Then, they voted on whether or not they could force people to move into the new villages. The vote was unanimous, and soon after that they began forcing people to move, sometimes by burning down their houses.

The next two months were a dark time. Stress and tensions rose. Witchcraft accusations ran rampant. Angry villagers on the brink of losing their homes campaigned vociferously to preserve their homes while those in favor of the government plan tried to sell their vision of future prosperity.

But what was perhaps most remarkable about this sequence of events was how it ended. As the bickering continued, the architects of the movement looked around at the changes they had created and did not like what they saw. They felt seduced by the counts in the census book into thinking of their friends, kin and neighbors as nothing more than numbers. They felt seduced by the clean lines of their village plans into creating villages that looked clean and rational but were not very functional. The doorways all faced the same way, whereas traditionally they could position their doorway in such a way as to be open to kin but private from passersby. They started to recognize that there were important reasons why they had lived as they lived, and they felt seduced by their new technologies into imagining an alternative way of life that they ultimately found that they did not want.

This is one of the great paradoxes of technology. It empowers people in ways they have never been empowered before, and those who master the technology seem to be the ones who benefit the most. But technologies often have unintended consequences, and in retrospect, it might be those who seem most empowered by the technology who are in fact overpowered and seduced by the technology itself.

I returned to the United States soon after these events in 2003. Wikipedia had just launched. Facebook would launch the following year, followed by YouTube, then Twitter, and the whole new mediascape we now call "social media."

Thinking about how new media had affected my friends in New Guinea, I wondered how these new media might affect us. How might we be seduced by the technology to promote changes we do not intend?

TELEVISION

When TV came into our homes over 50 years ago it immediately transformed our relationships in a way that can actually be seen in the arrangement of the furniture. Everything had to be arranged to face the box in the corner. For many people, this arrangement replaced the dining room, so instead of family dinners spent around a table, they were now spent around the box in the corner. And for 50 years, the most important conversations of our culture happened inside that box. They were controlled by the few (a few large TV networks) and designed for the masses (to win over a large audience). So they were always entertaining, even the serious ones. Our politics became entertainment and spectacle, made to fit between commercial breaks. In such ways, our media technologies shape our conversations, and taken altogether our conversations create our culture which Neil Postman grimly described in 1985 as one of irrelevance, incoherence, and impotence.

Postman recounts that the Lincoln-Douglas political debates of 1858 unfolded over the course of seven hours, with each candidate allowed an hour or more to respond in front of an attentive crowd. It was a true debate. Now we have sound-bites. If you can't state your argument in eight seconds or less, it's no good for TV. And in 1985 there was little you could do about it. Postman challenged his readers to imagine sitting in front of a television watching the most serious and "important" newscast available and ask yourself a series of questions, "What steps do you plan to take to reduce the conflict in the Middle East? Or the rates of inflation, crime and unemployment? ... What do you plan to do about NATO, OPEC, or the CIA?" He then says that he "shall take the liberty of answering for you: You plan to do nothing." In 1985, we had few options, and that was precisely Postman's point. There was no talking back to the media.

All media are biased, Postman noted. The form, structure, and accessibility of a medium shapes and sometimes even dictates who can say what, what can be said, how it can be said, who will hear it, how it will be heard, and how those messages may or may not be retrieved in the future. Postman coined the term "media ecology," noting that media become part of the environment all around us, transforming how we relate to one another in all aspects, from art to business, public politics to private family life. While any technology can have an effect on society, the change brought about by a change in media is especially profound, because a medium serves as the form through which all aspects of culture are expressed, experienced, and practiced.

A major new medium "changes the structure of discourse" Postman notes, "by encouraging certain uses of the intellect, by favoring certain definitions of intelligence and wisdom, and by demanding a certain kind of content."

Consider Postman's own narrative about how electronic media remade American culture. In the mid-1800s, the telegraph brought new forms of discourse to the nation. For the first time, information could travel faster than a human being and was no longer spatially constrained. The type of information was different, though, as the telegraph did not allow for lengthy exposition. People increasingly knew more *of* things, and less *about* them. Such news from distant lands could not be acted upon, so its value wasn't tied to its use or function, but to its novelty, interest, and curiosity. This created a discourse of "irrelevance, incoherence, and impotence" that we still recognize today on television. Postman pointed out that virtually all aspects of American culture—economics, politics, religion, and even education—had transformed into entertainment. We were, to borrow the title of the book, "*Amusing Ourselves to Death*."

Postman was writing in 1985, at the dawn of cable television, with its sudden onslaught of television options beyond traditional networks. In a famous novel written that year, Don Delillo describes a noxious cloud that may be seen to represent the mélange of decontextualized and disembodied information that began oversaturating our everyday experience, the phenomenon anthropologist Thomas de Zengotita simply called, "the blob."

"What do people do in relation to the nameless, the odorless, the ubiquitous?" asks DeLillo. "They go shopping, hunt pills ... " and ultimately find themselves coming together in the long lines of the superstore, "carts stocked with brightly colored goods ... the tabloids

... the tales of the supernatural and the extraterrestrial ... the miracle vitamins, the cures for cancer, the remedies for obesity ... the cults of the famous and the dead."

Postman's notion of media ecology reminds us that media become the environments in which we live. Humans are meaning-seeking and meaning-creating creatures, and the media we use populate our environment of meanings. It is in this environment of meanings that we search for our sense of self, identity, and recognition. "Onslaught," a famous Dove TV commercial , demonstrates what this is like for a young girl immersed in our current media environment. It shows a young girl bombarded by a flurry of media messages telling her to be impossibly thin with perfect skin, shining flowy hair, large breasts and buttocks, and more than anything, that how she looks is her primary measure of value. The commercial quickly progresses to a future in which the girl has low self-esteem, false body-image, and an unending desire to "fix" herself through the consumption of beauty products and plastic surgery. The lyrics underscore the point, "Here it comes la breeze will blow you away/all your reason and your sane sane little minds."

THE PROMISE OF THE INTERNET

The Onslaught video was made for the media environment of 1985 or 1995, but it was released in 2007. Large corporations no longer had a monopoly on visual media. Rye Clifton posted a remix of the commercial on YouTube called, "A message from Unilever." He points out that Unilever is the parent company for both Dove (the creator of this wonderful program rallying against the sins of the beauty industry) and Axe (the creator of many of the more objectifying and distasteful ads that are creating the problem in the first place). Using imagery from Axe as the "breeze that will blow you away," bombarding the young girl with objectifying imagery from Unilever's own ad campaign, thereby reveals their hypocrisy.

Another, created by Greenpeace (2008), shows a young girl in Indonesia taking in a flurry of images of the trees in the environment around her being destroyed to clear the way for palm plantations providing palm oil for Dove products. The song is the same, but with parody lyrics, "There they go, your trees are gone today, all that beauty hacked away. So use your minds." The video ends with the young Indonesian girl walking away from a recently cut down forest, and a subtitle that reads "98% of Indonesia's lowland forest will be gone by the time Azizah is 25. Most is destroyed to make palm oil, which is used in Dove products."

The video raced to over 1 million views on YouTube. Two weeks later, Greenpeace activists were invited to the table with senior executives at Unilever who then signed an immediate moratorium on deforestation for palm oil in Southeast Asia (Greenpeace 2009). Greenpeace noted that it was the single most effective tactic they had ever used.

Recall Postman's challenge in 1985. "What are you going to do about [major world issues you hear about on TV]… ?" He can no longer take the liberty of answering for us. We are no longer constrained to doing nothing. We can talk back. We can *create.*

While the mass media of television and major newspapers were one-way, controlled by the few, and made for the masses, the Internet offers a platform in which anyone can be a creator. It is not controlled by the few, and content can be created for niche audiences. More importantly, the Internet allowed us to experiment with new forms of collaboration and conversation. Wikipedia allowed anybody anywhere to contribute their knowledge to create the world's largest encyclopedia, just as eBay allowed anybody anywhere to sell to anybody anywhere else who had access to the Internet. Blogs allowed anybody anywhere to launch their own content platforms. YouTube allowed anybody anywhere to publish their own video channels.

In late 2007, four Kenyans came together to create Ushahidi, which means "witness" in Swahili. Ushahidi allowed people with ordinary cell phones to contribute important location-based information in times of crisis. They invented it in the chaos of riots that erupted after the Kenyan national elections. As traditional media outlets were overwhelmed and inadequate, Ushahidi allowed 45,000 people who didn't even know each other to work together as citizen reporters to provide key life-saving information. The creators of that platform then gave it away for free online so that others could use it. After the Haiti earthquake of 2010, some Tufts University students implemented Ushahidi Haiti and started receiving thousands of messages such as, "We are looking for Geby Joseph, who got buried under Royal University." These messages were then mapped, not on Google Maps – which was not good enough at the time – but on Open Street Maps, an open platform that allowed volunteers all over the world to trace satellite imagery to provide the most highly-detailed maps available. A U.S. Marine also sent a note to Ushahidi Haiti, to say, "I cannot overemphasize to you what the work of the Ushahiti/Haiti has provided. It is saving lives every day. I wish I had time to document to you every example, but there are too many... The Marine Corps is using your project every second of the day to get aid and assistance to the people that need it most."

Social media platforms have played key roles in major democratic uprisings around the world. In Egypt, protestors used Facebook, YouTube, and Twitter to inspire mass protests against President Mubarak, who had used his power to silence dissent and stay in office for over 30 years. After 18 days of mass demonstrations, Mubarak stepped down.

But social media can also be used by dictators and terrorists. In the wake of failed protests in Iran in 2009, the government posted pictures of protestors and offered rewards for identifying them, effectively using the Internet to extend their control and surveillance. And for several years, ISIS has effectively used slick video campaigns, radio shows, podcasts, and high-production-quality online magazines to attract young people from all over the world to join their cause.

We are discovering that a media environment that allows anybody anywhere to produce anything anytime and share whatever they find with anyone creates major challenges for our culture. Long-standing institutions such as major newspapers are closing. Essential occupations such as journalism are dwindling as many journalism majors now move into "content marketing" jobs, creating social media content to promote brands and products.

Just as the mediascape dominated by television favored content that was entertaining (even about serious topics), so does social media. But we now live in an "attention economy" in which our lives are so immersed in media that we simply don't have time to pay attention to it all. In the battle for our attention, content creators create shocking false headlines combined with surprising, shocking, or near-pornographic imagery as "clickbait."

Meanwhile, platforms like YouTube and Facebook use sophisticated algorithms to predict what we might like based on our friends, previous likes, and shopping history. We end up only seeing what Facebook thinks we will want to see, and end up living in what Eli Pariser has called "filter bubbles."

The 2016 US presidential elections magnified these problems. Democrats and Republicans lived in alternate media universes throughout the campaign season. They did not share the same basic facts about what was true and untrue, and both sides leveraged attacks at the other for producing "fake news." And since anybody anywhere can produce anything anytime, there was plenty of fake news going around, some of which was produced by people outside the United States with vested interests in the election outcome.

What can we do? There are online petitions to encourage Facebook and Google to stop personalizing our content in such a way that creates filter bubbles, and to create technologies that stop the spread of fake news. But some scholars, such as Evgeny Morozov, worry about such online petitions. Morozov worries that true activism that involved real people organizing in the streets is now being replaced by slacktivism, easy little "likes" and clicks done from the privacy of one's home that do not create lasting connections with real people who share similar activist goals.

Thirty years ago, scholars like Neil Postman worried that the major media corporations were using mass media to create a media environment that created a culture of irrelevance, incoherence, and impotence. Now, it seems that we might be doing it to ourselves.

THE INSTAGRAM EFFECT

Today, a new medium emerges every time someone creates a new web application. A little Tinder here, a Twitter there, and a new way of relating to others emerges, as well as new ways for contemplating one's self in relation to others. Listing our interests, joining groups, and playing games on Facebook; sharing photos and videos on Instagram or Snapchat; swiping left or right on Tinder; sharing our thoughts, ideas, and experiences on blogs; and following, being followed, and tweeting on Twitter are not only ways of expressing ourselves, they are new ways to reflect on who we are, offering new kinds of social mirrors for understanding ourselves. And because these technologies are changing so quickly, we are not unlike those villagers seeing a photograph of themselves for the first time. We are shocked into new forms of sudden self-awareness.

Unlike those villagers who barely know their own image, most kids today have grown up with parents posting their accomplishments on Facebook and then transitioned to having their own accounts in high school. They know how to craft their best self for the camera, and they're more comfortable than ever snapping picture after picture of themselves, crafting beautiful pages full of themselves and their likes and activities on Facebook and Instagram, and sending out little snippets of their lives on Snapchat. The era of the selfie is upon us.

I recently started noticing something strange about the profile pictures my students were using on the online portal for my course. They were all beautiful. When I face my students in person they look, on the whole, like you would expect any large group of more or less randomly selected college students to look. They look normal. On the whole, they look average. But online, they are magnificent! The women have flawless skin, bright white smiles, and beautiful hair. The men look as if they were cut right out of an adventure magazine. Upon closer examination, it becomes apparent that what I am seeing is *the filter.*

Most of these pictures have been lifted from their social media accounts, where one can find more of the filter. Blur effects filter out skin blemishes. Color filters make the images look professional and aesthetic. And of course, the only pictures that are posted are the ones that make it past their own critical eye, which serves as yet another filter. As a result, social media gives us a steady media stream of beautiful people doing amazing things, and those people are our friends.

And it isn't just young people. My Facebook feed is full of images of smiling families sharing a night out, going to school, playing at parks, and competing in their latest sporting events.

Television media gave us a steady stream of beautiful people doing amazing things, and this could sometimes make us feel inadequate or that our lives were not interesting or exciting. But we could always comfort ourselves in knowing that the imagery was fake and produced by a marketing machine.

But now every one of us is our own marketing machine, producing a filtered reality for our friends to consume. Essena O'Neill rose to Internet celebrity status on Instagram, and then suddenly quit, going back to re-caption all of her old images to reveal how they had been filtered. In one picture she sits on the beach, showing off sculpted abs. "NOT REAL LIFE," she writes. "Would have hardly eaten that day. Would have yelled at my little sister to keep taking them until I was somewhat proud of this. Yep so totally #goals." It can be inspiring to see your friends, or other people that do not seem so different from you, looking amazing and doing amazing things. But as Essena O'Neill discovered, it can also feed into a culture of feeling inadequate.

Sometimes the consequences are devastating. Madison Holleran, a track athlete at Penn, seemed to have it all. Smart, beautiful, athletic and at one of the top schools in the world, she seemed to have it made. And her Instagram account showed it. We see her smiling as she rides piggyback on a handsome boy. We see her proudly showing off her new Penn track uniform. We see her smiling in front of a row of beautiful houses, dressed in a beautiful dress. Indeed she seemed to have it all. The last entry is a beautiful array of floating lights over a park in the city. She took it just one hour before she took her own life.

Writing about the event for ESPN, Kate Fagan noted that she talked to her friends as they scrolled through Instagram, saying, "This is what college is supposed to be like; this is what we want our life to be like." Think of it as "the Instagram Effect" – the combined effects of consuming the filtered reality of our friends.

We have a tendency to compare our insides to people's outsides. Even before Instagram people were filtering their beliefs and appearances to put on a good show, but social media has the potential to magnify the effect. We see other people's lives through sophisticated filters, each image, post, and tweet quantified in likes. Seeing ourselves in a Polaroid is nothing new to us, but seeing ourselves with such a clear quantification of our "like"-ability and consuming a steady stream of filtered lives most definitely is.

"The constant seeking of likes and attention on social media seems for many girls to feel like being a contestant in a never-ending beauty pageant," reports Nancy Jo Sales in her book *American Girls*. A recent study shows that there has been a spike in emotional problems among 11- to 13-year-old girls since 2007, the year Apple's iPhone ushered in era of the always-on mobile social networking world. Since then, the "second world" of social media has become more important than the real world for many teens, as the complexities of teenage romance and the search for identity largely take place there.

A 2014 review of 19 studies found elevated levels of anxiety and depression due to a "high expectation on girls in terms of appearance and weight." Over half of American teenage girls are on unhealthy diets. The American Academy of Facial Plastic and Reconstructive Surgery reported an increase in plastic surgeries among teens due to a desire to look better on social media.

THE UNTHING EXPERIMENT

When Carpenter reported on the radical cultural changes that were in part brought about by people seeing their images in a Polaroid, he did so in hopes that we would analyze our own use of technology as well.

To analyze the effects of my tools on me, I once tried to avoid all visual images for a month. I stopped watching TV. I used an image blocker on my web browser (Wizmage for Chrome) and configured my phone to not load images. Of course, I couldn't avoid all images. I still caught a glimpse of a billboard or product box now and then. But I lived more or less without the supernormal stimuli of photoshopped and surgically enhanced beautiful people living apparently extraordinary lives beyond any life that I could ever imagine for myself.

Within just a few days, I started to notice a difference. I found ordinary people and ordinary life much more interesting, engaging, and beautiful. Three weeks later, I was in an airport and felt a surge of *joie de vivre* as I entered the mass of humanity. I was surrounded by beautiful people doing extraordinary things. Every one of them seemed to have an attractive quality and something interesting to say. Just a month earlier, I would have entered that same mass of people and seen nothing but overweight, unstylish, unkempt, and unattractive people. But within a few weeks removed from the onslaught of media, my consciousness had changed.

It struck me that media puts us in a state of passive consumption. In media worlds, people and their lives exist for our enjoyment. They are objects and characters to like or dislike, rather than complex people with complex histories and experiences to engage and interact with. As I stopped seeing people as objects, I saw beauty and worth in each of them. Without the distraction of media, I freed up several hours of my day that I spent exercising, talking to friends, and being out in the world.

LEARN MORE

- Amusing Ourselves to Death
  by Neil Postman
- Here Comes Everybody
  by Clay Shirky
- The Net Delusion: The Dark Side of Internet Freedom, by Evgeny Morozov
- What Made Maddy Run
  by Kate Fagan

Challenge Five: The UnThing Experiment

Your challenge is to give something up and live without a key technology for at least 48 hours.

Objective: Practice the art of seeing. See your seeing as you observe how this technology might shape your assumptions. See big – how it is an integral part of a larger cultural system. See small – how it might shape our most mundane routines (or even our bodies). See it all - how our lives and culture might be different (for better and for worse) without it.

Step 1. Give something up, like shoes, chairs, or cars. Or try giving up some form of virtual communication platform for at least 48 hours, and potentially a week or more.

Step 2. Post daily updates using #anth101challenge5, reflecting on the following:

- What do you miss about using the thing?
- What have you gained by not using it?
- How have you changed? Any insights? Do you see the world or other people any differently?

Step 3. Continue the experiment until you have some significant results. (Extend the time frame or move up a level if you do not have any significant insights.)

Step 4. Use your insights to reflect on the key lesson: "We create our tools and then our tools create us."

Learn more at anth101.com/challenge5

Lesson Six

Social Structure

Most of what we take as "reality" is a cultural construction – "realized" through our unseen, unexamined assumptions of what is right, true, or possible.

LOVE IN FOUR CULTURES

Nimakot Village, Papua New Guinea

Late one morning, a large argument broke out in the central clearing of the village. A young man and woman named Matius and Rona sat looking dejected and ashamed near the center of the scuffle. The two teenagers had been discovered sneaking off together the previous night, and had been dragged into the clearing by their families. Rona's brother sat next to her, armed with his 29-inch machete, and looked menacingly at Matius. Matius averted his eyes and stared down at the ground, picking at the grass with his fingers as the chaos of the argument swirled around him. Rona's mother stormed across the lawn, demanding that the boy's family give her a large pig. Others from the girl's family nodded with approval and encouraged her to continue. I sat with a group of locals about 20 meters away from the main action. One of the local women turned to me with a tear in her eye as the argument escalated. Crying with tears of joy, like a mother watching her own daughter on her wedding day, she said, "This is just like when I got married!"

There are no formal ritual "weddings" in this part of New Guinea, but events like this often mark the moment that a man and woman announce their commitment to one another. By the end of the vigorous discussion, the "bride price" had been set. Matius would need to give the bride's family 95 items such as string bags, clothes, and machetes. At a total market value of nearly $3,000 USD, the request was many times the amount of wealth of any typical villager. He would have to call upon his entire family for help, but even that would not be enough. The challenge of building such a tremendous amount of wealth would become an all-consuming and tremendously stressful task for the next several years of his life. At stake was his entire future – children, family, respect – even his most basic sense of manhood.

Maasai Boarding School, Kenya

When Esther was 14, she learned that her father planned to give her away in marriage to an older man. She ran away to her older sister's house, who helped her enroll in a school far away. But her father rushed the wedding plans, and her mother tracked her down and removed her from the school. Still hoping that she could escape the arranged marriage, she went to the District Officer, who told her about a rescue center sponsored by an international aid team that hopes to save young girls like Esther from early marriage and give her a chance at school.

Her father came to the rescue center to retrieve Esther, but the headmistress would not allow it, declaring Esther "a school child." Her father disowned her on the spot. He replayed the scene to anthropologist Caroline Archambault. "Esther will be your child," he told the school. "You will give her a husband and she will never set foot in my house again."

Madurai Village, Tamil Nadu, South India

For as long as Mayandi could remember, there was only one right girl for him, his cousin. As the firstborn boy in a Kallar family of the

Tamil, it was not only his right, but also "the right thing to do" to marry his mother's brother's daughter. The girl was quite literally the right girl for him, and they had a word for it, "*murai*."

Mayandi understood that it might seem cruel to an outsider unfamiliar with their customs that someone should be forced to marry someone. As he told American anthropologist Isabel Clark-Decés about their customs, he joked that the "right" person is not always "all right." Young Tamil girls would often tease each other about the "right" boys they were destined to marry. Mayandi struck the pose of a young girl talking to her girlfriend and joked, "Runny Nose is here to see you!" or "Eggshell Eyes is at your door!"

But Mayandi, like many other young Tamil, came to love and desire his "right" girl very much. It would bring status and honor to the family to marry her. His in-laws would not be strangers and would always feel welcomed in his house. He imagined a wonderful life for himself, his bride-to-be, and their growing family.

But tragedy struck as they approached marriageable age. The bride-to-be's father got involved in a deadly fight that sent him off to prison, and she had to move into the city. Mayandi was desperate to still make things work out and pressed his mother to arrange the marriage, but it wasn't to be. She married another man two years later.

Mayandi was devastated. He refused to marry for the next 20 years. Finally, after much pressure from his family, he relented and married his sister's daughter. They now have two children.

Edinburgh, Scotland

Rabih is not worried about collecting money so that he can pay for a bride. He is not worried about his sister being pulled out of school and being forced to marry a man against her will, and he would never dream of marrying his cousin. Rabih has his own set of troubles as he pursues love and marriage.

Rabih is "in love," as they say in his culture. As he sits in his room daydreaming about her, his mind wanders to fantasies of their future together. He lets his mind run free and wonders whether or not she might be "the One," his "soul mate" who will "complete him." It is his highest ideal, and the thing he wants more than anything in his life.

Feelings of passionate love are not unknown throughout the world. Anthropologists have documented them in nearly every culture they have studied, and have found evidence for romantic love going back thousands of years. But there is something historically and culturally unique about the feelings of people like Rabih. In the words of philosopher Allain de Botton, who tells the story of Rabih in *The Course of Love*, finding and falling in love "has been allowed to take on the status of something close to the purpose of life," and this feeling should be the foundation upon which a marriage should be built. "True love" is everlasting, and thought to be the most important part of a good marriage. If passion fades, it was not "true love."

This is precisely what worries Rabih. He has been in love before. He has hurt and been hurt. How can he be sure that this is the one? How can he make sure that their passion for one another will continue to burn?

In this chapter, we'll explore love and marriage in four different cultures. In order to understand their radically different ideas, ideals, and practices, we will have to use our anthropological tools for seeing our own seeing, seeing big, seeing small, and seeing it all. We'll have to examine many different dimensions of culture – infrastructure, social structure, and superstructure – to see how they all come to bear on ideas and practices of love and marriage.

Culture, as we have seen in the preceding chapters, is a powerful structure, but this structure is *con*-structed. The structure is nothing but the total sum of all of our actions, habits, ideas, ideals, beliefs, values and practices, no matter how big or small. A cultural structure is a powerful force in our lives. It provides the context and meaning for our lives. But, at the same time, our collective actions make the structure.

We make the structure.
The structure makes us.

This exploration will not only help us understand how different cultural realities get "real-ized," but might also help us understand our own realities in new ways. Such an exploration might even help speed us along on our own journeys toward understanding those perplexing questions about love that Rabih is trying to answer. As Alain de Botton notes, it will ultimately be Rabih's ability to see past his cultural conventions that will allow him to live up to his cultural ideals. He suggests that Rabih will need

> *"...to recognize that the very things that he once considered romantic – wordless intuitions, instantaneous longings, a trust in soul mates – are what stand in the way of learning how to be with someone. He will surmise that love can endure only when one is unfaithful to its beguiling opening ambitions, and that, for his relationships to work, he will need to give up on the feelings that got him into them in the first place. He will need to learn that love is a skill rather than an enthusiasm."*

A WORLD WITHOUT MONEY

Nimakot, Papua New Guinea

Matius had big plans for the day. He would be seeing one of his trading partners from a distant village, and hoped that he could ask him to support him in his quest to pay his bride price. It didn't bother Matius that his trade partner would be part of a planned attack on his village. In fact, he seemed excited by the prospect.

As word of the pending attack spread, all of the men from the village, along with a few close friends and kin from other villages, came in from their garden houses and hunting excursions, filling the village with a sense of intense anticipation. Men performed chants and dances in the village clearing, pumping themselves up for the attack, while women peeked out through the cracks and darkened doorways of village huts, anxiously awaiting what was to come.

We built a barricade of trees, limbs, and vines along the main path, but we knew this would do little more than slow them down.

Around noon, we heard a twig snap just beyond our barrier, and the village erupted into a frenzy of action. "Woop! Woop! Woop!" we heard the attackers call out, as dozens of them crashed our barricade and came rushing down the mountain into our village. Their faces were painted red and their hands dripped with what looked like blood, but they were not armed with spears or bows. They were armed instead with sweet potatoes dripping with delicious and fatty red marita sauce. They smashed the dripping tubers into our faces, forcing us to eat, attacking us with kindness and generosity.

They left as quickly as they came, but the challenge was set. We were to follow them back to their village and see if we could handle all the food they had prepared for us. We had to navigate a series of booby traps and sneak attacks of generosity along the way, sweet potatoes and taro being thrown at us from the trees. When we finally arrived at the edge of the village, their troops gathered for one last intimidating chant. They circled in and yelled as loudly as they could for as long as they could, letting the giant collective yell drown out in a thumping rhythmic and barrel-chested "Woop! Woop! Woop!" We responded in kind with our own chant, and then charged in for the food.

As we entered the village, we found a giant pit filled with red marita juice filled to the brim with hundreds of sweet potatoes and taro. It was bigger than a kiddie pool, no less than six feet across and nearly two feet deep. The marita seeds that had been washed to create this pool littered every inch of ground throughout the entire village. It was no wonder that the attack had taken several days to prepare.

We settled in for the feast with gusto, dozens of us taking our turn at the pit. But an hour in we were starting to fade, and the waterline of our pool of food seemed barely to budge. Our hosts laughed in triumph and started boasting about how they had gathered too much food for us to handle, giving credit to those among them who cleaned it, processed it, thanking each contributor in turn, and then proudly boasting again that their generosity was too much for us. We left, defeated, but already taking stock of our own marita produce and planning a return attack in the near future.

This is a world without money, banks, or complex insurance policies. Their items of value (like marita and sweet potatoes) cannot be stored indefinitely without spoiling. So large events like this serve a similar function as our banks and insurance companies. When they have a windfall of marita they give it away, knowing that when we have a windfall of marita we will return the favor. Such events strengthen social bonds and trade relationships, which are essential to survival in tough times.

For decades, most economists built their models on rational choice theory – the assumption that all humans are selfish and seek to maximize their own material gain. But these beliefs and values may be a reflection of our own socially constructed realities revolving around money in a market economy, rather than human nature. In these New Guinea villages, they struggle instead to demonstrate their generosity and minimize their material gain. They are not trying to accumulate wealth. Instead, they are trying to nurture relationships through which wealth can flow. This does not mean they are not rational, but when applied in New Guinea, rational choice theory has to account for the different motives and values created within the cultural context of different economic systems.

Anthropologists describe the difference between these economic systems as *gift economies* and *market economies.* In both economies, the same items might be exchanged and distributed, but in one they are treated as gifts and in the other they are treated as commodities.

Take, for example, a bag of sweet potatoes. In a gift economy, the bag of sweet potatoes is given with no immediate payment expected or desired. Instead, the giver hopes to strengthen the relationship between themselves and the recipient. The giver will likely give a brief biography of the potatoes, who planted them, tended them, harvested them, and so on, so that the recipient understands their connection to several people who have all contributed to the gift. In a commodity economy, that same bag becomes a commodity. It has a price, something like $5, and the recipient is expected to pay this price immediately. Once the price is paid, the transaction is over.

There are strong practical reasons for gift economies and market economies. Gift economies tend to thrive in small communities and where most things of value have a short shelf-life. Wealth is not easily stored, and there are no banks or currencies for them to store their wealth in either. The best way to "store" wealth is to nurture strong relationships. That way, when your own maritas are not ripe or your garden is out of food, all of those people that you have given to in the past will be there to give to you.

But beyond these practical reasons for the gift economy, are also some profound implications for the core values, ideas, and ideals that emerge in gift economies. In gift economies, people are constantly engaged in relationship-building activities as they give and receive gifts throughout the day. The constant reminders of where the gift came from and all the hands that helped give them a profound sense of interdependence. Along with this sense of interdependence comes a value on relationships rather than things. Most "things" are quickly consumed, rot, and fall apart. It is far more beneficial to have a strong network of relationships than a big pile of slowly rotting sweet potatoes.

It is only in this context that we can begin to understand the practice of "bride price" in New Guinea, and why Matius must face this seemingly impossible task of gathering $3,000 worth of items in exchange for his bride. From the Western perspective grounded in the logic of a market economy, this looks like he is "buying" a wife. But from the logic of a gift economy, he is building and strengthening a vast network of social relationships that will soon unite his network with the network of his bride.

The day turns out to be a great success for Matius. His trading partner has agreed to support him. His gift will join with the gifts of many others. And when Matius gives this bundle of gifts to his bride's family, they will spread those gifts throughout their network. By the logic of the gift economy, these people will give back, and a large cycle of giving will be created that unites two large networks that intersect at the new node created by the union of the bride and groom.

MARRIAGE WITHOUT LOVE

Maasai Boarding School, Kenya

A similar gift logic operates among the Maasai as well. When Esther's father arranged for her marriage at age 14, he was following a customary system in which the parents of both the bride and groom agree on the marriage terms for their children while they are still young. The bride price is paid over the course of the entire marriage. "There is probably no greater gift, as viewed by the Maasai, then having been given a daughter," notes Dr. Achimbault. "Marriage is understood and valued as an alliance of families."

Esther's father has three wives and 26 children. This practice of having many wives, known as polygyny, is common among pastoralists like the Maasai. This practice can be especially perplexing to any Westerner who believes in "true love." In a recent BBC program, a BBC reporter approached some Maasai teenage boys and asks directly, "What does love mean to you?" The boys laugh shyly and one of them rocks back and forth uncomfortably with a broad smile on his face. "That's a real challenge!" one exclaims and asks his friend to answer, who just giggles and turns away.

The reporter presses on the issue of polygyny. "When you do get married, are you going to take more than one wife or just one?" she asks. One boy answers matter-of-factly, "I will take one or two but no more than two."

She is taken aback by the nonchalance of his answer. She counters by joking with him, saying if he only takes one he can have her, but she would never be involved in a polygynous marriage. The man starts laughing. "But the work would be very hard for just one wife," the young man explains. "You would have to look after the cows, goats, water, and firewood – all on your own!"

Recent anthropological studies by Dr. Monique Borgerhoff Mulder support the man's argument and show that polygynous households among the Maasai have better access to food and healthier children.

One of the Maasai women wants to show the reporter that polygamy is actually good for them, and takes her to see the most senior wife of a polygynous family. She lives in a beautiful brick home, far superior to most of the other homes in the region. The economic incentive for polygyny seems clear, but the reporter is still skeptical about the quality of the marriage relationships. "Don't you get jealous of the other wives?" the reporter asks.

"No, no. Never."

"Do you argue?"

"No ... we're friends. We never fight. We are all the same age. We tell stories. We have fun."

Marriage practices like this are especially mystifying for people in the West. For many Westerners, love is our biggest concern and our strongest value, so when we find cultures that practice arranged marriage or polygamy, we find it strange and immediately infer that there may be a violation of basic human rights. But if we look at all humans through all time, it is *our* ideas about love that are strange.

Over 80 percent of all cultures worldwide practice polygyny (one man married to more than one woman) and a handful of others practice polyandry (one woman married to more than one man). As hinted at by the response from the Maasai teen that the work of a household would be very difficult for just one woman, the common reasons given for why these forms of marriage often come down to practicality. There is no mention of love.

Such marriages often make sense within the culture and environment. For example, in Tibet, where arable land is scarce and passed down through males, several brothers may marry one woman in order to keep the land together. As anthropologist Melvyn Goldstein has pointed out, if the land were divided among all sons in each generation, it would only take a few generations for the land to be too small to provide enough for the families.

Despite these apparent practical benefits, the value and romanticism we place on love makes the idea of young girls like Esther being married off at a young age unpalatable to most Westerners. When Esther's father attempts to remove her from school and arrange her marriage, he seems to be upholding oppressive patriarchal values.

But Esther's father is practical and he wants what is best for his children. He has sent most of his kids to school in hopes that they can find new ways to make a living. However, school is far away and expensive. Due to the dangers and difficulties of getting to school, most girls enter school late, just as they are reaching reproductive age. This creates a risk of early pregnancy, which will get them kicked out of school and greatly limit their marriage prospects. Furthermore, the schools have high drop-out rates and even those who finish are not guaranteed a job.

Pastoralism – the traditional way of making a living – has become more difficult due to frequent droughts brought about by climate change. Land privatization poses an additional problem, since a pastoralist is now constricted to the land to which he has a legal right. In times of drought and scarcity, movement across vast land areas is essential. One strategy for increasing the land one has access to is to create alliances between lineages through strategically arranged marriages. When Esther's father tried to pull her out of school, he did so because he saw an opportunity for her to have a secure future as a pastoralist with access to good land.

After laying out these essential pieces of context, Archambault makes the case that we should be skeptical of simple "binaries" that frame one side as "modern" and empowering of females and the other as "traditional" and upholding the patriarchy. Such binaries are common among NGOs promoting their plan to improve human rights. But through the lens of anthropology, we can see our assumptions, see the big picture, and see the details that allow us to understand the cultural situation, empathize with the people involved, and ultimately make more informed policy decisions.

LOVE WITHOUT MARRIAGE

Madurai Village, Tamil Nadu, South India

Sunil's marriage prospects looked good. In an arranged marriage among the Tamil, families carefully consider the wealth, status, reputation, and earning potential of potential marriage partners. Sunil had it all, and he was on his way to earning a prestigious law degree. But then he was struck by *katal* – an overwhelming sense of intense and dumbfounded longing for another person that we might call "love" in English. They say it is a "great feeling" that can "drive you crazy" and compels you to "do things you would not ordinarily do." It is a "permanent intoxication," as one 18-year old Tamil put it.

Love like this is known all over the world. Anthropologist Helen Fisher looked at 166 cultures, and found evidence of passionate love in 147 of them. As for the rest, she suspects that the ethnographers just did not pay attention to it. The Tamil are no different. The feeling of love may not be the foundation for their arranged marriages, but that does not mean the Tamil do not feel love.

Sunil described the girl as "smart, free, funny, and popular." He met up with her every day after class, and soon he was, as he says, "addicted" to her. Addiction might be the right word. Fisher studied brain scans of people in love and found that the caudate nucleus and ventral tegmental area of the brains lit up each time they were shown an image of their lover. These are areas of the brain associated with rewards, pleasure, and focused attention. Other studies have found that falling in love floods our brain with chemicals associated with the reward circuit, fueling two apparently opposite but mutually sustaining emotions: passion and anxiety. Overall, the studies reveal a chemical profile similar to someone with obsessive-compulsive disorder.

When two people share these feelings together, they can experience a shared euphoria like almost no other experience available to humankind. But when only one person feels this obsessive-compulsive form of passionate love – or when one person stops feeling it while the other still feels it – it can unleash a devastating psychological breakdown.

Sunil's romance was rocky. They started disagreeing and using harsh words with one another. After a fight one night, Sunil worried that she would leave him. His obsession gripped him with a flood of anxiety. He tried calling her at 2 am, but she did not answer. Desperate to talk to her, he went to her college early the next morning in hopes of catching her before her first class. "She was so happy to see me in the pathetic state I was in," Sunil lamented. When she called later to break off the relationship, Sunil completely broke down. He became an alcoholic and had to drop out of law school.

After two years of pain and trouble, he finally got over her, stopped drinking, and finished law school. But by then he had already missed out on his best opportunity for a successful arranged marriage with his favorite cousin. The perfect match, someone he had thought about marrying since the time he was a teenager, had come of age while he was drinking away his sorrows and had already married someone else (a different cousin).

Sunil's story represents an interesting tension at work as Tamil society continues to change. A more urban and mobile society creates more opportunities for young people to meet strangers and to feel *katal* for them. Education and career opportunities take young people far from home and family. The culture is starting to value individualism, free choice, and autonomy – all of which come together to make love marriages seem attractive. A common theme of Indian movies and television shows is the tension between love and arranged marriages.

However, most Tamil do not elope and create love marriages. From the standpoint of the family, the reasons are clear. As anthropologist Clark-Decés points out, "The basic explanation for this is that marriage is too important to be left to chance individual attraction – in fact, a child's marriage is the most important and often the most expensive decision a South Asian family ever has to make."

Worldwide, arranged marriages are especially common when a significant transfer of wealth is at stake, such as a large inheritance, bride price, or dowry. In India, marriage usually entails very large gifts between the families, often the equivalent of three years of salary or more. When the wealth of an entire extended family is on the line, everybody in the extended family has a vested interest in the union and arranged marriages are the norm and ideal.

It is not surprising then that the parents of bride and groom would prefer an arranged marriage. However, Clark- Decés and other anthropologists note that arranged marriage remains the norm and ideal among youth as well. Young men like Sunil want to achieve success and respectability within the ideals and values of their culture. They view marriage as the union of two families, not just two people. And ultimately, "for them, an arranged marriage is a sign of parental love."

This preference for arranged marriages has a profound impact on how people grow up. As Clark-Decés points out, the social category of "bachelor" is non-existent. Tamil youth do not spend a great deal of time in their teens and twenties worrying about who to date or how to date, since that is rarely the road toward marriage. Instead, they focus primarily on attaining significant status markers that confer wealth and prestige, such as their education. Whereas college in the United States is often seen as a place to meet a potential mate, college in South India is a place where one earns a degree to elevate their status for an arranged marriage.

It is not that love is absent or impossible in arranged marriages, but it is not the primary basis upon which marriages are formed. In a recent survey, 76% of Indians said they would marry someone if they had the right qualities, even if they were not in love. Only 14% of Americans would do so. As Leena Abraham found in a study of college students in Mumbai, love marriages are "seen as an arrangement beset with enormous insecurity."

ORIGINS OF LOVE MARRIAGE

Love marriage was once uncommon in the West as well. It was not until the Industrial Revolution and the broad cultural changes that came with it that love marriage became the norm. With the Industrial Revolution, individuals were no longer tied to land held in the family name. They became more mobile and less dependent on family and community for survival. People started orienting their lives more toward the market, and they could use the state for a safety net, weakening their dependency on relationships and family.

This increased individualism had two competing effects. On the one hand, it gave people more freedom. They became accustomed to making individual choices every moment of the day. But this freedom came with a cost. As they had more and more choices about what to buy, what to do, and how to act, they were also increasingly troubled with the question of whether or not they were choosing the right thing to buy, the right thing to do, or the right way to act. They came to suffer from a sense of what Emile Durkheim called *anomie*, a condition in which society provides little guidance and leaves people feeling lost and disconnected.

Feeling empowered by the power to choose, yet feeling lost and disconnected, romantic love marriage emerged as the perfect solution. We go searching for "the One" who can make us "feel whole" and "completes us." This is the key to understanding just how different we are from those Massai teens. They live in small, close-knit communities full of tight bonds to family and friends. Large, close-knit families are still the ideal in India as well. They do not need more intimacy. They have enough of it already. We, on the other hand, often feel alone, lost, and insecure. We crave intimacy. We crave a sense of validation. And we find that through love.

Unfortunately, this sets up an impossible situation. With the breakdown of family and community, we often turn to our lovers for intimacy, friendship, and economic support. One person is expected to provide all of this and passion at the same time. "We now ask our lovers for the emotional connection and sense of belonging that my grandmother could get from a whole village," notes family therapist Sue Johnson. But the security necessary for the intimacy and friendship we crave along with the everyday trials and mundanity of running a household can kill passion.

THE PARADOXES OF LOVE AND MARRIAGE

Edinburgh, Scotland

"For most of recorded history, people married for logical sorts of reasons: because her parcel of land adjoined yours, his family had a flourishing grain business, her father was the magistrate in town, there was a castle to keep up, or both sets of parents subscribed to the same interpretation of a holy text … what has replaced it – the marriage of feeling … What matters is that two people wish desperately that it happen, are drawn to another by an overwhelming instinct, and know in their hearts that it is right."

- Allain de Botton

In his book *The Course of Love,* philosopher Allain de Botton tells the love story of Rabih and Kirsten, along with his cutting observations about love and marriage. After a whirlwind romance, Rabih proposes to her, hoping to capture the feelings he and Kirsten have for each other and preserve them forever. Unfortunately, you cannot freeze a feeling, or marry one. You have to marry a person with whom you once shared a feeling. And feelings are not necessarily forever.

In *A Natural History of Love*, anthropologist Helen Fisher identifies two kinds of love: the burning fire of romantic passionate love, and the enduring intimacy and calm of companionate love. These two loves have very different chemical profiles in the brain. Romantic love is a rush of dopamine, a drop in serotonin, and a rise in cortisol that creates an intense passion and desire. Companionate love activates the attachment circuits of the brain. It is oxytocin-rich and induces a loving calm and sense of security. Unfortunately, this sense of calm and security can actually work against our feelings of passion. Passion thrives on insecurity. The reason for our obsessive ruminations and fluttering hearts is in part the very frightening idea that we might lose this person or that they might not return our love. The more we try to freeze the feeling by "locking in" the relationship through promises, proposals, or other means of entanglement, the more we drive it away. A desire for connection requires a sense of separation. The more we fuse our lives together, the less passionate we become.

This is not a problem in many cultures where passion in marriage is not required or expected. But in the West, there is a strong sense that "true love" burns with passion forever. If passion fades, it isn't "true love."

So as Rabih and Kirsten squabble in Ikea over which drinking glasses to purchase for their apartment, there is a lot more at stake than mere aesthetics. This will be one of thousands of little squabbles that are unavoidable when merging two lives, but they will always reflect deeper concerns and misgivings each one has about the other person. Such squabbles will be the main forum where they will try to shape and shift one another, make adaptations and compromises in who they are, and assess the quality of their relationship.

These negotiations are fraught with tension because of another ideal of "true love"—that it is unconditional, and that if someone truly loves you they will unequivocally accept you for all that you are and never try to change you. Each little push or prod feels like a rejection of the self.

Behind these feelings are deep and profound cultural assumptions about love itself. We tend to focus on love as a feeling. But according to a landmark book by psychologist Erich Fromm, our focus should not be on "being loved" so much as it should be on the *act of loving* and building up one's capacity to love. This insight runs counter to the cultural ideal of "true love" which says that when we find the right person, love will come easily and without effort. As a result of our misunderstandings about love, Fromm argues, "there is hardly any activity, any enterprise, which is started with such tremendous hopes and expectations, and yet, which fails so regularly, as love."

This basic insight is easy to accept intellectually, but it is quite another thing to incorporate it into your everyday life. For Rabih and Kirsten, it is the arrival of their first child that helps them understand love as something to give rather than something to merely feel and expect to be given. The helpless and demanding baby gives them ample practice in selfless love of another without any expectation of return.

Unfortunately for Rabih and Kirsten, their ability to love their child does not translate into an act of loving for one another. In the midst of sleepless nights, diaper changes, and domestic duties, there is little love left to give after caring for the baby. Over the coming years, Rabih and Kirsten admire each other greatly for the patience and care shown for their children, but also feel pangs of remorse and jealousy that such love and kindness had become so rare between them.

One would think that after so many years of marriage, people would stop needing a sense of validation from the other. But, de Botton notes, "we are never through with the requirement for acceptance. This isn't a curse limited to the inadequate and the weak." So long as we continue to care about the other person, we are unlikely to be able to free ourselves from concerns about how they feel about us.

Unfortunately, Rabih and Kirsten need very different things to feel a sense of validation. Rabih wants to rekindle the passionate love they once shared in sexual union. But after a long day of giving her body and self to her children, Kirsten does not want to be touched. She needs time to herself, and Rabih's "romantic" proposals feel like just another thing to put on her long "to do" list for others.

Allain de Botton's Story of Love recounts many twists and turns in the love story of Rabih and Kirsten. It is an honest portrayal of a true love story in which seemingly mundane arguments about who does more housework take their rightful place alongside more dramatic affairs and bouts of jealousy. Though they often feel distance between them, they go through everything – raising kids, watching their own parents grow old and die – together.

It is only after all of this – 13 years after saying their vows – that Rabih finally feels "ready for marriage." He is ready not because he is finally secure in an unequivocal faith in a perfect love with his soul mate for whom he feels an unbounding and never-ending sense of passion, but because he has given up on the idea that love should come easily. He is committed to the *art of loving*, not just a desire to *be loved*, and looks forward to all that his life, his wife, and his children might teach him along the way.

LEARN MORE

- "Ethnographic Empathy and the Social Context of Rights: 'Rescuing' Maasai Girls from Early marriage" by Caroline S. Archambault. American Anthropologist 113(4):632-643.
- The Right Spouse: Preferential Marriages in Tamil Nadu, by Isabelle Clark- Decés
- The Course of Love: A Novel by Alain de Botton

BECOMING OUR SELVES

Daniel has no eyes. Born with an aggressive eye cancer, they were removed before his first birthday. From an early age, Daniel realized that he could sense what objects are around him and where they are by clicking and listening for the echoes. Ever since then, like a bat, he uses echolocation to find his way around the world. It has allowed him to run around his neighborhood freely, climb trees, hike alone into the wilderness, and generally get around well as someone with perfect vision. "I can honestly say that I do not feel blind," he says.

In fact, he never thought of himself as "blind" until he met another boy named Adam at his elementary school. By then, Daniel was already riding bikes, packing his own lunch, and walking to school by himself. Adam, in contrast, had always attended a special school for the blind and had a constant supply of helpers to escort him through the world and guide him through his daily routines.

Daniel was frustrated with Adam's helplessness. He couldn't understand why Adam couldn't do things for himself or join in games on the playground. Even worse, the other kids started to mix Daniel and Adam up. They were "the blind boys." For the first time, Daniel felt what it was like to have society define him as "blind." And he was shocked and frustrated to discover that society did not expect any more from him than they did from Adam.

He had trouble making sense of it until he found a book by sociologist Robert Scott called *The Making of Blind Men.* In that book, Scott suggests that blindness is socially constructed. From the first powerful paragraph onward, Scott argues that "the various attitudes and patterns of behavior that characterize people who are blind are not inherent in the condition but, rather, are acquired through ordinary process of social learning."

To most people, this sounds shocking and farfetched. How can blindness be "socially constructed"? Blindness seems to be a matter-of-fact physical reality, especially in the case of Daniel, who has no eyes. But Scott doesn't mean to question this physical reality. Instead, he wants to challenge the assumptions that create a social role for blind people as "docile, dependent, melancholy, and helpless." Throughout his research, he meets many people like Daniel who defy these expectations, but finds others who have been conditioned to fit the stereotype. "Blind men are made," Scott declares emphatically, "by the same process of socialization that have made us all."

Scott moves the discussion beyond blindness to point out that we are all "made." Our self-concept is our estimation of how others see us given our culture's core beliefs, expectations, and values. This self-concept in turn shapes how we perceive the world and engage with it. In other words, most of what we take as "reality" is socially constructed, "real-ized" through our unseen, unexamined assumptions about what is right, true, or possible.

Scott reveals three processes through which our realities – such as "blindness" – are real-ized.

1. **Beliefs and expectations:** The first is the process of enculturation through which we learn the basic "common sense" beliefs and values of our culture.

From an early age, people learn a set of stereotypical expectations and beliefs about blind people as "docile, dependent, melancholy, and helpless." Blind people take on these beliefs and expectations as part of their self-concept.

2. **Behaviors and interactions:** Second, these beliefs become guidelines for our behaviors and interactions with others. In this way, even if a blind person has the fortitude to reject the stereotypes of blindness put upon them, they might be denied opportunities for more independence by the expectations of others who do not allow the blind person to take on a job or do other things for themselves.

3. **Structures and institutions:** Third, these beliefs and behaviors are woven into larger institutions and other social structures through which the beliefs and behaviors are reinforced. Institutionalized norms, laws, behaviors, and services shape our beliefs about what is right, true, and possible.

Scott found that blind people were encouraged to attend special schools and follow specific job tracks designed to accommodate their disabilities. They were offered free rides, escorted by hand through their daily activities, and had many of their daily tasks done for them. While these are all well-intentioned services, Scott also noticed that they reinforced the message that "blind people can't do these things." When Scott did the original research for his book in the 1960s, nearly 2/3 of blind American students were not participating in gym class. He worried that by treating blind people as helpless, they were becoming more helpless.

Many studies support this concern. Even rats seem to change their behavior based on what people think of them. In a remarkably clever experiment, psychologist Bob Rosenthal lied to his research assistants and told them that one group of rats was "smart" and another group "dumb." They were, in fact, the same kind of rats with no differences between them, yet the "smart" rats performed twice as well on the experimental tests as the "dumb" rats. Careful analysis found that the expectations of the experimenters subtly changed the way they behaved toward the rats, and those subtle behaviors made a big difference.

Other studies have found that teacher's expectations of students can raise or lower IQ scores and a study of military trainers found that their expectations can affect how fast a soldier can run. As psychologist Carol Dweck explains, we convey our expectations through very subtle cues, such as how far we stand apart and how much eye contact we make. These subtle behaviors make a difference in how people perform.

While we all understand the power of our own belief on our own behavior, these studies demonstrate that other people's beliefs can also affect us. This link between belief and behavior can become a vicious circle. A teacher's low expectations make a student perform poorly. The poor performance justifies and re-enforces the low expectations, so the student continues to perform poorly, and so on.

Daniel Kish was raised by a mother who refused to let society's expectations of blindness become Daniel's destiny. She let him roam free and challenged him to find his own way to make his way in the world. As a result, Daniel's mastery of echolocation allowed him to "see" and distinguish trees, park benches, and poles. He now enjoys hiking in the woods, bike rides, and walking around town without any assistance or seeing aids.

These abilities are reflected in his brain. Brain scans show that Daniel's visual cortex lights up as he uses echolocation. His mind is actually creating visual imagery from the information he receives through echolocation, so despite not having any eyes, he can see. Recent studies suggest that he actually *sees* with the same visual acuity as an ordinary person sees in their peripheral vision. In other words, he may not be able to read the words in a book, but he knows the book is there.

The story of Daniel Kish is a fitting opening for this lesson, because it reveals how a trio of forces – beliefs, behaviors, and structures – can shape how we see the world and ourselves. From an early age we are immersed in beliefs, behaviors and structures that tell us how to be a man or a woman, what it means to be "white," "black," or "Asian," and what qualifies as "handsome," "beautiful," or "sexy" among many other ideals and values that will form the backdrop against which we will form our sense of who we are.

GENDER: BIOLOGY OR CULTURE?

In the toy section of a store, you are likely to find an aisle of soft "girly" colors like pink and purple populated with dolls and playhouses. The next aisle has colder colors and sharper edges with guns and cars. Before they can put together a full sentence, most children will know which toys are for boys and which are for girls. Do these different interests of boys and girls reflect innate biological differences, or is the socialization of boys and girls so powerful that it already starts to appear at a very young age?

An issue of *Ladies Home Journal* in 1918 assigned blue to girls and pink to boys. It wasn't until the 1940s that American culture settled into the now familiar and taken-for-granted idea that pink is for girls and blue is for boys. But while the color of the toys is obviously a cultural construction, the boy's affinity for cars and trucks and the girl's affinity for dolls continues to be the subject of wide-spread debate in neuroscience, biology, psychology, and the social sciences.

In 1911, Thorndike suggested that the reason boys like trucks and girls like dolls is that men are more interested in "things and their mechanisms" and women are more interested in "persons and their feelings." Though highly controversial, a meta-study by Su, Rounds, and Armstrong in 2009 that analyzed dozens of studies on the topic found that men and women across multiple cultures see themselves differently, as "Women reported themselves to be higher in Neuroticism, Agreeableness, Warmth, and Openness to Feelings, whereas men were higher in Assertiveness and Openness to Ideas."

The differences were modest but statistically significant, and they seemed to confirm gender stereotypes. Other studies reveal similar results. Though there is no total scientific consensus, there is a strong contingent of scientists concluding that there are small but significant differences between men and women in their personality traits and interests. Conforming to the expectations of gender stereotypes, on average, women are slightly better than men when it comes to verbal reasoning, feeling, and empathy, while men on average are slightly better at systems thinking and spatial visualization. On average, women are more agreeable while men are more aggressive and assertive. The largest difference is that on average, women are more interested in people while men are more interested in things.

These differences are subtle, and there is a lot of overlap between men and women. If you were to pick a man or woman at random and try to guess if they would be above average in any of these traits, you would only improve your odds very little if you went with the stereotype. But even a small difference can matter a great deal when looking at what roles and careers people choose to pursue; indeed, a small difference in an average can make a big difference at the extremes. These subtle differences might potentially explain why women are so vastly under-represented in STEM fields but make up the majority of nurses and clinical psychologists (due to an interest in people vs. things). They might also explain why women are less well-represented in leadership positions (due, potentially, to men being more aggressive and less agreeable).

Are these differences real and permanent? Are they biological or cultural? The stakes of this debate are high. If these gender differences are real, innate, and unchangeable, then there may be little reason to suspect wide-spread discrimination and bias as the reason behind gender inequality. It might instead be a product of gendered choices and inclinations. Proponents of this position argue that we already have equal opportunity laws in place and a culture that promotes and champions the freedom to pursue your dreams. They suggest that perhaps the gender gap and apparent inequality is just a product of individual choices.

There are high stakes for men as well. Gender stereotypes that propose that men are more violent, courageous, and strong-willed, along with gender roles that ask men to provide for the family, serve the country, and sacrifice themselves for others while showing no signs of emotion or weakness, lead to many negative outcomes for men. While it is easy to look at the fact that 80% of all political leadership positions and 93% of the Fortune 500 CEOs are men and think that men have all the privilege, we should also consider the effect of gender stereotypes on the vast majority of men. Men's Rights Activists point out that men make up 97% of combat fatalities. They do more dangerous work, making up 93% of all work fatalities. Because they are stereotyped to be less nurturing, they lose custody in 84% of divorces. They also struggle more in school, making up just 43% of college enrollments. The problems start early, as they are nearly twice as likely as girls to repeat kindergarten.

With such high stakes, a constant flurry of articles, blog posts, YouTube videos, and message boards create a highly contentious and polarized cultural space where the origin and value of stereotypes is vehemently argued.

Contrary to what we would expect if these differences were biological and innate, they differ in magnitude across cultures. However, contrary to what we might expect if the differences were cultural, they are more pronounced in cultures where sex roles are more egalitarian and minimized, such as in European and American cultures. In Northern Europe, where gender equality is highest, gender differences in career choice are the most pronounced. Proponents of the biological thesis suggest that this is definitive proof that these differences are innate and not socially constructed.

But there are many critics of these studies. They point out a number of flaws in the studies that replicate gender stereotypes while offering little evidence that the stereotypes are actually true. For example, many of the most-cited studies ask participants to self-report on their level of empathy or respond hypothetically to prompts such as "I really enjoy caring for people" or "When I read the newspaper, I am drawn to tables of information, such as football league scores or stock market indices." Critics have found that in research situations in which people are reminded of their gender and gender stereotypes, the differences are magnified, but in situations where their gender is minimized the differences go away. A careful review of these studies by scholars like Cordelia Fine have found these self-report studies are unreliable in predicting actual behavior or actual ability, and the content of the questions themselves signal gender stereotypes (men like football and stock markets) that reveal little about how men and women actually think and more about how they have been culturally conditioned.

In short, the studies that attempt to suggest that gender differences are entirely rooted in biology continually come up short, but that is not to say there are not real biological differences. As biologists Anne Fausto-Sterling has summarized the situation, the brain "remains a vast unknown, a perfect medium on which to project, even unwittingly, assumptions about gender." But despite these unwitting assumptions, the cutting-edge research in psychology and neuroscience have demonstrated that there are real sex differences in the brain that should not be overlooked. Ongoing research is focusing less on whether gender is strictly biological or strictly cultural, and instead how biology and culture intersect in the creation of gender, trying to understand gender as a biocultural creation.

ARE GENDER STEREOTYPES UNIVERSAL?

Gender roles and stereotypes are pervasive in all cultures, and while there is some variation, there is also considerable overlap. All over the world and across almost all cultures, men hold more positions of leadership in economic, political, and religious domains, while women are most often the primary caregivers. Throughout much of human history, women would have been the primary source of sustenance for growing babies through breast feeding, leaving it to the man to do more work outside the home to bring home food. Men tend to be associated with public activities, while women are more associated with domestic activities. These differences usually also entail differences in status and power, so that globally we see pervasive inequality between men and women.

In Nimakot, Papua New Guinea, traditional religious beliefs practiced until the 1980s were centered around the great ancestress Afek. Temples throughout the region marked key places where she literally "gave birth" to the key elements of the culture. Women's reproductive powers were highly revered and feared. Menstrual blood was seen as dangerous and polluting. During their periods, women were required to stay in a small menstrual hut away from the main village, and women were never allowed into the men's house, where the most sacred rituals surrounding the ancestress took place. So while it may appear that women are given a lofty status in light of the culture revolving around an ancestress, in practice women were locked out of positions of sacred and political power, and forced into confinement for three days of every month.

There are a wide range of approaches and opinions on these matters, even within the same culture or religion. Some Muslim women, for example, see the wearing of the *hijab* head-covering as oppressive, refuse to wear it, and encourage other women to give it up as well. But other Muslim women argue that it is their right and choice to wear the *hijab* as an expression of their submission to God, and that it gives them the freedom to move about in public without the leering and objectifying eyes of men. Some of these same Muslim women argue that it is the scantily-clad Instagram model obsessed with her looks, morphing her body through diets, postures, and surgery, who is truly overcome and controlled by the gaze of men.

There is also considerable cultural variation in the total number of genders. The socialization of "men" and "women" starts at a very young age. By the time we are making the wish-list for our fifth birthday, we already take it for granted that there are two distinct categories of children: boys and girls. But a quick review of gender roles and categories around the world demonstrates that many of our ideas about gender are socially constructed and can exist in very different ways in different cultures.

It is commonly assumed that one is just born male or female, and while it is true that there are important biological differences formed at birth and ongoing differences that emerge throughout life, these are not easily put into a simple binary of male and female.

To understand this complexity, anthropologists find it useful to distinguish between sex and gender. Sex refers to an individual's biological traits while gender refers to cultural categories, roles, values, and identities. In short, sex is biological. Gender is cultural.

In India there is a third gender called the Hijra. Hijra are people who were usually born male but live their lives as a third gender, neither male nor female. Some are born intersexed, having both male and female reproductive organs. Texts dating back 4,000 years describe how Hijra were thought to bring luck and fertility. Several Native American cultures have also traditionally recognized a third gender and sometimes ascribed special curing powers to them. The Bugis on the island of Sulawesi recognize five genders. What we call "transgendered men" or "transgendered women" have a ready and identifiable role and place in their society. To these they add a fifth, the Bissu. Bissu are androgynous shamans. They are not merely thought to be gender neutral or non-binary. A better translation is that they are "gender transcendent." They are thought to have special connections to the hidden world of "batin." The Bugis believe that all five genders must live in harmony.

These more complex systems that move beyond the simple binary of male and female may be better suited for the realities of human variation. Over 70 million people worldwide are born intersexed. They have chromosomes, reproductive organs, or genitalia that are not exclusively male or female. In societies where such variations are not accepted, these individuals are often put through painful gender assignment surgeries that can cause psychological troubles later on if their inner identity fails to match with the identity others ascribe to them based on their biology.

"MAKING GENDER"

To understand how gender might be socially constructed, we can remove the references to blindness from the example in the opening story and create a sort of "Mad Libs" for the social real-ization of gender. You could fill in the blanks below with the expectations associated with either gender to create a short summary of how that gender is socially constructed.

1. **Beliefs and expectations:** From an early age, people learn a set of stereotypical expectations and beliefs about men/women as "__________." Men/women take on these beliefs and expectations as part of their self-concept.
2. **Behaviors and interactions:** Second, these beliefs become guidelines for our behaviors and interactions with others. In this way, even if a man/woman has the fortitude to reject the stereotypes put upon them, they might be denied opportunities for ____________ by the expectations of others who do not allow the men/women to ________.
3. **Structures and institutions:** Third, these beliefs and behaviors are woven into larger institutions and other social structures through which the beliefs and behaviors are reinforced. Institutionalized norms, laws, behaviors, and services shape our beliefs about what is right, true, and possible.

Together, these three concepts make up a trio of real-ization, with each element relating to and re-enforcing the others. You could draw the relations between them like this:

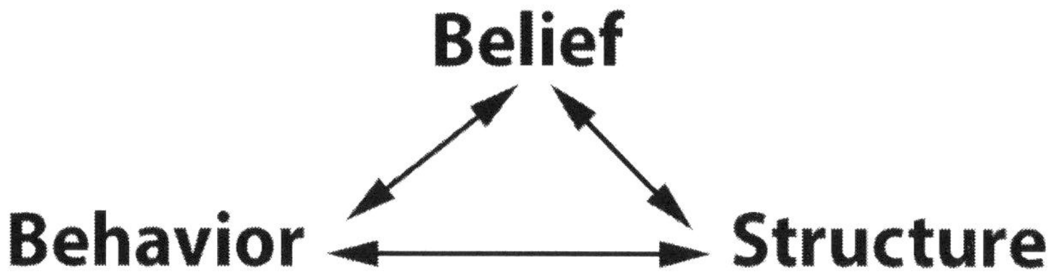

In a landmark set of essays called "Making Gender," anthropologist Sherri Ortner explores the relationships between these domains as a way of exploring how gender roles, stereotypes, and relationships might change or get reproduced in our everyday actions. She notes that this involves "looking at and listening to real people doing real things ... and trying to figure out how what they are doing or have done will or will not reconfigure the world they live in." For her, the anthropological project consists of understanding the cultural constraints of the world, as well as the ways in which people actively live among such constraints, sometimes recreating those same constraints, but sometimes changing them.

Consider the first element: beliefs and expectations. Cordelia Fine asks you to imagine that you are part of a study in which the researcher has asked you to write down what males and females are like according to cultural lore. You might resist the idea that people can be stereotyped, but you would have no trouble reproducing the stereotype. "One list would probably feature communal personality traits like compassionate, loves children, dependent, interpersonally sensitive, nurturing ... On the other character inventory we would see agentic descriptions like leader, aggressive, ambitious, analytical, competitive, dominant, independent, and individualistic." She concludes by noting that you would have no trouble knowing which one matches which gender.

Unfortunately, even if you don't buy into these stereotypes, you can't help but take them into account in forming your own self-concept. They are part of the cultural framework and meaning system upon which we craft our identity and sense of self. Even if we explicitly choose to craft an identity against these stereotypes, we do so in full acknowledgment that we are doing so, and that we may need to be prepared for how the world might receive us. A woman who demonstrates an aggressive leadership style will likely be perceived more negatively than a man with the same approach, while a stay-at-home dad who shows emotion easily may be openly ridiculed for not properly providing for his family. In short, we do not craft our identities in a social vacuum and must account for cultural stereotypes as we navigate the world.

In this way, beliefs and expectations shape the second element; behaviors and interactions. We have probably all experienced ourselves bending our personalities ever so slightly to accommodate a particular situation. If we are around people we think might hold stronger traditional gender stereotypes, we are likely to change our behavior to match their expectations. Controlled studies by Stacy Sinclair in which women are told that they are about to meet with a charming but sexist man led these women to self-assess themselves as more stereotypically feminine.

Other studies prime students with gender stereotypes and then give them moral dilemmas to see how they will respond. For example, in a study by psychologist Michelle Ryan, one group of participants was asked to brainstorm ideas for debating gender stereotypes and another was not. Then they were asked to solve a moral dilemma. Among those who had brainstormed the ideas for debating gender stereotypes, women were twice as likely to respond to the moral dilemma by offering empathy and care-based solutions in line with gender stereotypes.

In other words, whenever the gender stereotype is in mind, people shape their behavior in relation to that stereotype. It is surprisingly easy to bring the stereotype to mind. When researchers at American University added a small checkbox to indicate your gender as male or female to the top of a self-assessment, women started rating their verbal abilities higher and math abilities lower than when the checkbox was not on the form.

Psychologists who study "stereotype threat" call this "priming." It is a technique used in the lab to "prime" research participants with a gender stereotype, role, or identity before doing another task to see how it effects the outcome. But these effects go far beyond the lab, because while the "priming" done in the lab is often very subtle, we live our lives completely immersed in situations that can prime these gender stereotypes. As evidence of this, consider the constant barrage of advertisements we see online, on TV, and in our social media feeds that reproduce gender stereotypes and consider their effect. When researcher Paul Davies showed research participants advertisements of women in beauty commercials or doting over a brownie mix and then asked them to take an exam, he found that women attempted far fewer math problems than they did if they were shown more neutral ads. They also were less likely to aspire to careers in STEM fields after seeing these commercials. Psychologists Jennifer Steele and Nalini Ambady conclude that "our culture creates a situation of repeated priming of stereotypes and their related identities, which eventually help to define a person's long-term attitude towards specific domains."

As a result of the stereotypes and behaviors they influence, we end up creating the third element: structures and institutions. Women who resist the stereotype and pursue STEM fields, attempt to climb corporate ladders, or pursue political success will find fewer and fewer other women alongside them as they move up the ranks. They find themselves in male-dominated institutions that reinforce and reproduce the stereotypes. Despite the progress made over the past 50 years, they may still face discrimination in hiring and promotion, or they may find that their ideas or opinions are not often accepted, or they may find themselves immersed in a masculine culture where they find it difficult to fit in and be effective.

Meanwhile, in Armenia, women make up about half of computer science majors (vs. 15% in America). Hasmik Gharibyan suggests that this is because Armenians do not expect to have a job they love. Jobs are for financial stability. Joy is to be found in family and friends, not a job. We see a similar pattern in other developing countries, so that contrary to many expectations, those countries with more traditional views of gender have less gender inequality.

As mentioned earlier, many of those who favor a biological explanation take this as evidence that men and women have innately different interests and abilities leading them down different career paths when they have total freedom of movement. However, sociologists Maria Charles and Karen Bradley argue that these differences result from our strong cultural emphasis on individual self-expression. Unlike developing countries, self-expression plays a large role in career choice over practical considerations. Being an anthropology major or an engineering major is as much an identity as it is a career.

In this way, a culture that values self-expression may exaggerate and exacerbate the stereotypes and frameworks that provide the raw material from which people construct their selves. While the impact of stereotypes may seem small in any particular situation, we are never not in a situation, and these effects add up and result in substantially different and gendered behavioral patterns, interests, and worldviews. These behaviors, interests, and worldviews then become a part of the social world that others must navigate, thereby perpetuating the stereotypes.

We do not know yet how this social construction interacts with biological processes in the brain, but as anthropologists, sociologists, psychologists, biologists, and neuroscientists continue their explorations into how gender is made, we will likely see many important new discoveries in the field demonstrating the complexities of this biocultural creation.

RACE AS A BIOCULTURAL CONSTRUCTION

Most Americans publicly proclaim that they are not racist, but all Americans know the common stereotypes and how they map on to each racial category. The idea that there are "blacks" "whites" and "Asians" goes largely unquestioned. But many anthropologists propose that when we look at the entire global human population, the notion of race is a myth. It is a cultural construction. As biological anthropologist Alan Goodman notes, "what's black in the United States is not what's black in Brazil or what's black in South Africa. What was black in 1940 is different from what is black in 2000." Scientists like Goodman note that if you lined up all the people on the planet in terms of skin color you would see a slow gradation from light skin to dark skin and at no point could you realistically declare the point at which you transition from "black people" to "white people."

How did our skins get their color? Skin color is an adaptation to sun exposure. Populations in very sunny areas along the equator have evolved to produce more melanin, which darkens the skin and protects them from skin disorders as well as neural tube defects that can kill unborn children. Populations in less sunny areas have evolved with less melanin so that their lighter skins can absorb more Vitamin D, which aids in the absorption of calcium, building stronger bones.

When anthropologists argue that race is a myth, they are pointing out that variations in skin color cannot be neatly categorized with other traits so that people can be clearly separated into clear types (races) along the lines created by our cultural concept of race. For example, some populations in the world that have dark skin have curly hair, while others have straight hair. Some are very tall, and some are very short. Humans have a tendency to create categories based on visual traits like skin color because they're so prominently visible. But, as anthropologist Marvin Harris notes, organizing people into racial types according to skin color makes as much sense as trying to organize them according to whether or not they can roll their tongues. Skin color, like tongue-rolling, is highly unlikely to correlate with any complex behavior such as intelligence, discipline, aggression, or personality, in part because these complex behaviors are strongly shaped by culture and therefore the racial categories and stereotypes in any given culture will have a profound effect on those behaviors.

This is not to say there is not significant human variation across populations, but cutting-edge DNA studies from revolutionary studies in genetics have shown that the boundaries of what might be considered "populations" have always been changing. As geneticist David Reich points out, there were different populations in the past, but "the fault lines across populations were almost unrecognizably different from today." So while different populations differ in bodily dimensions, lactose tolerance, disease resistance, and the ability to breath at high altitudes, these differences do not fall into neat, fixed, unchanging, and scientifically verifiable racial categories.

Currently, most anthropologists maintain that race is a social construction with no basis in biology. However, some anthropologists are now arguing that our social constructions are having a real impact on biology. For example, if someone is socially classified as "black," they are more likely to live in conditions with limited access to good nutrition and healthcare. In short, as Nancy Krieger recently noted, "racism harms health," and this means that different races have different biology, but this biology is in part shaped by social forces.

At the root of these health inequalities is continued racial segregation. Why, 50 years after the Civil Rights movement, are our cities still segregated? Why do white families have over 10 times the net worth of black families? Why are whites almost twice as likely to own a home? Why are blacks twice as likely to be unemployed? Why are black babies 2.5 times more likely to die before their first birthday?

Race is real-ized through the same triad of forces that real-ize gender and blind men in the previous examples.

At the level of beliefs, studies show that Americans hold implicit biases even when they claim to deny all racial biases. For example, Yarka Mekawi and Konrad Bresin at the University of Illinois recently did a meta-analysis of the many studies involving the "shooter task" in which people are asked to shoot at video images of men with guns but avoid shooting men who are not holding guns. They found that across 42 studies, people were found to shoot armed black men faster than armed white men, and slower to decide to not shoot unarmed blacks. Such studies are increasingly important in an age of social media that has brought several police shootings of unarmed blacks under public scrutiny and inspired widespread protests such as the Black Lives Matter movement. These studies reveal that the stereotype that blacks are prone to anger and violence lays a claim on the consciousness of whites *and* blacks, even when those individuals are committed to overcoming racial bias.

Our beliefs, conscious and unconscious, affect our behavior. When researchers sent out identical resumes with only the names changed, they found that resumes with "white-sounding" names like Greg and Emily were 50% more likely to receive a call-back versus resumes with "black-sounding" names like Jamal and Lakisha.

These biases are often shared across races, so that blacks and whites hold the same stereotypes, and these stereotypes affect how they act and perform. For example, Jeff Stone at the University of Arizona set up a mini-golf course and announced to the players that it was specially designed to measure raw athletic ability. Black players outperformed white players. Then, without changing the course at all, he announced that the course was specially designed to measure one's ability to see and interpret spatial geometry. White players outperformed black players.

But we fail to see how the ideas become real-ized without also looking at structure and the impact of institutionalized racism. Institutionalized racism is often misunderstood as institutions and laws that are overtly racist, or as an institution that is permeated with racists people or racist ideology. These misunderstandings lead people to claim that a city and its institutions cannot be described as having institutionalized racism if the city or its institutions are operated by blacks.

Institutionalized racism is better viewed not as the willful creation of racists or racist institutions, but as the cumulative effect of policies, systems and processes that may not have been designed with racism in mind, but which have the effect of disadvantaging certain racial groups.

For example, consider the insurance industry. Insurance companies do not usually have racist policies or overt racists working within them. In fact, when they are found to have any racist policies or racist employees, they face legal sanctioning. Nonetheless, they do have a set of policies that disadvantage blacks disproportionately to whites. They charge for auto-insurance based on ZIP code, which includes a calculation for how likely it is that your car might be stolen or damaged. Since more blacks live in poor, high-crime areas, this policy has the effect of disadvantaging them.

In many states and cities, school funding is also tied to ZIP code. It is also much more difficult to get a loan in some ZIP codes. Therefore, one of the most powerful forces that continuously re-creates racial prejudices is a structure that includes black poverty and segregated cities created after hundreds of years of slavery and official segregation. Even though official segregation is now a thing of the past, its legacy lives on as black families are more likely to live in poverty and in impoverished neighborhoods where it is more difficult to find and receive loans, a good education, and good opportunities. On average, blacks continue to have less wealth, less education, fewer opportunities, and live in impoverished areas with higher crime rates. These characteristics then get associated with blackness, thereby supporting the stereotypes that inform the practices that continually re-create the structure of segregation.

As Stokely Carmichael and Charles Hamilton argued when coining the term "institutional racism," we all rightly protest and take action when someone dies as the victim of a racist hate crime, but fail to see the problem when

> *"...five hundred black babies die each year because of the lack of power, food, shelter and medical facilities, and thousands more are destroyed and maimed physically, emotionally and intellectually because of conditions of poverty and discrimination in the black community ..."*

That was written over 50 years ago, in 1967. Black poverty in the inner city remains a problem, exacerbated by many historical trends and forces. Recognizing the triad of forces involved in real-ization (beliefs, behaviors, and structures) is essential to overcoming racim. If we only try to rid ourselves of our biased beliefs, we run the risk of not addressing important practices and structures that perpetuate those beliefs.

This potential to raise awareness, liberate our thinking, see our seeing, and potentially build a better world is why social scientists have been so excited about the idea of the social construction of reality for the past fifty years. But given that the future of reality is at stake, such discussions can become highly politicized and contentious, especially when the discussions might impact public policy or social norms.

This kind of investigation allows us to see into the processes through which our culture is made, and may even give us an opportunity to push back and re-make culture. But how far can this go? Can we really see the makings of our own realities and then just re-make them? This is not something to be answered in a single book, but to be continually discussed and debated in our everyday lives. Indeed, such a debate is the engine of culture and cultural change itself. However, we can make three important points of departure:

1. Socially constructed realities shape and are shaped by physical reality in many complex ways.

2. Because the future of reality is at stake, discussion and debate about socially constructed realities tend to be highly politically charged and contentious.

3. Socially constructed realities are "made up" but they are still "real" and have real consequences. "Time" and "money" may be social constructions, but they are still really real. The fact that 2:30 pm is a social construction and part of a larger cultural set of beliefs emphasizing order and efficiency doesn't mean you can blow off your 2:30 pm appointment to protest this set of social constructions and not face any social consequences.

LEARN MORE

- Invisibilia Podcast: How to Become Batman
- The Making of Blind Men by Robert A. Scott
- Delusions of Gender: How Our Minds, Society, and Neurosexism Create Difference, by Cordelia Fine
- Skin: A Natural History by Nina G. Jablonski
- Race – The Power of an Illusion, www.pbs.org/race

Challenge Six: Get Uncomfortable

Your challenge is to do at least one hour of fieldwork, immersing yourself in a cross-cultural or sub-cultural experience – a place, event, activity that makes you uncomfortable. Do fieldwork and write up a "thick description" of your experience.

Objective: Experience more, experience difference, and experience differently – to practice using communication, empathy, and thoughtfulness to really experience the world from a different cultural position.

1. Stretch yourself to experience a different cultural or subcultural reality. For example, if you are atheist, go to church. If you are Christian, go to a Buddhist retreat. In short, do something you would probably never otherwise do and open yourself up to the experience.

2. Make sure that it is "cultural" in that it involves engaging and interacting with people.

3. After the event, write up a "thick description" of your experience. A thick description is an exquisitely detailed description of the setting, participants, activities, interactions, and social dramas playing out that allow the reader to feel ad if they are really there.

Go to ANTH101.com/challenge6 for additional tips and information.

Lesson Seven

Superstructure

We fail to examine our assumptions not just because they are hard to see, but also because they are safe and comfortable. They allow us to live with the flattering illusion that "I am the center of the universe, and what matters are my immediate needs and desires."

BIG QUESTIONS ABOUT MORALITY

The ideal marriage among the Sumbanese of Indonesia is for a woman to marry her father's sister's son, and for a man to marry his mother's brother's daughter. Like the marriages among the Tamil, these cousin marriages are arranged by elders and thought to be far too important to be left up to individual choice. These marriages create alliances between clans which are further reinforced through ceremonies involving an elaborate exchange of valuables such as horses, pigs, ivory, and gold. For the Sumbanese, this is simply the right thing to do.

One day, the anthropologist Web Keane was discussing these matters with an elder Sumbanese woman when she turned the tables and asked him about American marriage practices. Keane told her that individuals choose their own partners, that we rarely or never marry cousins but otherwise there are no rules, and that we do not host an elaborate exchange of goods like the Sumbanese. "She was visibly appalled," Keane notes. With a sense of shock she exclaimed, "So Americans just mate like animals!"

On the surface, this story is a reminder of the vast differences between us. Our cultures seem to encapsulate very different morals, ethics, and values. Marriage practices are just one expression of what at root seem to be vastly different ideas and ideals. The American marriage system rests on ideals of individualism, freedom, liberty, and choice. If we really stop to imagine a young girl marrying her cousin at the behest of her elders, we can't help but feel as appalled as the Sumbanese woman above. The Sumbanese system seems to be denying her most fundamental right to live a free life, fall in love, and pursue happiness under her own terms. But beneath the surface we might also perceive a few important similarities. First, both systems are supported by moral and ethical values. Americans may disagree on the specifics of the ethical system, but we recognize it as an ethical system and understand the value of such constraints. We might even agree with the sentiment that, as Keane summarizes it, "being ethical makes you human."

The problem of different morals and ethics raises some challenging questions. As noted earlier, *great questions can take us further than we ever thought possible.* But questions can be disconcerting too, especially those that might lead us to question our moral and ethical foundations. Are there universal principles of right and wrong? Where does our morality come from? Does it have natural or divine origins? Are we born with a sense of morality or do we learn it? The implications of how we answer these questions will impact everything about how we live and find meaning and purpose in life. The stakes are high.

Morality provides many benefits to human societies. They keep people in line and allow us to live in relative peace and harmony. They can provide a sense of direction, meaning, and purpose. And they often put us in accord with the natural world around us as well, providing rules and directions for how to treat the world and the other creatures with whom we live.

But morality can also drive us apart. Many of the most intense conflicts and wars stem from real or perceived moral differences.

Even within a single culture there can be virulent conflict over moral principles. As I write these words there are several protests planned in America today in the ongoing battles that have been dubbed the "culture wars." The culture wars pit ardent conservatives against progressive liberals on issues of abortion, women's rights, LGBTQ rights, free speech, political correctness, racial inequalities, global warming, and immigration, among many others. Over the past few years, the culture wars have become even more explosive, with protests and counter-protests often erupting into violence.

In the midst of these conflicts there is a growing sense that we simply cannot talk or have a civil discussion anymore. We live in different media worlds inside the filter bubbles created by social media. One person's facts are another's "alt-facts." Is there any hope to find common ground?

In this lesson, we will be exploring the roots and many flourishing branches of morality, but ultimately our goal will be to use the anthropological perspective to try to see our own seeing, see big, and see small, so that we can "see it all" – see and understand our own moral foundations as well as those of others in hopes that we can have productive conversations with people who see the world differently. To do this, we will have to open ourselves up to the anthropological method to experience more (other moral ideas and systems), experience difference (by truly understanding the roots and foundations of those systems), and experience differently (by allowing ourselves to imagine our way into a new way of thinking, if only temporarily, to truly understand a different point of view).

IS THERE A UNIVERSAL MORALITY?

Imagine the following dilemma: A woman is dying and there is only one drug that can save her life. The druggist paid $200 for the materials and charges $2,000 for the drug. The woman's husband, Heinz, asked everyone he knows for money but could only collect $1,000. He offered this to the druggist but the druggist refused.

Desperate, Heinz broke into the lab and stole the drug for his wife. Should he have done this?

This is the famous Heinz dilemma, created by Lawrence Kohlberg to analyze how people think through a moral dilemma. Kohlberg was not interested in whether or not people thought Heinz acted morally. He wanted to know how they justified their answer. From their responses he was able to construct a six-stage theory of moral development proposing that over the course of a lifetime, people move from a "pre-conventional" self-centered morality based on obedience or self-interest to a more "conventional" group-oriented morality in which they value conformity to rules and the importance of law and order. Some people move past this "conventional" morality to a "post-conventional" humanistic morality based on human rights and universal human ethics.

Kohlberg proposed that these are universal stages of moral judgment that anyone in any culture may go through, but still allowed for a wide range of cultural variation in the group-oriented conventional stages based on local rules, customs, and laws. His post-conventional stages represent a universal morality but only a very few people can see their way past their own cultural conventions to see and act on them. In his studies, just 2% of people responded in a way that reflected a model of morality based on universal human ethics, and in practice he reserved the highest stage of moral development to moral luminaries like Gandhi and Mother Theresa.

However, some saw Kohlberg's "universal" morality as biased toward a very specific model of morality that was culturally and politically biased in favor of liberal American values. By placing this "humanistic morality" as beyond and more developed than morality based on conformity or law and order he was placing his own cultural values at the pinnacle of human moral achievement. Kohlberg's stage-theory model provided justification for a liberal secular worldview that championed questioning authority and egalitarianism as more advanced and developed than religiously-based moral worldviews that valued authority and tradition.

Then Kohlberg's former student Elliot Turiel discovered that children as young as five often responded as "conventional" in some contexts but "post-conventional" in others. When children were asked whether or not it was okay to wear regular clothes to a school that requires school uniforms, kids said no, except in cases in which the teacher allowed it. The kids recognized that these rules were based on social conventions. But if you asked them if it was okay if a girl pushed a boy off a swing, the kids said no, and held to that answer even in cases in which the teacher allowed it or there were explicitly no rules against it. In this case, the kids were not basing their moral reasoning on social conventions. Turiel suggested that these were moral rules, not conventional rules, and moral rules were based on a universal moral truth: *harm is wrong.*

This moral truth discovered by Turiel as he analyzed the discourse of children reflects the wisdom of "The Golden Rule," which is found in religious traditions all over the world. The words of Jesus ("Do unto others what you would have them do unto you.") are echoed in the Analects of Confucius ("Do not do to others what you do not want them to do to you."), the Udana-Varga of Buddhism ("Hurt not others in ways that you yourself would find hurtful.") and the Hadiths of Islam ("None of you truly believes until he wishes for his brother what he wishes for himself."), as well as many others. But evidence of a universal human morality might go beyond what is written in our texts. It might be written in our DNA.

THE NATURE OF HUMAN NATURE

Two dominant theories of human nature have been debated for centuries. One suggests that we are inherently good, peaceful, cooperative, empathic and nurturing. The other argues that we are inherently evil, violent, competitive, and selfish. In the 17th Century, Thomas Hobbes argued that our societies are composed of selfish individuals and that without a strong social contract enforced by government we would be engaged in a "war of all against all," that we would be unable to cooperate to build technologies, institutions, and knowledge, and that ultimately our lives would be "solitary, poor, nasty, brutish, and short." Against this conception stood Jean-Jacques Rousseau with his image of the Noble Savage living in accord with nature in peaceful and egalitarian communities beyond the corruption of power and society.

Many early popular anthropological accounts of indigenous people aligned with Rousseau's vision. Countering popular stereotypes of violent "savages," work such as that of Margaret Mead and Elizabeth Marshall Thomas portrayed indigenous people like the !Kung San as "The Harmless People" – hunter-gatherers living peaceful lives despite the absence of formal laws and governments.

However, over the past few decades anthropologists have acquired more detailed statistics on these groups, and the rates of violent death among hunter-gatherers appears much higher than what we find in large state-based societies, even when massive atrocities like the World Wars are taken into account. Violent death rates among males of the Jivaro and Yanomamo have been reported to be over 45%. Adding more data to the side that humans are inherently violent, anthropologist Carol Ember estimated that 64 percent of hunter-gatherer societies are either in a war or will be in one within the next two years. Under the weight of this evidence, linguist Steven Pinker declared that the "doctrine of the Noble Savage" had been "mercilessly debunked."

But proponents of a better human nature note that just because we are naturally aggressive does not mean that we do not also have other important traits. Looking to our closest primate ancestors we find ample evidence of violent territorial behavior, but primatologist Franz de Waal sees a softer side as well. After a violent skirmish among chimpanzees he watched as the two fighters retreated to the tree tops. Soon one of them held out a hand in the direction of the other. They slowly moved closer to one another and reconciled with a hug. He had originally been tasked with studying aggression and conflict among chimps, but it was clear to him that chimpanzees valued their relationships and found ways to repair them when they were damaged.

In further field observations and lab tests, de Waal pieced together a vast array of evidence suggesting that primates exhibit two pillars upon which a more complex human morality can be built: empathy and reciprocity.

In one simple field test, he showed a looping video of a chimp yawning to see if chimps experience yawn contagion. Other studies among humans had shown that yawn contagion correlates with empathy. When chimps see a video of a chimp they know yawning, they "yawn like crazy" he says. This mimicry is a basic building block of empathy, an ability to imagine our way into another's emotions and perspective.

This perspective-taking is of utmost necessity when cooperating on complex tasks and we find it not only in primates but other mammals as well. Chimpanzees and elephants are able to cooperate on the task of pulling in a food tray to obtain food. And chimpanzees will cooperate with another chimp even when there is nothing in it for them, showing that these actions go beyond mere selfishness.

In another study they let a chimpanzee purchase food with tokens. If the chimp paid with a red token, only they got food. If they paid with a green token, both the chimp and another chimp next door received food. If chimps were purely selfish, we would expect random selection of tokens, so that over time 50% would be red and 50% would be green. However, chimps tend to make prosocial choices by selecting the green token that fed the other chimp as well.

These pro-social tendencies extend into more elaborate notions of fairness as well. In a study of capuchin monkeys one monkey was paid in cucumber and the other in grapes. By the second round of payments the first monkey was furious and demanded fairness, throwing the cucumber back at the researcher and demanding the grape. Among chimpanzees the same test elicited even more complex behavior. The chimp receiving the grapes refused grapes until the other chimp also received grapes.

For decades, de Waal found himself struggling against a strong consensus among scientists that deep down, humans are violent, cruel, aggressive, and selfish. They proposed that only a thin veneer of human-made morality kept the world from falling apart. But his work was leading him somewhere else. Each experiment revealed that our evolutionary history had placed deep within us the capacity for empathy, cooperation, reconciliation, and a sense of fairness. "Our brains have been designed to blur the line between self and other," de Waal noted on our capacity for empathy. "It is an ancient neural circuitry that marks every mammal, from mouse to elephant."

De Waal seemed to be confirming Turiel's findings. Turiel had found a basic universal morality in five-year-old children that showed that we place an innate value on fairness and see harm to others as inherently wrong. De Waal now found this same basic morality among monkeys and apes, suggesting that the foundations of our morality run very deep in our biology and evolutionary history.

THE PROBLEM OF CULTURAL VARIATION

Despite these apparent universals in the domains of harm and fairness, anthropologists did not need to look far to see a vast array of different moral standards reflected in the beliefs, practices, taboos, and rituals around the world. Aside from the most titillating accounts of human sacrifice, head-hunting, and ritualized cannibalism were many others that defied categorization into a simple scheme that placed principles of harm and fairness as the two pillars of morality.

In the 1980s, anthropologist Richard Shweder started working with Turiel to examine the cross-cultural evidence for a universal morality. Together, they determined that there was simply not enough evidence yet. They recognized that the five-year-olds may have simply picked up the principles of fairness and harm through socialization. They needed a more thorough study of moral development in other cultures to determine if these moral principles were made by nature or culture.

Shweder knew a great way to get started. He had done extensive fieldwork in the Hindu temple town of Bhubaneswar in India. As he describes it, it is

> *"...a place where marriages are arranged, not matters of 'love' or free choice, where, at least among Brahman families, widows may not remarry or wear colored clothing or ornaments or jewelry; where Untouchables are not allowed in the temple; where menstruating women may not sleep in the same bed as their husbands or enter the kitchen or touch their children; where ancestral spirits are fed on a daily basis; where husband and wives do not eat together and the communal family meals we find so important rarely occur; where women avoid their husbands' elder brothers and men avoid their wives' elder sisters, where, with the exception of holy men, corpses are cremated, never buried, and where the cow, the first 'mother,' is never carved up into sirloin, porterhouse or tenderloin cut."*

Note that it isn't just the practices that strike the Western reader as strange, there are whole categories of persons and activities that run against our ideals of fairness and equality. The notion that there could be a whole class of people known as "Untouchables" runs counter to Western Enlightenment ideals of equality. To see what this could tell us about the possibility of universal morality, Shweder set up a study to compare the moral reasoning of Hindu Brahmans from Bhunabeswar with the people of Hyde Park, Illinois.

Shweder came up with 39 scenarios that he thought would be judged very differently between the two groups. For example, among the 39 scenarios the Brahman children thought the most serious moral transgression was one in which the eldest son gets a haircut and eats chicken the day after his father's death. The second worst was eating beef, which was ranked worse than eating dog, which was only slightly worse than a widow eating fish. Other serious breaches as judged by the Brahman children included women who did not change their clothes after defecating and before cooking, a widow asking a man she loves to marry her, and a woman cooking rice and then eating it with her family. None of these, with the exception of eating dog, were seen as breaches by the children of Hyde Park.

Some of the disagreements between Brahmans and Americans reflected deeper and broader differences in basic moral vision. For example, Brahmans were deeply concerned about people modeling the behavior prescribed for them by their social role and position, while Americans prioritized equality and non-violence. Brahmans approved of beating a disobedient wife or caning a misbehaving child, while Americans found nothing wrong with the Brahman-disapproved behaviors of a woman eating with her husband's elder brother or washing his plates.

So does this mean there is *not* a universal morality based on the foundations of harm and fairness? Turiel was not convinced. He pointed out that there was still strong agreement among Brahmans and Americans when it came to matters of harm and fairness. Both groups agreed that breaking promises, cutting in line, kicking a harmless animal, and stealing were wrong. As for the differences, Turiel argued that they could still fit within his model of universal morality because the cultural differences were just social conventions.

But Shweder's research indicated that the locals did not see it this way. They saw their "social conventions" as moral imperatives. They were as real and obvious as Turiel's foundations of harm and fairness. Behind these differences, Shweder argued that there was a profound difference not only in how Brahmans viewed morality, but also in how they think about the self, the mind, and the world.

Shweder proposed that the Brahmans were using three different moral systems as they evaluated different scenarios. The first he called the "ethic of autonomy." This is the most familiar system to people in the West and the dominant ethic in individualistic cultures. The central idea is that people are autonomous individuals who should be able to pursue happiness so long as it does not impinge upon the happiness of others. Turiel's "universal morality" is based in this ethic. Shweder's point is that this apparently "universal" morality, while shared universally, is not the dominant moral system in other cultures.

The second moral system is the "ethic of community." This one may take priority over the ethic of autonomy in more socio-centric cultures that emphasize the solidarity and well-being of the society, group, or nation over and above the individual. To maintain social order, this ethic emphasizes social roles, duties, customs, and traditions. Hierarchies are important, as are the values of respect and honor that may be required to uphold them. The emphasis on the ethic of community is what leads Brahmans to disagree with Americans on beating a disobedient wife or caning a misbehaving child.

The third moral system is the "ethic of divinity." This system sees people as part and parcel of a world that requires constant and conscientious reverence to taboos, rules, and behaviors in line with a sacred worldview. Behaviors are judged not just in terms of whether or not they violate individual rights, but for how they might upset or fall in line with sacred rules, taboos, and prescriptions. This system explains the vast majority of differences between Brahmans and Americans, such as the food and behavior taboos.

Turiel and Shweder argued about how to interpret these cultural differences. Turiel continued to advocate for the idea that the behaviors Shweder categorized in these alternative ethical systems could be understood within a single, more simplified system based on rational assessments of individual harm and fairness if we just account for how Brahmans think. For example, he pointed out that the Brahman idea of reincarnation meant that they might be reasoning that breaking a taboo is wrong because it could lead to harm in a future life. If Brahmans were indeed doing this kind of calculation, the underlying moral decision would still be based on individualistic notions of harm and fairness.

WEIRD MORALITY

Jonathan Haidt had an idea about how to settle this debate. He invented scenarios that he called "harmless taboo stories" and shared them with research subjects of different backgrounds and education levels in Brazil and Pennsylvania to get their reactions. One story is about a man who purchases a chicken and has sex with the carcass before eating it. Another is about a woman tearing apart an American flag and using it to clean her house. Another is about a family eating a dog. Another is about a brother and sister having sex. In each case he is careful to arrange the facts in the story so that it is clear that there is no harm done to anyone, yet he also knows that it will trigger people's sense of disgust and thereby create a moral dilemma as to whether or not it is write or wrong. If Turiel is right that all morality is ultimately based on harm and fairness, people should be able to see that their disgust is simply based on cultural conventions and ultimately reason that the people in the stories have done nothing wrong.

Out of 12 groups, all but one saw these "harmless" acts as moral violations. The rest were using different moral models based on community and divinity, supporting Shweder's claims. The only one group that held true to Turiel's model of moral reasoning was upper-class Americans at the University of Pennsylvania.

Cultural psychologists Joe Henrich, Steve Heine, and Ara Norenzayan would later call this group of people "the weirdest people in the world," using the acronym WEIRD to define them as Western, Educated, Industrialized, Rich and Democratic. Haidt's study showed that the WEIRDer you are, the more likely you are to stick to Turiel's model of moral reasoning based solely on the ethic of autonomy when making a moral decision. But it turns out that if you want to make inferences about human nature, WEIRD people may be the least typical and representative sample of humans on the planet.

As Haidt summarizes it, the key difference between WEIRD people and most other cultures is that WEIRD people "see a world full of separate objects, rather than relationships." This includes the individual, who is seen not in terms of their relationships but instead as an entity separate and unto itself. As anthropologist Clifford Geertz has noted,

> The Western conception of the person as a bounded, unique, more or less integrated motivational and cognitive universe, a dynamic center of awareness, emotion, judgment, and action organized into a distinctive whole and against its social and natural background, is, however incorrigible it may seem to us, a rather peculiar idea within the context of the world's cultures.

Richard Shweder proposed that this "egocentric" or individualistic view of the world and the moral reasoning that went along with it were historically and culturally rare, fostered during the Western Enlightenment and rising to prominence in the 20th Century. Most cultures are more "sociocentric," emphasizing the need for social order, solidarity, rules and roles above individual needs and desires.

Haidt wanted to immerse himself in a more sociocentric culture to better understand their morality, so he teamed up with Shweder and went to Bhunabeswar. Emulating the open-minded anthropologists that inspired his trip, Haidt immersed himself in local life, and very soon felt the feelings of dissonance and shock that can come when someone crosses over into a very different cultural world. He immediately felt the conflicts between his moral world and the one he had just entered. His egalitarian ethos made him uncomfortable with having servants. He had to be told to be stricter with them and stop thanking them. "I was immersed in a sex-segregated, hierarchically stratified, devoutly religious society," he writes, "and I was committed to understanding it on its own terms, not mine."

Tourists often move about among other tourists. A tourist in India might briefly interact with the local culture, but will often find themselves on that same day telling a story about the interaction, and falling back into common Western assumptions to explain and describe what they saw. Full cultural immersion over several weeks or months allowed Haidt to start to see the world more as the locals saw it.

He credits his ability to break past his WEIRD biases and assumptions on a simple fact: he liked the people he was living with in India. They were helpful, kind, and patient, and they became his friends. So even though he would normally reject their hierarchical rules as oppressive and sometimes sexist, he found himself leaning in a little further to understand them, rather than immediately discounting them.

As he did, he saw a completely different set of assumptions and values supporting the system. Rather than equality and individual rights as sacred values, it was the honoring of elders, rules, and gods that mattered most. Rather than striving to express one's unique identity, they strove to fulfill their respective roles. He had understood Shweder's argument intellectually, but now he began to *feel* it. "I could see beauty in a moral code that emphasizes duty, respect for one's elders, service to the group, and negation of the self's desires." He was not blind to the downsides of their system – the potential abuse of women, Untouchables, and others who were low in the hierarchy – but it also made him aware of the downsides of his own moral system. "From the vantage point of the ethic of community, the ethic of autonomy now seemed overly individualistic and self-focused."

THE FOUNDATIONS OF MORALITY

Haidt noticed something peculiar as his research subjects responded to his harmless taboo stories. All of them, even the WEIRD ones, had immediate responses of disgust. Only after these initial responses did they start struggling to come up with moral reasonings to support their feelings. It was as if they were making quick and intuitive moral judgments and then searching for reasons after the fact. At the time, most research had assumed that morality was based in moral reasoning. It was assumed that people consciously considered their moral values and then made decisions based on these conscious deliberations. Haidt suspected that morality was more intuitive, and that the seat of morality rested in the emotions, not in the intellect.

In one study, he had his research team stand on street corners with fart spray. They would spray a little bit and then pose moral dilemmas to passers-by using his harmless taboo stories. It turns out that when people are immersed in a cloud of fart, they make harsher moral judgments. Haidt proposed that the fart spray was triggering the emotion of disgust. The intellect then tried to explain this emotion using moral reasoning. Contrary to popular belief, Haidt was showing that reasoning does *not* lead to moral judgment. It is the other way around. We use reasoning to explain our judgments, not to make them. He modeled it like this:

Intuition ➔ Judgment ➔ Reasoning

Haidt found additional support for his "intuitionist model of morality" in the studies of primates by Frans de Waal. After all, if conscious moral reasoning was necessary for morality, how could monkeys demand fairness or empathize with someone who has been harmed? Other studies showed that moral philosophers, people who spend their whole lives studying and sharpening their capacities for moral reasoning, are no more moral than anyone else. Just as one does not need to know and name the specific rules of grammar that make a language work in order to speak a language, people (and other apes) do not need moral reasoning to act morally.

If these moral intuitions lie deeper in the brain and our moral reasoning is at least partially shared by our primate cousins, it would follow that our moral capacities are innate and part of our evolutionary heritage. But instead of proposing a universal morality, Haidt and his colleagues proposed that humans may have universal moral "taste receptors." Using the metaphor of the tongue and its taste receptors, Haidt pointed out that humans all share five tastes (salty, sweet, bitter, sour, and umami) and yet build a wide-range of different cuisines to satisfy them. Similarly, moral "taste receptors" could serve as the backdrop upon which thousands of different moral systems could develop. Breaking through the nature-nurture debate, Haidt found a model that accommodated the exciting findings of primatologists that suggested a universal human morality while still making room for the vast range of cultural variation found by anthropologists.

Haidt and his colleagues proposed six foundations of morality that developed through the process of evolution as our ancestors faced the challenges of living and reproducing.

1. **Care/harm.** Emotions: Empathy, Sympathy, Compassion. Developed to protect and care for vulnerable children, we feel compassion for those who are suffering or in distress.

2. **Fairness/cheating.** Emotions: Anger, Gratitude, Guilt. Developed to reap the benefits of reciprocity, we feel anger when somebody cheats, gratitude when they cooperate, and guilty when we deceive others.

3. **Loyalty/betrayal.** Emotions: Pride, Rage, Ecstasy. Developed to form coalitions that could compete with other coalitions, we feel a sense of group pride and loyalty with our in-group and a sense of rage when someone acts as a traitor. Group rituals also give us a

sense of ecstasy and make us feel part of something bigger than ourselves.

4. **Authority/subversion.** Emotions: Obedience, Respect. Developed to forge beneficial relationships within hierarchies, we feel a sense of respect or fear toward people above us in a hierarchy, fostering a sense of obedience and deference.

5. **Sanctity/degradation.** Emotions: Disgust and Aversion. Developed to avoid poisons, parasites, and other contaminants, we feel a sense of disgust toward the unclean, especially bodily waste and blood.

6. **Liberty/oppression.** Emotion: Righteous anger/reactance. Developed to maintain trust and cooperation in small groups, we feel a sense of righteous anger and unite with others in our group to resist any sign of oppression.

Think of these as our moral "taste receptors." Just as people have different personal tastes that develop within larger cultural systems, so it is also true for morality. We all grow up within a certain moral culture that shapes our moral tastes, but we also have personal differences in tastes.

UNDERSTANDING OTHER MORALITIES

One of the greatest gifts of ethnographic fieldwork, immersion in a foreign culture, and careful study of the human condition is that it allows you to see your own culture in a new way. Haidt was raised in a liberal household in a liberal city and went to school at a liberal college. By his own account, he was immersed in a liberal bubble. The Left was his native culture. "I was a twenty-nine-year-old liberal atheist with very definite views about right and wrong," he writes. But after his visit to India and his ongoing studies of morality, he started to see Republicans and other conservatives with a more open mind.

He had always been a liberal, because he saw it as the group that advocates for equality and fairness for all individuals regardless of their background. *How could anyone be against equality?* he wondered. He assumed that conservatives must just be selfish, prejudiced, and/or racist. Why else would conservatives want to lower taxes and strip away funding to help the poor?

But when he came back from India and started researching the foundations of morality, he found that he was starting to understand why people on the religious right would fight for more traditional values and social structures. He had gone to the other side of the world to get a glimpse of people with a radically different morality to his own. Now he realized that such people were all around him. And with the culture wars heating up as Democrats and Republicans yelled right past each other into gridlock, Haidt wanted more than ever to understand the roots of these alternative moralities to see if he could help both sides understand one another a little better.

He set up a questionnaire to assess how people varied in their moral "tastes," and thanks to some good press about his project in the *New York Times*, over 100,000 people participated. The results showed substantial differences in what factors and values liberals and conservatives consider when making moral decisions.

In short, liberals focus primarily on just three foundations (Care, Fairness, and Liberty) while conservatives equally consider all six. Moreover, liberals see the other three (Loyalty, Authority, and Sanctity) as potentially immoral, because they constrain their pursuit of their most sacred value: caring for victims of oppression. If we want equality for all, we have to dissolve groupishness (Loyalty), undermine hierarchy (Authority), and never press one group's sacred values upon others (Sanctity).

However, until Haidt did his study, he (like other liberals) did not even recognize these other three moral foundations, and this led him to misunderstand and misjudge conservatives. Conservative stances against immigrants, programs to help the poor, gay marriage, feminism, and the rights of oppressed groups lead many liberals to assume that conservatives are simply heartless and selfish. However, these mis-judgments arise because liberals judge conservative morality on the basis of just three of the six foundations, which makes it seem like the conservatives do not care about other races and ethnicities, poor people, immigrants, women, and gay people.

To test this idea, Haidt asked his liberal study participants whether conservatives would agree or disagree with the statement "One of the worst things a person can do is hurt a defenseless animal." Liberals thought conservatives would disagree, demonstrating that liberals think conservatives are heartless and selfish. They fail to see that conservatives are pursuing a broader range of positive moral values, and that there may be some merit to what they bring to our political discussions.

Ultimately, Haidt sees that at the root of these opposing moral visions are two very different views of society and human nature, and they are the same two views that we have been arguing about for centuries that were presented in the opening of this chapter. Stephen Pinker calls them the Utopian Vision and the Tragic Vision. The Left takes the utopian view. We are good in our core, but the biases and assumptions of our cultures and societies corrupt us. We are limited from achieving a better world by socially constructed rules, roles, laws, and institutions that are oppressive to some groups and identities among us. We can create a more just, free, and equal society by recognizing how these things are constructed, thereby setting ourselves free from bias, bigotry, and oppression.

The Right takes a more tragic view of society and human nature. They see humans as constrained and limited in their moral capacities and abilities. We are naturally prone to violence, tribalism, and selfishness. If we eliminated hierarchies, we would just re-create them in new forms because of our will to power and desire for self-preservation. The only thing that keeps the world from falling apart into violent chaos is the system of rules, traditions, moral values, and social institutions. We should be careful in our attempts to mess with these precious (and for many, divine) moral institutions that hold our fragile society together.

As Haidt started to see, understand, and empathize with the conservative perspective, he found himself "stepping out of the Matrix" and taking "the red pill." He did not "turn red" and become a conservative, but he could now genuinely appreciate their perspective and actually listen to their views with true understanding. This opened him up to many new and exciting ideas for solving major social problems that he had never considered before.

From his work we can find five good reasons to challenge ourselves to open up and try to understand and even appreciate the arguments coming from the other side of the political aisle.

1. Both sides offer wisdom.

On the Left, the wisdom centers on caring for the victims of oppression and constraining the powerful. The Left seeks to offer equal opportunity for all, which has obvious merit based on universal principles of harm and fairness. But there is also an important utilitarian aspect to the argument. There is tremendous wasted human potential right now in disadvantaged places (impoverished inner cities, rural towns, migrant worker camps, refugee camps). Providing adequate support and opportunity in these places could add tremendous value to society by unleashing the potential of more people.

The Right offers the wisdom of markets. Societies have grown beyond the capacity for any one person or small group to understand and manage. Markets allow millions and sometimes billions of people to participate in the essential, minute decisions of production, pricing, and distribution of goods. What emerges is a super-organism that is greater than the sum of its parts.

The Right also offers the wisdom of moral order and stability. Societies function best when there is a sense of solidarity and trust among members, and this can be nurtured through shared values, virtues, norms and a shared sense of identity.

2. They each reveal the blind spots in the other.

Liberals have a blind spot that makes it difficult for them to see the importance of shared moral principles, values, and virtues that uphold our traditional practices and institutions. Pushing for change too fast can be dangerously disruptive and divisive. On the other hand, conservatives fail to see how these traditional practices and institutions might oppress certain groups or identities and may need to reform or change along with other cultural changes.

3. Our political differences are natural and unavoidable.

Our moral judgments are based in our intuitive emotional responses that are beyond conscious control. Since our emotional responses vary along with our personalities, we cannot expect everyone to agree, and it should not seem unusual to find that a two party political system would so consistently break somewhere close to 50/50 in every election.

Furthermore, studies of identical twins separated at birth and raised in different households suggest that our genetics can explain one-third to one-half of the variability of our political attitudes. Genes shape our personalities, which in turn shape which way we will lean politically. This genetic effect is actually stronger than the effect of how and where we are raised.

4. Our political differences are an essential adaptation.

Humans have not survived and thrived alone. We have survived as a species with many different personality types, and *because* we are a species with many different personality types. Some personalities are open to new experiences and people. Others are more careful and fearful. We have survived through many millennia thanks to the balance of these traits. We should be grateful to those who are different from us, for they offer important checks and balances against our own limited vision and understanding.

5. There are many dangers to Us vs. Them thinking.

Our tendency to create in-groups lead us into political "bubbles" where we only encounter the safe and familiar ideas of our political "tribe." When we encounter an idea that is associated with the other tribe, our immediate reaction is one of disgust. We then use our moral reasoning to explain our reaction, finding reasons to reject the idea even if it is a good one that could serve our highest ideals. Likewise, we will have warm feelings toward any idea put forth as one that supports our political leanings. We will then search for reasons to accept the idea. In the age of Google, it is all too easy to find research and reasons to support any idea, thereby strengthening our biases and assumptions.

As Haidt so eloquently and concisely states, "morality binds and blinds." Our moral inclinations bind us together and then blind us to the other.

LEARN MORE

- The Righteous Mind, by Jonathan Haidt
- Thinking Through Cultures: Expeditions in Cultural Psychology, by Ricahrd Shweder
- Ethical Life: Its Natural and Social Histories by Webb Keane

THE DYNAMICS OF CULTURE

All cultures are dynamic and constantly changing as individuals navigate and negotiate the beliefs, values, ideas, ideals, norms, and meaning systems that make up the cultural environment in which they live. The dynamics between liberals and conservatives that constantly shape and re-shape American politics is just one example. Our realities are ultimately shaped not only in the realm of politics and policy-making, but in the most mundane moments of everyday life.

Anthropologist Clifford Geertz famously noted, echoing Max Weber, that "Man is an animal suspended in webs of significance he himself has spun." These webs of significance create a vast network of associations that create the system that brings meaning to the most minute moments of our lives and dramatically shape the decisions we make. Due to these "webs of significance," even the simple decision of which coffee to drink can feel like a political decision or some deep representation of who we are as a person.

In a recent BuzzFeed video, a woman sits down for a blind taste test of popular coffees from Dunkin' Donuts, Starbucks, McDonalds, and 7-11. As she sits, the young woman confidently announces her love for Dunkin Donuts coffee. *"Dunkin' is my jam!"* she says, declaring not only her love for the coffee but also expressing her carefree and expressive identity. But as she takes her first sip from the unmarked cup of Dunkin' Donuts coffee she nearly spits it out and screams, *"This is the worst!"* and then confidently proclaims that that cup had to be *"7-11!"* She eventually settles on the 4th cup from the left as the best. When she is told that she has chosen Starbucks, it seems to create a minor identity crisis. She covers her head in shame, *"Oh my god, I'm so against big business."* Her friend, who has also chosen Starbucks, looks to the sky as if having a revelation about who he is. *"We're basic,"* he says. *"We're basic,"* she repeats, lowering her head in shame and crying with just enough laugh to let us know that she is kidding, but only kind of kidding.

Another woman, elegantly dressed in a black dress with a matching black pullover and a bold pendant, picks McDonald's – obviously well "below" her sophisticated tastes. She throws her head back in anguish and then buries her head in her hands as she cries hysterically, but a little too hysterically for us to take it too seriously. She wants us to know that this violates her basic sense of who she is, but that she is also the type of person who can laugh at herself.

The point is that what tastes good to us – our taste for coffee, food, music, fashion, or whatever else – is not just a simple biological reaction. There is some of that, of course. We are not faking it when we enjoy a certain type of music or drink a certain type of coffee. The joy is real. But this joy itself is shaped by social and cultural factors. What tastes good to us or strikes us as beautiful or "cool" is shaped by what it means to us and what it might say about us.

The simple "high school" version of this is to say that we are all trying to be cool, and though we may try to deny it as we get older, we never stop playing the game. We are constantly trying to (1) shape our taste to be cool, or (2) shaping "cool" to suit our taste. Replace the word "cool" with "culture" and you see that we have one of the fundamental drivers of cultural change. We shape our taste (which could include our taste in food, politics, rules, roles, beliefs, ideals) to be acceptable, while also attempting to shape what is acceptable (culture) to suit our tastes.

WHY SOMETHING MEANS WHAT IT MEANS

In 2008, Canadian satirist Christian Lander took aim at the emerging cultural movement of "urban hipsters" with a blog he called "Stuff White People Like." The hipster was an emerging archetype of "cool" and Landers had a keen eye for outlining its form, and poking fun at it. The blog quickly raced to over 40 million views and was quickly followed by two bestselling books.

In post #130 he notes the hipster's affection for Ray-Ban Wayfarer sunglasses. "These sunglasses are so popular now that you cannot swing a canvas bag at a farmer's market without hitting a pair," Lander quips. He jokes that at outdoor gatherings you can count the number of Wayfarers "so you can determine exactly how white the event is." If you don't see any Wayfarers, "you are either at a Country music concert or you are indoors."

Here Landers demonstrates a core insight about our webs of significance and why something means what it means. Things gather some of their meaning by their affiliation with some things as well as their distance from other things. In this example, Wayfarers are affiliated with canvas bags and farmers markets, but not Country music concerts. The meaning of Wayfarers is influenced by both affiliation and distance. They may not be seen at Country music concerts, but part of their meaning and significance depends on this fact. If Country music fans suddenly took a strong liking to Wayfarers, urban hipsters might find themselves disliking them, as they might sense that the Wayfarers are now "sending the wrong message" through these associations with Country music.

A quick quiz can demonstrate how this plays out in the American Culture Wars. Imagine you are sitting in traffic behind a Toyota Prius. In the left lane in front of you is a pickup truck, jacked up with extra-large tires. Both are covered in bumper stickers and you can overhear the music playing inside. Can you match the stickers and music with the vehicle?

Peace Sign	NRA
American Flag	Country Music
Obama - OneBigAssMistakeAmerica	CNN – Communist News Network
Rainbow Flag	Indie Music
War is Terrorism	Obama bin Lyin'
TRUMP-PENCE	COEXIST
Yellow Ribbon	

Of course you can. Symbols hang together. They mean what they mean based on their similarity and differences, their affiliations and oppositions. So the meaning of OneBigAssMistakeAmerica gains some of its meaning from being affiliated with the truck and not with the Prius. The cultural value of the truck and Prius depend on their opposition to one another. They may be in very different regions of the giant web of culture, but they are in the same web. It isn't that there are no Indie music fans who hate Trump and drive trucks. Some of them do. But they know, and you know, that they are exceptions to the pattern.

The meaning of symbols is not a matter of personal opinion. Meanings are not subjective. But they are not objective either. You cannot point to a meaning out in the world. Instead, cultural meanings are *intersubjective.* They are shared understandings. We may not like the same music or the same bumper stickers, but the meanings of these things are intersubjective, or in other words, *I know that you know that I know* what they mean.

At some level there is broad agreement of meanings across a culture. This facilitates basic conversation. If I gesture with my hands in a certain way, I can usually reasonably assume that you know that I know that you know what I mean. But the web of culture is also constantly being challenged and changed through the complex dynamics of everyday life. The web of culture does not definitively dictate the meaning of something, nor does it stand still. We are all constantly playing with the web as we seek our own meaningful life.

We use meanings and tastes as strategic tools to better our position in society and build a meaningful life, but as we do so, we unwillingly perpetuate and reproduce the social structure with all of its social divisions, racial divides, haves and have-nots. This is the generative core of culture. In Lesson Six, we explored the idea that "we make the world." In this lesson we start digging into the mystery of *how* we make the world.

TASTE AND DISTINCTION

Why do you like some music and hate others? Why do you like that certain brand of coffee, that soft drink, those shoes, clothes, that particular car? In a famous study published in 1979, French anthropologist Pierre Bourdieu put forth the idea that our tastes are strategic tools we use to set ourselves apart from some while affiliating with others. Taste is the pursuit of "distinction," the title of his book.

Bourdieu needed to invent new concepts to explain how taste and distinction work within a society. He pointed out that tastes have cultural value. The right taste can be an important asset as you make your way through society and try to climb the social ladder. So he invented the notion of "cultural capital" to refer to your cultural knowledge (what you know), "social capital" to refer to your social network (who you know) and pointed out (importantly) that *what* you know and *who* you know play a strong role over the course of a lifetime in *how much you own* (economic capital) and your social status.

Cultural capital includes your ability to catch the passing reference to books, movies, and music of the cultural set you aspire to be a part of during a conversation. It includes your capacity to talk with the right words in the right accent about the right things. It includes your ability to dress right, act right, and move right. And it includes your taste, an ability to enjoy the right music, foods, drinks, movies, books, and fashion, among other things.

What is "right" for one person is not necessarily "right" for another. If you aspire to be an affluent urban intellectual hipster, the cultural capital you will set about accumulating is very different from the cultural capital sought after by someone pursuing acceptance as authentically Country. Importantly, this distinction between the two sets is essential to the vitality of each. As Carl Wilson explains, "you want your taste affirmed by your peers and those you admire, but it's just as vital that your redneck uncle thinks you're an idiot to like that rap shit. It proves that you've distinguished yourself from him successfully, and you can bask in righteous satisfaction."

THE CYCLE OF COOL

Cultural capital, like economic capital, is scarce. There is only so much time in a day to accumulate cultural capital, and most of us spend a great deal of our time pursuing it, recognizing its importance in our overall social standing. But cultural capital – what is "cool" – is always on the move. Capital attains its value by being scarce. Cultural capital – "what is cool" – maintains this scarcity by always being on the move. Being cool is a full-time job of carefully watching for trends and movement in the webs of significance we are collectively spinning.

Market researchers try to keep up with what is cool by tracking down trend-setting kids to interview them, study them, and follow them on social media. Once market researchers get in on a trend, they can create products to serve this new taste; but as soon as the mass consumer picks up on it, the trend-setter can no longer like it without being associated with the masses. Doug Rushkoff calls this the "cycle of cool." Once that "cool" thing is embraced by the masses, it's not cool anymore, because it's no longer allowing people to feel that sense of distinction. Trend setters move on to the next cool thing, so that the mark of what is "cool" keeps moving.

Market researchers are also employed by media companies producing movies, TV shows, and music videos that need to reflect what is currently popular. In *Merchants of Cool*, a documentary about the dynamics of cool and culture in the early 2000s, Doug Rushkoff asks, "Is the media really reflecting the world of kids, or is it the other way around?" He is struck by a group of 13-year-olds who spontaneously broke out into sexually-laden dances for his camera crew the moment they started filming "as if to sell back to us, the media, what we had sold to them." He called it "the feedback loop." The media studies kids and produces an image of them to sell back to the kids. The kids consume those images and then aspire to be what they see. The media sees that and then crafts new images to sell to them "and so on ... Is there any way to escape the feedback loop?" Rushkoff asks.

He found some kids in Detroit, fans of a rage rock band called Insane Clown Posse. They thought they had found a way to get out of the media machine by creating a sub-culture that was so offensive as to be indigestible by the media. With his cameras rolling, the kids yell obscenities into the camera and break out singing one of their favorite and least digestible Insane Clown Posse songs, "Who's goin ti**y f*in?" one boy yells out and the crowd responds, "We's goin ti**y f*in!" They call themselves Juggalos. They have their own slang and idioms, and they feel like they have found something that is exclusively theirs. "These are the extremes that teens are willing to go to ensure the authenticity of their own scene," Rushkoff concludes. "It's a double dog dare to the mainstream marketing machine," Rushkoff notes, "Just try to market this."

They did. Before Rushkoff could finish the documentary, the band had been signed by a major label, debuting at #20 on the pop charts.

WHY WE HATE

Growing up in a small town in Nebraska, I learned to hate Country music. One would think it would be the opposite. Nebraskans love Country music. But that was precisely the point. By the time I was a teenager, I had aspirations of escaping that little town. I wanted to go off to college, preferably out of state, and "make something of myself." The most popular Country song of that time was by Garth Brooks singing, "I've Got Friends in Low Places." I didn't want friends in low places. I wanted friends (social capital) in other places, high places, so I tuned my taste (cultural capital) accordingly. I hated Garth Brooks. I hated Country music.

I loved Weezer. Weezer was a bunch of elite Ivy League school kids who sang lyrics like, "Beverly Hills! That's where I want to be!" It was like a soundtrack for the life I wanted to live. "Where I come from isn't all that great," they sang, "my automobile is a piece of crap. My fashion sense is a little whack and my friends are just as screwy as me." It seemed to capture everything I was, and everything I aspired to become.

My hatred for Country music bore deep into my consciousness as I associated it with a wide range of characteristics, values, beliefs, ideas, and ideals that I rejected and wanted to distinguish myself from. The hate stuck with me so that years later, I still could not stand to stay on a Country music station for long. I once heard a bit of a Kenny Chesney song about knocking a girl up and getting stuck in his small town. "So much for ditching this town and hanging out on the coast," the song goes, "There goes my life." *Ha!* I thought. *I got out.* Then I changed the channel.

Of course, nurturing such hatreds is not especially conducive to being a good anthropologist, or a good human being for that matter. What can we do? Is it possible to overcome our hatreds? And if we can do it with music, can we do it with hatreds of more substance and importance? Can we get beyond hatreds of others, other religions, other cultures, other political beliefs? And can we do it without giving up all that we value and hold dear?

Carl Wilson, a Canadian music critic, decided to do an experiment to explore these questions. He called it "an experiment in taste." He would deliberately try to step outside of his own taste-bubble and try to enjoy something he truly hates. His plan was to immerse himself in music he hates to find out what he can learn about taste and how it works.

As he thought about what he hated most, one song immediately came to mind: Celine Dion's "My Heart Will Go On." The song rocketed to international popularity as the love song of the blockbuster movie *Titanic* in 1998. The song, and Celine Dion herself, have enjoyed global success that is almost unrivaled by any other song or celebrity. She sells out the largest venues all over the world. As the US entered Afghanistan in 2003, *The Chicago Tribune* noted that Celine was playing in market stalls everywhere, her albums being sold right beside Titanic-branded body sprays, mosquito repellant ... even cucumbers and potatoes were labeled "Titanic" if they were especially large.

As a Canadian music critic with a vested interest in being cool among affluent urban intellectual hipsters, Wilson could not think of any song he hated more. In general, urban hipsters like Wilson love to bash Celine, and especially this song. Maxim put it at #3 in its ranking of "most annoying song ever" and called it "the second most tragic event to result from that fabled ocean liner."

Wilson quotes Suck.com for calling *Titanic* a "14-hour-long piece of cinematic vaudeville" that teaches important lessons "like if you are incredibly good-looking, you'll fall in love."

Wilson's hate for the song crystallized at the Oscars in 1998. Up against Celine's love ballad was Elliot Smith's "Miss Misery" a soul-filled indie love song about depression from *Good Will Hunting* that you would expect to hear from the corner of an authentic hip urban coffee shop. Smith was totally out of place at the Oscars. He didn't even want to be there. It wasn't his scene. He reluctantly agreed to sing when the producers threatened to bring in '80s teen heart throb Richard Marx to sing it instead. As a compromise, he performed the song alone with nothing but his guitar. It wasn't his kind of scene, but he would still do his kind of performance.

Then Celine Dion came "swooshing out in clouds of fake fog" with a "white-tailed orchestra arrayed to look like they were on the deck of the *Titanic* itself." Elliot's performance floated gently like a hand-carved fishing boat next to the Titanic performance of Celine. Madonna opened the envelope to announce the winner, laughed, and said with great sarcasm, "What a shocker … Celine Dion!" Carl Wilson was crushed, and his hate for Celine, and especially that song, solidified.

Wilson did not need to probe the depths of his consciousness to know that he hated that song, but he still did not know *why* he hated that song. Perhaps Bourdieu's terminology could help, he mused. Turning to the notions of social and cultural capital, he started exploring Celine Dion's fan base to see if he was using cultural capital to distinguish himself from some groups while affiliating himself with others.

He was not the first to wonder who likes Celine Dion. He quoted one paper (*The Independent on Sunday*) as offering the snarky musing that "wedged between vomit and indifference there must be a fan base: … grannies, tux-wearers, overweight children, mobile-phone salesmen, and shopping-centre devotees, presumably." Looking at actual record sales, Wilson found that 45% were over 50, 68% female, and that they were 3.5 times more likely to be widowed. "It's hard to imagine an audience that could confer less cool on a musician," Wilson mused. It was no wonder he was pushing them away by pushing away from the music.

But he also noted that the record sales showed that they were mostly middle income with middle education, not unlike Wilson himself. Wilson aspires to be an intellectual and tries to write for an intellectual audience, but he has no clear intellectual credentials such as a Ph.D., and his income reflects this.

This brings up an important point about the things we hate: We often hate most that which is most like us. We have elevated anxieties about being associated with things that people might assume we would like, so we make extra efforts to distinguish ourselves from these elements. So Wilson pushes extra hard against these middle-income middle-educated Celine fans while attempting to pull himself toward the intellectual elite.

This is not as simple as an intentional decision to dislike something just because it isn't cool. It works at a much deeper level. The intellectual elite that Wilson aspires to be associated with talks and acts in certain ways. They have what Bourdieu calls a certain "habitus" – dispositions, habits, tastes, attitudes, and abilities. In particular, the intellectual elite tend to over-intellectualize and deny emotion. Nurturing this same habitus, Wilson hears a simple sappy love ballad on a blockbuster movie loved by the masses and immediately rejects it. It doesn't feel intentional. He truly hates it, and that hatred is in part born out of this habitus.

HOW TO STOP HATING

Wilson pressed forward with his experiment. He met Celine's fans, including a man named Sophoan, who was as different from Wilson as possible. He is sweet-natured and loves contemporary Christian music, as well as the winners of various international Idol competitions. "I'm on the phone to a parallel universe," Wilson mused about their first phone conversation. But by the end of it, he genuinely likes Sophoan, and he is starting to question his own tastes. "I like him so much that for a long moment, his taste seems superior," Wilson concludes. "What was the point again of all that nasty, life-negating crap I like?"

As Wilson explored his own consciousness a bit deeper, he started to realize just how emotionally stunted he had become. He had just been through a tough divorce. It wasn't that he felt no emotion; it was that his constant tendency to over-intellectualize allowed him to never truly sit with an emotion and really feel it. Instead he would "mess with it and craft it … bargain with it until it becomes something else."

Onward with the experiment. Wilson decided to listen to Celine Dion as often as possible. It took him months before he could play it at full volume, for fear of what his neighbors might think of him. He had developed, as he put it, a guilty pleasure. And the use of the word "pleasure" was intentional. He really was starting to enjoy Celine Dion.

"My Heart Will Go On" was more challenging, though. It wasn't just that it had reached such widespread acceptance among the masses. It was that it had been overplayed too much to enjoy. "Through the billowing familiarity," he writes, "I find the song near-impossible to see, much less cry about."

That is, until it appeared in the TV show *Gilmore Girls*. After the divorce, Wilson found himself drawn to teenage drama shows. His own life was not unlike that of those teenage girls portrayed in the shows. Single and working as a music critic, he often goes out to shows and parties where he always struggles to fit in, find love, and feel cool among people who always seem to be a little cooler than him.

In the last season of *Gilmore Girls*, the shihtzu dog of the French concierge dies. The concierge is a huge Celine fan, and requests "My Heart Will Go On" for the funeral. The whole scene is one of gross and almost ridiculous sentimentality, but a deep truth is expressed through Lorelai, the lead character, as it dawns on her that her love for her own husband is not as deep or true as the love this concierge has for his dog. She knows it's time to move on and ask for a divorce. Wilson starts to cry:

> Something has shifted. I'm no longer watching a show about a teenage girl, whether mother or daughter. It's become one about an adult, my age, admitting that to forge a decent happiness, you can't keep trying to bend all the rules; you

> aren't exempt from the laws of motion that make the world turn. And one of the minor ones is that people need sentimental songs to marry, mourn, and break up to, and this place they hold matters more than anything intrinsic to the songs themselves. In fact, when one of those weepy widescreen ballads lands just so, it can wise you up that you're just one more dumb dog that has to do its best to make things right until one day, it dies. And that's sad. Sad enough to make you cry. Even to cry along with Celine Dion.

I think back to my own experience with that Kenny Chesney song – the one about the guy getting stuck in the small town after getting a girl pregnant. After I became a father, I was driving home from a conference, back to be with my wife and infant son in Kansas. (We felt drawn back to small town life, and decided to settle close to home to start our family.) The singer describes his little girl smiling up at him as she stumbles up the stairs and "he smiles … There goes my life." I, of course, am weeping uncontrollably at this point. I'm a different person. The song speaks to me, and completely wrecks me in a later verse as the chorus is invoked one last time in describing his little girl going off to college. *There goes my life. There goes my future, my everything, I love you, Baby good-bye. There goes my life.* (I can't even type the words without crying.)

Like me, Wilson once hated that sappy music. But now, he says, "I don't see the advantage in holding yourself above things; down on the surface is where the action is." By opening himself up to experiencing more, experiencing difference, and experiencing differently, Carl Wilson became more. He expanded his potential for authentic connection—not just to music, but also to other people. In his efforts to be cool, he spent a great deal of time trying to not be taken in by the latest mass craze, unaware that he was "also refusing an invitation *out*." The experiment allowed him to move beyond this, open up to new experiences and more people. He started to see that the next phase of his life "might happen in a larger world, one beyond the horizon of my habits."

LEARN MORE

- Distinction: A Social Critique of the Judgement of Taste, by Pierre Bourdieu
- Let's Talk about Love: Why Other People Have Such Bad Taste, by Carl Wilson
- Merchants of Cool. PBS Frontline Documentary
- Generation Like. PBS Frontline Documentary

RELIGIONS AND WISDOM OF THE WORLD

"In the day-to-day trenches of adult life, there is actually no such thing as atheism. There is no such thing as not worshipping. Everybody worships. The only choice we get is what to worship. And the compelling reason for maybe choosing some sort of god or spiritual-type thing to worship – be it JC or Allah, be it YHWH or the Wiccan Mother Goddess... – is that pretty much anything else you worship will eat you alive. If you worship money and things... then you will never have enough, never feel you have enough. ... Worship your body and beauty and sexual allure, and you will always feel ugly. ... Worship power, you will end up feeling weak and afraid. ... Worship your intellect, being seen as smart, you will end up feeling stupid, a fraud, always on the verge of being found out. But the insidious thing about these forms of worship is not that they're evil or sinful, it's that they're unconscious. They are default settings. They're the kind of worship you just gradually slip into, day after day, getting more and more selective about what you see and how you measure value without ever being fully aware that that's what you're doing."

-- David Foster Wallace

In the ancient village of Kapilavastu, India, Kisa's baby was not waking up. She lovingly nudged him and waited for his eyes to open, but he remained still. He had died during the night, but Kisa could not accept this. She had recently lost her husband, and her baby meant everything to her. She picked up the baby and rushed for help. The Buddha was staying nearby, so she went to him for medicine.

The Buddha, seeing that Kisa's son had died, told her that in order to make the medicine, he would need mustard seed from a house that had not known death. Kisa rushed back to the village to find such seed. At each house she asked if they had known death, and each time she heard story after story about loved ones lost. Everywhere, the answer was the same. No house did not know death. She listened to their stories, and she started to understand.

She returned to the Buddha understanding that death is an essential element of life. Instead of trying to comfort her with the idea that all who die go to heaven, he offered instead the idea that learning to understand the true nature of the inevitable sufferings of life could bring her peace, joy, and enlightenment.

This story illustrates the profound similarities in the trials, challenges, problems and paradoxes of life that we all must face by virtue of being human. Consider the following list.

All humans:

- are born incomplete and dependent on others.
- must form social relationships to survive.
- must learn to deal with death and suffering.
- must deal with envy, jealousy, and change.
- encounter a world much bigger and more powerful than themselves and must deal with forces – physical, social, economic, and political – that are out of their control.
- must grow and change physically, emotionally, intellectually, and psychologically as they transition

> from childhood to adulthood, from dependency to parenthood, and on into old age and death.

The trials of life along the way are many, and often devastating. A core tenet of all of the major religions is the simple truth of unavoidable human suffering. What can be the meaning of an existence that is so fragile and temporary?

Many people assume religion is simply a superstitious belief system attempting to explain the world based on ancient understandings of the world. Religion is ridiculed for being an outdated science and justification for backwards or regressive morality. While this is certainly true for many people (not only today, but throughout human history), when we immerse ourselves into the religious worlds of different cultures and religions around the world, we also find that religion is doing a lot more than just trying to explain or moralize the world.

In this lesson we will explore what renowned mythologist Joseph Campbell calls the four "functions" of religion:

1. **The Cosmological Function:** It provides a framework for relating to the world in a deeply meaningful way.
2. **The Sociological Function:** It brings people together and gives them guidelines for staying together.
3. **The Pedagogical Function:** It provides wisdom for navigating the inevitable challenges and trials of life.
4. **The Mystical Function.** It allows people to feel connected to something bigger than themselves, giving them a sense of awe, peace, and profound significance.

UNDERSTANDING DIFFERENT WORLDVIEWS

Unlike the current Christian notion that if you believe in God and accept Christ as your personal savior, you can be saved and live for eternity in heaven, the Buddha did not ask his followers to believe in anything. Instead, he asked them to practice virtue, understanding, mindfulness, and meditation so that they could achieve enlightenment.

This difference reminds us that starting from a Western perspective on religion can lead us to miss out on a full understanding of how others see the world. In much of the world, religion is not about "belief."

In New Guinea, there were spirits everywhere, and keeping yourself right with them was a matter of life or death. We occasionally brought an offering of pig to different spirits – the spirit of the mountain to our east, or the spirit of that grove down the hill – and invited them to feast. But these spirits were not supernatural to them. They insisted that they did not simply "believe" in them. They were just part of nature. They were not something you *believed* in because they were not something you would ever question. They just were. Therefore, faith and belief were irrelevant to them.

Living with them made me realize that many of the most basic questions we have about religion are culturally bounded and ethnocentric due to this focus on "belief" as the core of religion. For example, most of us would think that the proper question to ask when understanding other religions would be something like, "What god or gods do they believe in?" But this question only makes sense coming from a religious background of the Abrahamic faiths (Judaism, Christianity, and Islam). These faiths all focus intensively on faith or belief in a single omnipotent god. But what about all of the other religions – which number in the thousands – that are not based on a single god, or any god, or even on the notion of faith and belief?

Questions based on what people believe are culturally biased because they end up defining other people's religions in our terms. Hinduism, a richly textured religion full of rituals, practices, contemplation, meditation, and stories aimed toward helping people live a balanced fulfilling and meaningful life, is diminished to become nothing more than "polytheism" - belief in more than one god. The rich world of spirits my friends in New Guinea experience, and the complex rituals and practices they engage in to relate to them, becomes nothing more than "animism" – belief in spirits.

Another problem with focusing on "belief" is that in many languages, there may not be a concept that conveys exactly what is meant by the English word "believe." Anthropologist Rodney Needham documented several examples of this, and notes that early linguists like Max Müller found it difficult to find the concept in several languages when they started documenting indigenous languages in the late 1800s.

This problem with the word "belief" strikes at the heart of just how differently cultures may view the world. As Dorothy Lee notes so powerfully, "the world view of a particular society includes the society's conception of man's own relation to the universe, human and non-human, organic and inorganic, secular and divine, to use our own dualisms." The key phrase here is, "*to use our own dualisms.*" Remarkably, Lee is recognizing that our most basic assumptions are culturally bounded. Other people do not make the same distinctions between the human and non-human or secular and divine that we do. They may not make those distinctions at all. She points out that the very notion of the "supernatural" is not present in some cultures. "Religion is an ever-present dimension of experience" for these people, she notes, and "religion" is not given a name because it permeates their existence. Clyde Kluckohn notes that the Navaho had no word for religion. Lee points out that the Tikopia of the Pacific Islands "appear to live in a continuum which includes nature and the divine without defining bounds; where communion is present, not achieved, where merging is a matter of being, not of becoming."

Furthermore, the division of the world into economics, politics, family and religion is a Western construction. As Lee notes, for many indigenous peoples, "all economic activities, such as hunting, gathering fuel, cultivating the land, storing food, assume a relatedness to the encompassing universe, and with many cultures, this is a religious relationship."

Our focus on "belief" as the core of religion leads us to emphasize belief over practice, and mind over body. In Christianity you have to *believe* to be saved. Westerners tend to see other religions as different versions on this theme, so we approach the study of religion as an exploration of what others believe. But the Christian emphasis on "belief" is itself a modern invention. A careful textual analysis of writings from the 17th Century by Wilfred Cantwell Smith found that the word "believe" was only used to refer to a commitment of loyalty and trust. It was the notion of "believing in" something, not believing whether or not a statement was true. In other words, according to Smith, faith in the 17th Century was a matter of believing *in* God (putting trust and loyalty in him) not believing *that* God exists. He turns to the Hindu term for faith, *sraddha*, to clarify what he means. "It means, almost without equivocation, to set one's heart on." Similarly, the Latin "credo" is formed from the Latin roots "cor" (heart) and "do" (to put, place, or give). The emphasis on belief as a matter of truth only became an issue as the belief of God's existence became more fragile and open to question with the rise of science. As a result, most of us are used to wrestling with big ideas about the big everything, and the big question of what to believe looms large in our consciousness.

WHERE BELIEF DOES NOT MATTER

To examine a religion that does not focus on belief in more detail, we can look to the philosophical Hinduism that emerged about 2,500 years ago in India. The fourth Brahmana of the Upanishads, a sacred text of Hinduism dated to this time period, describes the beginning of time as beginning with nothing but "the Great Self" or the "Brahman." The Self was all that there was. Seeing that he was alone, the Self felt afraid, but then he thought, "There is nothing but myself, why should I fear?" But then he felt lonely and he longed for a companion. So he split himself in two, man and woman, and embraced the woman. From that union, all humans were born.

The woman hid herself as a cow, so the man turned into a bull and embraced her, and all cattle were born. She turned herself into a mare, and he into a goat, and all goats were born, and so on until all the creatures of the world were created. "And thus he created everything, down to the ants." In contrast to the story of Genesis, in which God stands outside of creation and creates the world, the Hindu Self (Brahman) has become everything everywhere. The Brahman is the ultimate reality that permeates all of reality. It is beyond all dualities and cannot be properly named, because to name is to make distinctions between this and that. As the Upanishads say, "He who worships him as one or the other, does not know him."

As a result, the core problem in Hinduism is not to believe in God, have faith in God, or to form a relationship with God as an external being. It is instead to recognize one's own divine nature within. The world of separate things is an illusion called Maya, and as long as we are trapped in this illusion, we are trapped in Samsara, the endless cycle of death, rebirth, and reincarnation.

Since the divine oneness was fractured by the original fear and desire, this means overcoming fear and desire to recognize one's oneness with all of creation. The core problem is not salvation, as it is in Christianity. The core problem is how to achieve enlightenment by transcending the illusory dualities of the world.

One cannot achieve enlightenment by knowledge or belief alone. One must actually experience the unity of all things. In one of the most famous stories of the Upanishads, a young man comes home after studying for many years. He is very proud of his knowledge until his father asks, "Svetaketu, my child, you are so full of your learning and so censorious, have you asked for that knowledge by which we hear the unhearable, by which we perceive what cannot be perceived and know what cannot be known?"

The boy was humbled and asked to learn more. The father told him to put some salt in a glass of water and come back tomorrow. When he returned the father asked him for the salt. Svetaketu noted that the salt had dissolved and no longer existed. His father asked him to taste the water. "How does it taste?" he asked. "Salty," he replied. "Now taste from the bottom," his father asked. "Salty," he replied again. "It is everywhere, though we do not see it. So it is with the Self. It is everywhere, though we do not perceive it. And thou art that."

That line "thou art that," translated by Alan Watts emphatically as "You're it!" is the key idea of Hinduism and Buddhism. It means that all is one and all is divine, but it is not a doctrine to believe in dogmatically. It is an experience that one must constantly work to achieve through practices such as meditation, overcoming selfish desires, and serving others.

THE COSMOLOGICAL FUNCTION

Religious cosmologies can be so profoundly different as to constitute entirely different visions of time and space. Let's dive into the terraced landscapes of Bali to get a glimpse into a worldview that allows the people to relate to their world in a way that is good for the environment and the people.

The terraced rice landscapes in the mountains of Bali form some of the most beautiful landscapes in the world. Look closer, and you will see a landscape permeated with religion. Every rice farmer in Bali has a small shrine where irrigation water enters his fields. At this shrine he carries out daily offerings and rituals. A little upstream, there is a small temple where the irrigation canal first enters the local region. Groups of farmers meet here to perform collective rites and hold meetings. Still further upstream there is yet another temple, where the irrigation canal splits off from the main channel. And at the very top of the system there is the main temple at Lake Batur, dedicated to the supreme goddess of water, Dewi Danu, as well as 146 other deities. Water is essential to rice farming, and therefore to the health and vitality of the people, so in addition to these temples there are additional shrines and temples at every pond, lake, spring, and the headwaters of every river. There are additional temples downstream, positioned not to worship water but to act as defense against pests and other threats to the harvest. Together, this pan-regional network of temples creates a religious landscape permeated with the notion of water bringing life and vitality from upstream against the forces of death and destruction that might come from below.

Notions of time are also different, and organized around this cosmology. They have a complex system of three calendars. First there is the 210 day calendar called Uku, which is broken up into 30 seven-day weeks and six 35-day "months," matching the length of the growth cycle of their first rice planting. The second is a lunar/solar calendar, in which each month is directly tied to the moon, and an extra month is added once every two or three years to keep it in line with the solar calendar. Brahman priests oversee the coordination of the calendars, and make the decisions about when to add an additional month.

Each year, the high priest of the central Batur Temple sends a formal invitation to the 204 regional temple congregations to a special festival to mark the full moon of the tenth month. Each temple is instructed to bring specific items as offerings to the water goddess and other deities. This is no small matter. The priests must carefully plan this event to match the growth cycle of the rice. Rice needs a lot of water as it is maturing, followed by a great deal of sun as it reaches maturity. Ideally, a rice harvest comes to maturity right at the end of the rainy season.

For many decades, outside researchers thought that the water temple network was based merely on religious superstition and served no practical purpose. Even worse, it was thought that the priestly requirements to plant at certain times and to not plant at others was likely detrimental to maximizing rice yields.

In the 1970s, scientifically engineered planting strategies known as the "Green Revolution" were adopted by the Indonesian government. The power of the water temple priests was stripped away. They continued their rituals and offerings, but they no longer controlled the water. Soon, pest populations soared, along with the spread of diseases. Imported pesticides were used widely to contain the problem but also killed eels, fish, and according to local hospital reports, some farmers as well.

Within a few years, there were widespread calls to put the priests back in charge. Anthropologist Stephen Lansing ran a computer model to demonstrate how the priestly system of water management worked to maximize yields while minimizing pests. What he found was that the short fallow periods dictated by the priests starved pests and contained disease. These fallow periods had to be carefully coordinated and synchronized across a wide area so that the pests could not just go from one farm to another. Lansing's computer model showed that not only was the priestly system effective, it was the most effective solution possible.

Lansing ends his study of the Balinese rice fields with a haunting image showing the contrast between the competing systems of the priests and the scientists.

> *Downstream, foreign consultants dispatch airplanes to photograph Bali's rivers from above, and draw topographic maps of new irrigation systems. Upstream, a group of farmers drop frangipani flowers in their canals before beginning a new ploughing. The new subak prepares for the dedication of its Ulun Swi temple, two subaks arrive at the master water temple for advice on dealing with the brown plant-hoppers which have destroyed half their crop, and half a dozen men with picks and shovels shore up the sides of a field that has produced two crops of rice each year for the past eight centuries.*

THE SOCIOLOGICAL FUNCTION

Traditionally, Australian Aborigines spent much of their time roaming wide areas of land, hunting and gathering their food. They lived in small family groups and rarely encountered other people. The landscape itself was sacred. Every rock formation, valley, and river were the footprints and marks left behind by the culture heroes of the Dreamtime, the time before time when all was created. People find their way by singing ancient songs which sing the stories of these culture heroes. The songs are like maps showing the way. "If you know the song, you can always find your way across the country," wrote Bruce Chatwin in his book *Songlines.*

But sometimes Aborigines came together in larger groups for a large ritual. We all know the feeling of gathering in large groups of people for a special event like a big game or concert. As Emile Durkheim famously described these gatherings of Aborigines, "a sort of electricity is generated from their closeness and quickly launches them into an extraordinary height of exaltation. Every emotion expressed resonates ... echoing the others ... like an avalanche that grows as it goes along." He uses the term "collective effervescence" to describe this feeling, which is one that can lift a person so high as to feel a brief moment of something akin to enlightenment – a true lightness of being – or ecstasy – a feeling of being outside of one's self. This collective effervescence is a key element of ritual, and something all humans continue to seek out, even if they are not religious.

That humans everywhere can experience this kind of "collective effervescence" is a sign of our shared humanity, a product of our social nature. Such experiences help us build or repair social bonds and communities, overcome conflicts, and work together to survive, thrive, and find joy in our lives.

THE PEDAGOCIAL FUNCTION

Religions also give wisdom and guidance for the challenges and changes of life. One of the most dramatic changes all humans must go through is the transition from dependency in childhood to the state of independent adulthood. In many cultures this transition is marked by an initiation ritual. These rituals show remarkable similarities across cultures, capturing some deep wisdom about what it takes to be a successful adult.

Though initiation rituals vary greatly, they all flow through three primary stages which Arnold Von Gennep identified as separation, liminality, and incorporation. The stages represent the movement of the initiate from one stage of life to another. In the separation phase, they are removed from their childhood. This often involves a dramatic removal from the mother and is accompanied by symbols of death, representing that the child is "dying," to be reborn as something new. The initiate is then placed in a secluded place with other initiates as they enter the stage of liminality, a stage marked by ambiguity and disorientation. Initiates are meant to feel as if they have lost their place in society and now stand apart, not knowing who they are or how they should act.

College serves this function in modern Western societies. Each year, millions of teenagers leave the familiar surroundings of their childhood homes to live alone for the first time. On college campuses they take on some adult responsibilities, but not all of them, thereby living in a state betwixt and between childhood and adulthood. It can be a turbulent time as they try to figure out who they are and how they want to emerge as full adults. In the meantime, their relationships with parents can become strained due to the ambiguity between their continued partial dependency and their emerging adulthood. Like initiates all over the world, they are no longer classified as child and not yet classified as adult, so there are no clear roles or rules to follow.

In indigenous rituals, the old child-self is now "dead" to ordinary society, so they are sometimes treated as a corpse would be treated, indicating the death to their former selves. They might be buried or required to lay motionless. But at the same time, they are about to be reborn, so they may be treated as embryos or seedlings. Among the Min groups of New Guinea, initiates have their hair made into a bun that resembles a taro tuber, representing a seed that will grow. With symbols of both death and birth, the secluded space itself is often thought of as both tomb and womb.

Before they can be reborn, they have to endure trials and tests to see if they are ready. The Satere-Mawe of Brazil put on gloves filled with stinging bullet ants and have to dance with the gloves on, enduring the pain until they pass out. The Kaningara of New Guinea must lie still while their elders cut hundreds of deep cuts into their bodies, covering them in their own blood, and then endure stinging nettles that make the gashes swell into lasting scars. By the time they heal, their skin looks like the scaly flesh of the crocodiles they revere. Painful body modification is common in initiation rituals, providing a test to demonstrate their ability to overcome fear, quell their desire for comfort, and show that they are ready for the challenges and sacrifices of adulthood.

In the final phase of incorporation, the initiates are revealed to the society and announced as full adults. There are often images of rebirth. For example, in some New Guinea societies, initiates crawl through the spread legs of the elder men as if to be reborn into society. They emerge from the "womb" of the initiation as a new man.

These rituals can have a profound effect. For example, among the Kalenjin of Kenya, the male initiates are required to endure a painful circumcision without anesthesia. Their bodies are covered with dried mud so that if they flinch even the slightest bit, the mud will crack to reveal their weakness. If this happens, the initiation is considered a failure. They are not real men and are not allowed to marry. Some have suggested that this ritual is the reason why Kalenjin are so strong and able to endure pain. The Kalenjin are world-renowned long distance runners. Consider that only 17 Americans have ever run a marathon in under 2 hours and 10 minutes. Thirty-two Kalenjin did it in just one month in October 2011. The Kalenjin make up only .06% of the world population, yet they consistently dominate long distance running events worldwide.

If initiates are able to overcome fear and quell their desires, the secrets of adulthood are revealed. Sometimes the revelations are profound and overturn everything they thought they knew. For example, the Keraki of New Guinea grow up hearing terrifying monstrous sounds emanating from the forbidden regions of the forest. They are told that these are the sounds of the great crocodile spirit. During the initiation, their eyes are covered by senior men as they wait for the spirit to come. They hear the terrifying sound come closer and closer until it is right upon them and about to swallow them up. Then the men uncover their eyes to reveal that it is the men themselves spinning bull-roarers that makes the sound. They are then appointed keepers of the secret and protectors of the bull-roarers, which are not viewed as "tricks" but as sacred divinities in their own right.

As horrific as some of these rituals may sound, they serve all of the religious functions. First, they serve a sociological function of creating social solidarity and providing roles and rules for living together. In this case, the process itself is a strong bonding experience for initiates, and the end of the process gives them a firm understanding of themselves as adults and establishing their role for the rest of society. Second, rituals and religions serve a pedagogical function of teaching people how to live and endure the inevitable challenges and changes of life. In this case, the ritual lays out the rules and expectations of adulthood while teaching the initiates important lessons about how to overcome fear, quell desire, and live up to their full potential. Third, rituals and religions serve a cosmological function, providing a comprehensive worldview that explains why the world is the way it is. In this case, the rituals reveal secrets of the world that can inform their lives and bring meaning to it. And finally, there is also a mystical function served by such rituals. The ritual provides a time to sit with and contemplate the mysteries of being and the awe of existence itself.

THE MYSTICAL FUNCTION,

THE PERENNIAL PHILOSOPHY, AND "REAL FREEDOM"

Despite the remarkable diversity of religious traditions around the world, some mythologists, philosophers, and anthropologists propose that there are some profound similarities shared across all traditions, especially in how they all inspire a sense of profound awe and can lead to religious experiences of intense wonder and ecstasy. This perspective is most prominently known by Aldous Huxley's collection of religious texts and statements from all over the world, which he called *The Perennial Philosophy*.

Huxley arranges the texts into 27 sections to demonstrate 27 core ideas or themes that all religious traditions address in similar ways. When laid out as such, it is remarkable to consider the similarities. Nearly all human groups everywhere have religious objects which are worshiped, create sacred spaces, have cosmological notions of good and evil, a philosophy of grace and free will, emphasize the importance of self-knowledge, recognize the inevitability of human suffering, engage in prayer, ritual, and other spiritual exercises, and encourage charity.

According to Huxley, the Perennial Philosophy can be simplified into five statements that all major religious traditions adhere to philosophically:

1. There is a transcendent something bigger than us.
2. We are or seem to be separated from it.
3. We can re-unite with it.
4. This unity is the ultimate purpose of our existence.
5. There is a law, dharma (sacred teaching), or way that must be followed to achieve this end.

Huxley proposes that the ultimate goal of the major wisdom traditions is for humans to recognize their inherent connection to the world. He uses the phrase "Thou art that" from the Hindu salt water story as the central tenant of this idea. The basic human problem is that we do not feel this sense of unity with God or the universe. We feel fundamentally alone, separate, and vulnerable.

In the Abrahamic faiths of Judaism, Christianity, and Islam, we were once living in a heavenly paradise, but we ate of the Tree of Knowledge of Good and Evil and were expelled from the Garden. The imagery is a powerful portrayal of Huxley's vision of original unity followed by separation from God. Each tradition offers a pathway to build a relationship back to God.

In Eastern traditions such as Hinduism and Buddhism, the problem is slightly different. Humans are not separated from God, but are actually made up of the same stuff as the divine and really are divine in themselves. However, we do not feel that sense of divinity. We make distinctions into this and that and identify with somethings and not others. We live in a world of illusions (maya) in which we see ourselves, others, and the things of this world as separate, failing to see that we are actually all connected and united as one. We have to engage in certain practices to "wake up" to our "true self." The "true self" is the one true self that makes up the entire universe, the *Atman.*

While Abrahamic and Eastern traditions differ in how they conceptualize transcendent reality, both suggest that we are somehow separate from it but can be re-united with it through divine love, divine union, or awareness of divinity within us.

Widely regarded as one of the greatest writers of our time, David Foster Wallace demonstrates how these core ideas from the world's wisdom traditions can inform our everyday lives in a graduation speech which has become one of the most popular graduation speeches of all time, watched millions of times on YouTube and published as a bestselling book called *This is Water.*

Wallace points out that our everyday experience leads us to make three false assumptions:

1. *I am always right.* We tend to live with a perpetual certainty that we are right and others have it wrong. We have

remarkable abilities to confirm our biases by seeking out only friends and information that confirm us and avoiding truly listening to and understanding other ideas and perspectives.

2. *I am the center of the universe.* We see through our own eyes, feel through our skin, and hear through our ears – all of which gives us the constant visceral experience of being the actual center of the universe. The evidence bombards us at every moment of our lives. When we allow the assumption to guide us we close ourselves off to empathy and the ability to imagine our way into another person's perspective.

3. *I don't need to think about how to think.* Most of us rarely stop to think about how we think or where our thoughts come from. This lack of reflection keeps us locked inside our assumptions and stunts our growth.

Together, this trio makes up what Wallace calls "our natural default setting." They are constantly operating on us, unconsciously, in the most mundane experiences of everyday life – sitting in traffic, shopping in a crowded supermarket, waiting in a checkout line. Wallace points out that it is easy to experience these inconveniences through our automatic default setting as being "all about *me* ... about my hungriness and my fatigue and my desire to just get home, and it's going to seem for all the world like everybody else is just in my way."

But, if we really learn how to think – how to be open to others and their experiences, how to consider alternatives to our own assumptions – we can experience these situations differently. We can imagine our way into the perspective of others. When we are initially annoyed by a screaming kid in the checkout line, or a big SUV blocking our way in traffic, or some form of bad behavior, we can use our capacities of imagination and empathy to see them as fellow humans struggling through many of the same struggles that we have.

Echoing the words and ideas of the great wisdom traditions, Wallace notes that, "It will actually be within your power to experience a crowded, hot, slow, consumer-hell type situation as not only meaningful, but sacred, on fire with the same force that lit the stars: love, fellowship, the mystical oneness of all things deep down."

In this lesson, we have explored how moving past our own moral assumptions or our own likes and dislikes in music can lead to greater understanding of others and may even offer us a richer and fuller experience of life by opening us up to enjoying different kinds of music. By digging in and exploring ourselves and our own tastes, values, and ideals a little more deeply, we can move ourselves toward what David Foster Wallace calls "real freedom" – the "real freedom" to open ourselves up to other people, challenge our own biases and assumptions, and live richer and fuller lives.

"It is unimaginably hard to do this," Wallace concludes, "to stay conscious and alive in the adult world day in and day out." But, he says, "that is real freedom. The alternative is unconsciousness, the default setting, the rat race, the constant gnawing sense of having had, and lost, some infinite thing."

LEARN MORE

- The World's Religions: A Concise Introduction
  by Huston Smith
- God is Not One: The Eight Rival Religions that Run the World, by Stephen Prothero
- Light at the Edge of the World: A Journey through the Realm of Vanishing Cultures, by Wade Davis
- The Serpent and the Rainbow
  by Wade Davis
- Perfect Order: Recognizing Complexity in Bali
  by Stephen Lansing

Challenge Seven: The Other Encounter

Your challenge is to understand and empathize with somebody as different from you as possible, preferably with religious, political, or identity differences that are especially difficult for you to understand.

Objective: Practice the art of seeing your way into another person's perspective. This requires seeing your own seeing to move past your assumptions, seeing big to see the historical and cultural conditions that led to your differences, and seeing small to see the specific details of your differences.

1. Find an other. This may be someone in your class or someone you know or meet outside of class, but they should have beliefs, ideas, or ideals that you find **very difficult** or even impossible to understand. *This exercise works best when you really challenge yourself by meeting with an other whose beliefs really bother you in some way.*

2. Big Talk. Set aside at least one hour to have a very deep conversation with them. Select questions from the list at anth101.com/challenge7 to get you started.

3. Reflect on all you have learned about who they are and who they are becoming, where they have been and where they are going, what they have done and what they will do, who they have touched and who they will touch.

4. Take a picture together or an artistic portrayal of what you learned and share your experience. #anth101challenge7

Lesson Eight

Globalization

Our failure to move beyond such a view has led to the tragedy of our times: that we are more connected than ever yet feel and act more disconnected.

THE TRAGEDY OF OUR TIMES

A woman in Haiti wipes sweat from her brow as she sifts through pile of trash. This small pile sits upon a larger pile which is itself on top of what can only be described as a mountain of trash, extending several hundred meters in every direction. Most of the trash in that mountain has been shipped thousands of miles from other countries. A fire fuming with black toxic smoke burns in the background, where there is a small, emaciated cow looking for something to eat. The woman picks through rotting meat, blood-stained needles and shards of broken glass looking for anything of value – maybe a bit of metal or, if she is very lucky, a piece of discarded jewelry that she can exchange for money.

The products she sifts through have their own remarkable story to tell. Most of them are pieced together from materials extracted from all over the world, put together by humans in other places around the world, shipped to still other places in the world to be used and consumed, and in some cases handed down and around to others in other parts of the world, until finally they end up here. She rummages through the tattered clothing and fabrics to see if there is anything worth saving. She is not particular about the style, color, brand, or even the size – anything reasonably clean and whole can be worked into something worth keeping. There are empty soda cans, plastic bags, bottles and other plastic waste, each with their own global story to tell.

If we could hear the stories, we would have a pretty good picture of the world as it is today. Take for example just a single T-shirt, as NPR's Planet Money did in 2013. They followed the birth of a T-shirt from a cotton farm in Mississippi. The cotton from this farm is shipped to Indonesia to be transformed into yarn, and then into fabric. The fabric then goes to Bangladesh to be sewn into a T-shirt by women paid about $80/month. The finished T-shirt is packed into a shipping container bound for Miami. The long journey from Bangladesh to the United States costs just seven cents. The labor to sew the shirt costs 12 cents. The cotton in the shirt costs 60 cents to produce. After adding in profit margins, insurance, and duties, the O'Rourke Group found that a retailer will pay about $5.67 for the shirt and put it up for sale for about $14.

But what is the true cost of that shirt? What did it cost the environment to make that shirt? How much water? How many tons of CO2? What did it cost the workers? What was the total impact on their health and well-being? The story of our world is sewn into the fabric of that shirt and woven into the tragedy of our times: that we are more connected than ever, yet feel and act more disconnected. Products seem to appear on the shelves and racks of stores or arrive at our doorstep from Amazon as if by magic, revealing no hints at where they came from, or the relationships that are necessary to create them. Karl Marx famously referred to this as "commodity fetishism" – the relationships that tie us together to the people who produce the things we buy are captured in a single number, the price. And so we consume at an ever-increasing rate, with little regard for our connections to the Earth that provides the materials or to those people in faraway lands who transform them into products. The average American will throw away 80 pounds of clothing this year.

Some of that will end up in a pile of trash somewhere in Haiti, where a woman wipes sweat from her brow as she sifts through the pile. She is dark-skinned, clearly of African descent, speaks French, and lives on an island in the Caribbean, thousands of miles away from both France and Africa. How do we end up with an African woman speaking French living on a pile of trash in Haiti? To answer that, we have to unravel 600 years of world history and rethink a few of our assumptions about how the world works.

REDEFINING "POWER"

A procession of over two million people stretching out greater than five miles long mourned the loss of Mahatma Gandhi in January 1948. He held no official power and had very little money and few possessions. He preferred to wear sandals and a simple white cloth that he made himself. He was a diminutive man who carried no weapons. In short, he had none of the traditional trappings of power as we normally think of it, yet he was a man of tremendous power—and he would redefine "power" itself. It is this redefinition of power that is essential to understanding global inequality today.

Gandhi swayed millions with writings and actions that helped free India from British rule and would ultimately inspire hundreds of millions of others throughout the world to find their own inner strength and power to throw off the shackles that bounded them. The fight for civil rights in the United States, the struggle against apartheid in South Africa, the fight to overthrow a brutal genocidal dictator in Serbia, and the struggles for democracy in the Middle East all bear the imprint of his inspiring actions and revolutionary philosophy of power. When *Time* magazine listed the Top 100 most influential people of the 20th Century, they put him at Number Two. Only the discoverer of that massive power of atomic energy, Albert Einstein, was deemed more influential. Einstein himself noted of Gandhi, "Generations to come will scarcely believe that such a one as this ever in flesh and blood walked upon this earth." A multiple

Academy Award-winning film made over 30 years later would recount that he had "become the spokesman of all mankind. He made humility and truth more powerful than empire."

Gandhi became an extraordinary public speaker and powerful revolutionary, but he did not start out that way. He actually liked being part of the British Empire as a boy and set off for London at age 18 to study law. He came back to India a lawyer, wearing a fine British suit, but completely froze in his first courtroom case and struggled to find work after that. Two years later, he received an offer to do legal work in South Africa.

It was in South Africa that Gandhi would find his true calling. He was shocked by the racism against Indians in South Africa. One night, he purchased a first-class ticket for the train. A white passenger complained, but Gandhi refused to move—so he was forcibly thrown off the train at a remote station. As he sat alone on the train platform that night, he vowed to fight the "disease of color prejudice" no matter what the cost.

Using his knowledge of the law and skill in writing, Gandhi was able to draw international attention to the plight of Indians in South Africa. More importantly, he started to discover a new way of thinking about power, and new ways of fighting back against a mighty power like the British. When the British declared that Indians would have to register and carry passes at all times, Gandhi called a meeting and convinced the people not to fight back with force, but to simply not cooperate with the British law. Over 95% of Indians heeded Gandhi's call and refused to register. Later, they made a dramatic public showing of their protest, burning over 2,000 registration certificates in a public bonfire.

Gandhi was experimenting with a revolutionary idea of power. His idea was that power is not "held" by those in power; rather, it is "given" by those who are not in power. If the people refuse to cooperate, the power ceases to exist. At that point, those in power are required to use force, but Gandhi saw that if he and his fellow Indians could stand with dignity as they received the blows, those giving the blows would hurt more than those receiving them, for it would awaken their hearts to the injustice of their actions.

These revolutionary ideas had their roots in ancient wisdom – the Hindu doctrine of ahimsa (non-violence) as well as the Christian notion of turning the other cheek. Gandhi was reading widely in world religions at the time, and was especially inspired by Leo Tolstoy's *The Kingdom of God is Within You.* Tolstoy believed that when you turn the other cheek and receive the blows of an enemy, you are also turning their hearts, awakening them to the truth that all people and things are worthy of dignity and respect.

Tolstoy explicitly applied his ideas to the case of India in "A Letter to a Hindu," which Gandhi published in his own newspaper. In that letter, Tolstoy refers to the fact that India had been settled by the British East India company when he notes, "A commercial company enslaved a nation of two hundred million people." He goes on, with words that Gandhi would later repeat as especially striking to him, "What does it mean that 30,000 men – not athletes, but rather weak and ordinary men – have subdued 200 million vigorous, clever, capable, and freedom-loving people? Do not the figures make it clear that it is not the English who have enslaved the Indians, but the Indians who have enslaved themselves?"

Gandhi saw in these words a confirmation of his own intuitions about the true nature of power, and he found in Tolstoy's non-violence a powerful method. He called the method Satyagraha, Sanskrit for "holding firmly to the truth." Gandhi himself defined it as "the Force which is born of Truth and Love."

Returning to India, Gandhi brought the Satyagraha method with him and called for peaceful protests and strikes to protest unjust British laws. In response, the British implemented martial law, forbidding people to gather in large groups.

On April 13, 1919, over 1,500 men, women and children gathered in a large walled garden to celebrate a traditional Punjabi festival. British troops moved into the arena and started firing without warning. Official counts by the British reported 379 dead and over 1,000 wounded, but later investigations suggest much higher casualties. General Dyer, leader of the British on that day, reported that 1,650 rounds had been fired. Nearly every one of them hit a man, woman, or child.

Reports of the massacre were devastating to Britain's global reputation, and global sentiment turned toward Gandhi and his movement. Gandhi was beginning to show the world that there was more than one kind of power, especially in a world that was growing increasingly connected by a vast communications network of telegraph, radio, and newspapers. The British clearly had the upper hand in terms of economic power and physical force. Political Scientist Joseph Nye would later call these coercive forms of power "hard power." But Gandhi also recognized another form of power: the capacity to influence others and shape their ideas, what Nye would later call "soft power." Long before political scientists like Nye would name these two forms of power, Gandhi was putting them into action.

Gandhi came to realize that these two forms of power do not necessarily work together, and in fact when a regime with great hard power exercises that power without good reason, they can lose soft power. In studying Gandhi's methods, Gene Sharpe would call this effect a form of "political jiu-jitsu" in which the strength of an opponent could be used against them by generating soft power.

After the massacre, Gandhi turned firmly against the British and became fully committed to Indian independence. He started to recognize the economic power Britain held over India by extracting cheap raw materials and cheap labor, and providing a large market for British-produced commodities such as fine clothing. Gandhi gave up all British goods and took to the loom to fashion his own simple clothing, calling on others to do the same.

Gandhi was discovering a third form of power, one that has immense importance to anthropologists studying inequality in the world today. Eric Wolf would later call it "structural power," power that is embedded in the structure of economic, social, geographic, and political relationships. This, Wolf notes, is the power that forms the background of Michel Foucault's influential notion of power as the ability "to structure the possible field of action of others." As Wolf says, "structural power shapes the social field of action so as to render some kinds of behavior possible, while making others less possible or impossible."

As global markets have extended to virtually every space on Earth, anthropologists have turned to ideas of structural power to understand how the forces of the global economy shape the social fields they study, and "render some kinds of behavior possible, while making others less possible."

Though he did not have the idea of "structural power" to help him, Gandhi saw that there was a structure of power oppressing him and his fellow Indians. He carefully studied the structural relations between India and Britain, trying to discover why Britain was so rich and India was so poor, and what they could do about it.

YALI'S QUESTION

Why are some countries so rich and others so poor? Gandhi's question has been asked by many, including a man named Yali. Yali was a famous local politician in New Guinea in the early 1970s. In 1972, he ran into Dr. Jared Diamond on a New Guinea beach and asked him a series of probing questions about the history of humankind, building up to the key question: "Why is it that you white people developed so much cargo (material goods and technologies) and brought it to New Guinea, but we black people had little cargo of our own?"

It took Diamond nearly three decades to formulate an adequate response. In his Pulitzer Prize winning book, *Guns, Germs, and Steel,* he starts by carefully dismantling racist arguments suggesting that Europeans might be genetically superior or more intelligent. Instead, he works backwards through history to discover why, by the early 1500s, Europeans had so many advantages over people in the Americas that allowed them to conquer the Aztec and Incan empires.

By then the Europeans had domesticated horses, and possessed guns and steel swords, ocean-going ships, large-scale political organizations, and phonetic writing systems, as well as resistance to several deadly epidemic diseases. In short, Diamond argues, guns, germs, and steel gave them the key advantage.

But those were just the proximate factors enabling their success. Diamond then spends the rest of the book digging into the deeper ultimate factors that led to Europeans having these advantages over others. As a geographer, he pays especially close attention to the environment and the shape of the continents, pointing out that Europe is on the western edge of the massive Eurasian landmass. This landmass has 13 of the 14 large mammals that have ever been domesticated, along with nearly all of the major grains with the exception of corn. This combination of large domesticated mammals and domesticated plants meant that by 6,000 years ago, the Eurasians were using large draft animals to power their plows, providing more calories and fueling population growth.

In addition, the Eurasian landmass is very wide from east to west, creating a large, continuous stretch along the same line of latitude where people could share their farming innovations and other ideas and technologies. Being along the same line of latitude meant that they would share a similar climate and environment, so innovations in one area along this line were likely to work in other areas along this line as well.

As a result of this massive exchange of innovations and ideas, the whole of Eurasia, from Europe to China, was home to many of the largest early empires. Their innovations and the ability to share them led to still more innovations. A positive feedback loop emerged:

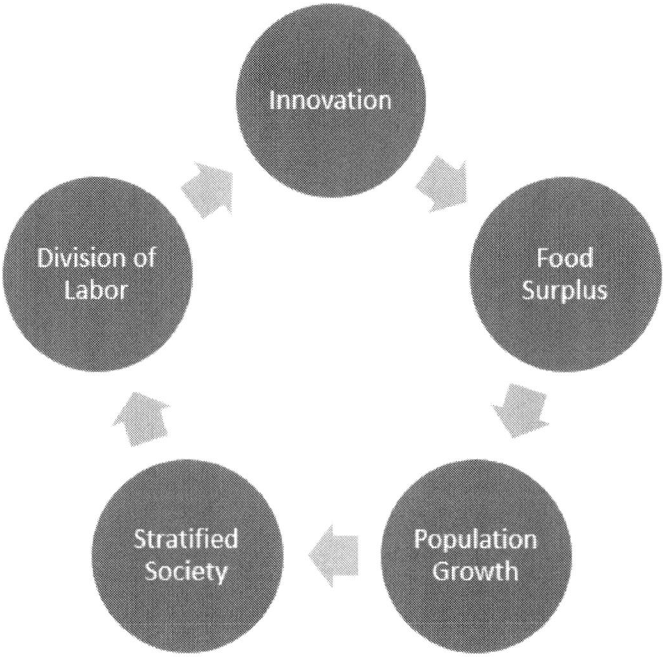

Innovations create a food surplus which allows for population growth. As population grows, society becomes more complex and stratified. More job types are created, increasing the division of labor. With more and more people engaged in work other than the manual labor of production, more innovations become possible. Some of these innovations will increase food surplus, and the cycle continues.

Meanwhile, since many of the worst diseases that have plagued humankind originate in domesticated animals, the people of Eurasia were exposed and built resistance to a wide range of diseases that would be new to people in the Americas.

When Europeans first came to the Americas in the late 1400s, these diseases came with them. By some estimates, nearly 95% of all indigenous Americans died from these diseases. Smallpox, measles, and chicken pox spread from original European contacts and traveled faster than the Europeans themselves. Key leaders of major

American civilizations, such as Incan Emperor Huayna Capac, died from these diseases, setting off wars of succession before Europeans actually walked into these empires themselves. Among the Aztecs, the Spanish were able to exploit tensions that had been exacerbated by disease to get some Aztecs to fight on their side. By 1531, the most significant American empires, the Aztec and the Inca, had both been defeated. Spain and other European countries set off on an age of exploration to see what they could learn about and acquire from this new world.

WORLD SYSTEMS

Jared Diamond's Guns, Germs, and Steel argument is often criticized by anthropologists for focusing too much on Europe's technological advantages and overlooking the relationships and interconnections formed between societies since the early first contacts he describes in the book. In short, Diamond's book gives an excellent argument for why some countries were rich and others were poor up until 1492, but little to help us understand why some countries are rich and others poor after over five hundred years of global trade and exchange.

In 1972, Frances Moore Lappe' was contemplating the same question as Diamond, but came to a very different conclusion. She realized that she had always assumed that the world was divided into "two worlds." One included those countries where agricultural and industrial revolutions had propelled their people to prosperity, and the other included those countries that, due to lack of resources, proper climate, corruption, or a lack of work ethic had not undergone these revolutionary changes. But the more she researched the history of these separate "worlds," the more she recognized that the two worlds were not separate at all. She came to question the notion of a "First World" and a "Third World" as separate worlds and started to tear down the "two worlds" perspective. She came to understand that the "two worlds" have been connected for over five hundred years, and that the poverty of one might in fact be necessary for the wealth of the other. They are the result of an ongoing historical process with its roots in colonialism.

As Europeans colonized the world, they transformed societies that were growing food for their own subsistence into exporters of cash crops for European consumption. They used their military might to capture lands and then levied taxes or created large plantations that forced locals to produce cash crops like sugar, coffee, cocoa, and tobacco. Or they put colonized peoples to work in dangerous mines, extracting precious metals such as gold and silver. The silver mines at Potosi in present-day Bolivia fueled Spanish trade and conquest. The fertile lands of the Caribbean were turned over to sugar production to serve the sweet tooth of European's growing consumer class. The American South turned to cotton and tobacco production.

European colonization brought together the old and new worlds into a global economy and a global ecology. Foods, plants, and diseases spread throughout the world, along with ideas, values, technologies, money, and commodities.

As Lappe' considered these interconnections, she realized that thinking about why rich countries are rich and poor countries are poor might be a biased way of framing the question. These are not two separate worlds. They are part of a single world system. The wealth of the so-called "First World" is directly dependent on the poverty of the "Third World." In a famous essay addressing the question, "Why can't people feed themselves?" Lappe joined Joseph Collins to argue that the problem is not that some countries are underdeveloped. Instead, these countries might be better understood as being in a constant process of *being underdeveloped* within a world system that profits from their lack of development.

Sociologist Immanuel Wallerstein has developed this idea into a model that has been highly influential in anthropology. Wallerstein argues that the world system is made up of a core, semi-periphery and a periphery. Cheap labor and raw materials provide the core with the means to produce high profit consumption goods which then flow back to the periphery.

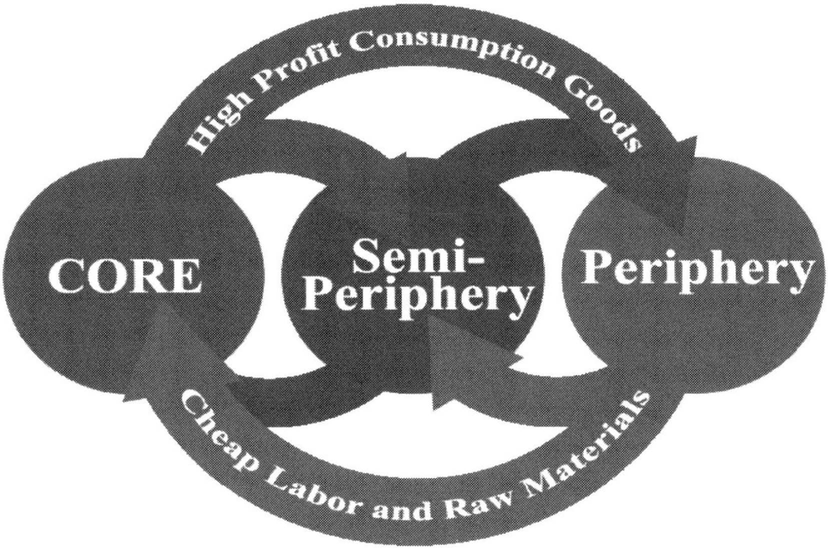

Wallerstein's World System Theory Model

The slave trade was perhaps the most profound example of this world system in action. Due to the decimation of indigenous Americans by European diseases, there was ample land for Europeans to settle, but not enough labor. Meanwhile, Africans, by virtue of sharing the same continuous land mass with Europeans, had already built up resistance to European diseases and had a few of their own, like Malaria and Dengue Fever, that made Africa difficult to conquer and settle. So instead of settling Africa, Europeans traded with the more powerful African nations. The most notable "commodity" they traded was people: African slaves. The slaves were brought to the Americas to work in the vast sugar, cotton, and tobacco plantations.

This brought about what is sometimes referred to as the triangle trade. Slaves from Africa were shipped to the Americas to produce sugar, cotton and other raw materials, which were shipped to Europe to produce rum, clothing and other manufactured goods, which were then shipped back to Africa to trade for more slaves which were brought to America to produce more sugar and so on. Europe grew rich on the hard labor of African slaves, not simply on their technological superiority.

The world systems model demonstrates a very different kind of feedback loop than the one driven by technology and innovation we saw earlier. In this model, the rich colonizers get richer at a rate far greater than the poor laborers that fueled the economy. The growing wealth set the stage for the Industrial Revolution in Britain.

The Industrial Revolution only elevated the need for raw materials, while also increasing the European's capacity to conquer new lands and rule over them. Remote regions of Africa and the Amazon that had been impenetrable and difficult for Europeans to settle started to come under European control behind the onslaught of machine guns and armaments shuttled in on a growing network of train tracks.

By the late 1800s, the European powers were engaged in the "scramble for Africa," strategically colonizing every bit of land they could grab, laying down train tracks that would slowly drain Africa of its natural resources in rubber, copper and other precious materials.

As had occurred in the Americas and Asia, local subsistence farmers in Africa were forced to transform their production to serve the global market. Northern Ghana shifted production from nutritious yams to cocoa. Liberia produced rubber; Nigeria, palm oil; Tanzania, sisal; and Uganda, cotton. All of them became dependent on global trade for their subsistence.

But perhaps the worst was the Belgian Congo, which was transformed into a massive slave plantation 76 times the size of Belgium itself. There African slaves were forced to meet quotas harvesting rubber to serve the growing demands of the new auto manufacturers. If a village failed to reach their quota, some of the villagers would be killed. Severed hands of the dead were offered as proof of death, which in turn created a trade in severed hands. At least two million and as many as 15 million Congolese lost their lives during the rubber boom - a genocide that rivals the holocaust of World War II. International outrage led to the ouster of King Leopold from the colony in 1908, and the nightmare was over. But the colonial history of the Belgian Congo and other African nations continues to shape the global economy and the massive inequalities we see today.

GANDHI'S GAMBIT

Mahatma Gandhi could see the same "World System" pattern operating in India. Indians were sending loads of cheap cotton picked with cheap labor to Britain, where it was woven into cloth and sold back to India at a huge profit. India was a cheap place for Britain to obtain raw materials and cheap labor, as well as an emerging market for the goods they produced.

In 1930, he announced a plan for massive non-cooperation. He would simply not cooperate with the British laws prohibiting the collection and sale of salt. It does not sound so revolutionary on the face of it, unless you understand the web of structural power that he was planning to tear apart. Gandhi saw the British monopoly on salt production as the perfect representation of British structural power. The British had simply claimed ownership of a natural mineral existing on Indian soil and banned all Indians from processing it. Gandhi's plan was to simply not obey the ban and start processing salt, which he could freely pick up on a salt beach.

The march started off modestly from his home, 240 miles from the coast where he would collect the salt. He stopped in each town along the way to speak about his plan, to explain why he was doing it—and thousands upon thousands joined in the march. By the time he reached the beach, he was surrounded by tens of thousands. He picked up the salt, breaking the unjust law that held Indians back from harvesting their own abundant natural resource and declared,

"With this salt, I shake the foundations of the British Empire." The action inspired millions of Indians to protest and over 60,000 were arrested, including Gandhi, but not before he could arrange for his satyagrahis to march on the nearby salt works factory.

The satyagrahis marched toward the salt works as if it belonged to them, unarmed and unflinching. Webb Miller, a United Press reporter, stood witness as the police turned violent against the thousands of quiet and calm protestors. "They went down like tin pins. I heard the sickening whacks of the clubs on unprotected skulls." His report was read out loud in the U.S. Senate and published in over 2,000 newspapers worldwide.

Sensing the inevitability of Independence, Gandhi was invited to London to discuss terms. But the breakout of World War II delayed the process, and Gandhi was imprisoned many more times as he became more and more resolute that Britain must "Quit India." Finally, in 1947, Independence was granted.

HOW WE MAKE THE WORLD

Gandhi's methods and the story of his success spread throughout the world. There was a growing recognition that power can be resisted through dignity and non-violence. Martin Luther King would call Gandhi "the guiding light of our technique of nonviolent social change." Gandhi's vision of awakening a recognition of the truth of human dignity through the force of love lived on through non-violent protests all over the world. "There is something about this method," King said, "that has power. They try to handle it by throwing us in jail. We go into the jails of Jackson, Mississippi and transform these jails from dungeons of shame into havens of freedom and human dignity."

Beyond Gandhi's remarkable and revolutionary revelations about the nature of power was a deeper insight: *We make the world.* He understood that the world is nothing more or less than the sum of all of our interactions. He used the power of "seeing big" to understand that the world he lived in was formed by a vast history of larger structural and global forces. He saw the structural power that shaped his circumstance and understood the history that created that power. He also used the power of "seeing small" to understand how we make the world through even our smallest actions. His refusal to wear British clothing, or picking up a lump of salt, may seem like small gestures, but he understood that even small things are manifestations of larger structures and that he was indeed shaking the foundations of the empire.

Gandhi was very well-read, but he also knew that he could not just think his way into a new way of living—that he would have to live his way into a new way of thinking. From an early age, he started engaging with what he called "experiments in truth," which became the title of his remarkable autobiography. These experiments are not unlike our own 28 Day Challenges or the Unthing Experiments we did earlier in this class. From an early age, he experimented with different foods and lifestyles. And throughout his life he experimented with giving up foods, British clothes, and even sex as he continually experimented with his mind and body, working his way toward a deeper understanding of himself, his body, and the world. As he remade himself, he grew in his understanding of how to remake the world, for if the world is nothing but what we make of it, we are the first that must change.

Gandhi understood that the world around us is largely invisible, like the water the fish is swimming in, but his daily practices allowed him to make his assumptions fragile and see the world with new eyes. Such renewed vision opens up new possibilities for envisioning a better world. Philosopher Maxine Greene calls this the social imagination, "the capacity to invent visions of what should be and might be in our deficient society." She goes on to explain that "there must be restlessness in the face of the given, a reaching beyond the taken for granted."

This is nothing short than a prescription for what David Foster Wallace called "real freedom." When we ask deep and hard questions about our own biases and assumptions, see big to understand where they come from, and see small to understand how they shape our everyday lives, we are then set free to re-imagine them, and to re-imagine what is right, true, and possible.

A STORY OF RICH AND POOR

Let's look at two communities on opposite ends of a world system today. Rüschlikon, a small village in Switzerland, received over 360 million dollars in tax revenue from a single resident, Ivan Glasenberg, in 2011. That amounts to $72,000 for each of the village's 5,000 residents. It is one of the richest communities in the world. Glasenberg is the CEO of Glencore, one of the most powerful companies in the world, specializing in mining and commodities. If we follow the commodity chain back to its source, we find copper mines like the Mopani copper mine in Zambia, where 60% of people live on less than $1/day, the residents struggle to find adequate food and health care, education is difficult to attain, and the air and water are frequently polluted by the mines. The GDP per capita in Switzerland is the highest in the world at just over $75,000. Zambia is among the lowest at under $2,000. In fact, Glencore's revenues alone are ten times the entire Gross Domestic Product of Zambia.

Over a 10-year period in the early 2000s, $29 billion dollars' worth of copper was extracted from Zambia, yet Zambia only collected $50 million/year in taxes while spending over $150 million/year to provide electricity for the mines. Zambia was actually losing money on their own resources. How did this happen?

During the "scramble for Africa" the region was proclaimed a British Sphere of Influence administered by Cecil Rhodes and named "Rhodesia." When copper was discovered, it became one of the world's largest exporters of copper; but the wealth did little to improve the lives of Africans. By the time Zambia gained independence in 1964, they were rich in resources but lacked the knowledge and capital to mine those resources. Nonetheless, they successfully operated the mines under national control for over a decade, and their economy grew on their copper profits. By the mid-1970s, they were one of the most prosperous countries in sub-Saharan Africa. But their entire economy depended on that single commodity, and in the 1970s, the price of copper dropped dramatically as Russia flooded the market with copper. Like many other countries who depend on exports of natural resources, their economy collapsed along with the prices.

The Zambian economy was in crisis and had to look to the International Monetary Fund and World Bank for big loans. But soon they could not keep up with their loan payments. Like other developing countries, the loans that were supposed to save them became crippling. For every $1 they were receiving in aid from rich countries, they were spending $10 on loan interest. By the year 2000, with copper prices falling again, Zambia was in crisis and could not receive any more loans. The copper mines were privatized and sold to companies like Glencore.

They were trapped in a system that left them no more options. They wanted to demand a higher price for their copper, but their impoverished neighboring countries would just undersell them.

Over the next decade, the cost of copper soared and Glencore made massive profits. But the lives of Zambians did not improve, because none of that money found its way into Zambia. As a large multinational corporation, Glencore was able to avoid paying taxes in Zambia through a practice called "transfer pricing." Glencore is made up of several smaller subsidiary companies. Their Zambian subsidiaries sell the copper very cheaply to their subsidiaries in Switzerland, which has very low taxes on copper exports. Then the Swiss company marks up the price to its true market value and sells the copper. On paper, Switzerland is the largest importer of Zambian copper (60%) and one of the world's largest exporters of copper, yet very little of this copper ever actually arrives in (and then leaves) Switzerland. This little accounting trick is in part why copper accounts for 71% of the exports from Zambia, but only contributes 0.2% to their GDP.

Meanwhile, it is the residents near the mines that must pay the tax on their environment and health. Occasionally the sulphuric acid used in the mines seeps into the ground water, turning their tap water blue and sending hundreds into the hospitals. Residents complain of respiratory infections from the sulphur dioxide in the air.

This is obviously unfair, but Zambia does not have the financial resources to fight Glencore's army of lawyers. This is just one more chapter in a long history that consistently places Zambia on the weaker end of power. At the dawn of colonization, they faced the military might of the British and lacked the power to defend their land. They entered at the bottom of an emerging global economy and have never had the resources to educate their public and prepare them for success. They now find themselves trapped in cycles of poverty. Without a strong tax base, they cannot support strong institutions that could raise health and education to create jobs that could create a strong tax base.

STRUCTURAL POWER & COMMODITY CHAINS

In 2004, I was applying for my first professional job and purchased my first suit for my first big job interview. The interview went well, and the suit became one of my most prized possessions. It reminds me of that successful day when I landed my first "real job." But I wonder, who else contributed to that wonderful day that served as the culmination of my education? Who harvested the wool for my suit, and where did it come from? Who wove that wool into fabric? Who sewed that wool into the suit itself? Who brought it to the store?

For such a task, Wallerstein developed the idea of the "commodity chain" to map out the "network of labor and production processes whose end result is a finished commodity." To counter the extent to which the true cost of commodities are often hidden from view, he meticulously maps out all the inputs that go into a commodity at each stage of its production, from the equipment, tools, energy, and labor right down to the food the workers eat to produce the energy that allows them to work.

My suit's label says it was made in Canada, but a documentary produced about the company that made the suit shows that it is a global garment, touched by hands all over the world. The wool comes from Tasmania, an island off the cost of Australia that is covered in sheep. But the sheep are not native to the land. They were brought there by Australian colonizers in the 1800s. Violence, along with the new diseases brought by the colonizers, nearly wiped out the entire native population. Of the 6,000 original inhabitants, just 200 survived by 1830, when a missionary moved the remaining Tasmanians to a new island in hopes of saving their lives. More disease and malnutrition ultimately led to their complete extinction. Their genocide is part of the story of my suit.

It would seem most efficient to just produce the suit right there in Tasmania or somewhere else in Australia, but cheaper labor can be found elsewhere. So after the wool was harvested from Tasmanian sheep, it was sent to Amritsar, India where workers were paid about $3/day to transform the wool into fabric. Again, it would seem to make the most sense to just complete the suit in India, where the fabric is produced, but there is even cheaper labor available.

The shoulder pads were made in Korea, the lining in China. Only the buttons on my "Canadian" suit were made in Canada. All of these parts came together in Germany, where they were shipped east until they found the cheapest labor they could find in Russia, where the workers were paid about $2/day.

When asked about the low labor costs, the CEO of the company posed a question in response: "Are we exploiting this labor market or are we helping them? I mean, that's the $65,000 question." Economists almost unanimously agree that despite the low wages, these low wages are better than nothing, and are essential for helping the people and their countries rise out of poverty. The workers themselves are grateful for the work, but still fight for better wages.

There are encouraging signs over the past 20 years that the vast human efforts to end poverty and improve human well-being are paying off, and that these positive indicators are driven not only by charities, international aid, government programs and idealistic non-profits, but also by the jobs created through the spread of the global economy. As summarized by Max Roser, OurWorldinData.org shows that in just the past 24 hours:

- Life expectancy increased by 9.5 hours worldwide.
- The number of people in poverty fell by 137,000.
- 295,000 people received access to electricity.
- 620,000 people got online for the first time.
- 305,000 gained access to safer drinking water

But even with these positive signs of change, it's hard to overlook the desperate impoverished conditions of the global working poor living on less than $3/day.

The CEO himself does not feel like he has much power to change the situation. On the one hand, he has consumers demanding a particular price point. If he pays higher wages and has to raise his price, another company will offer the lower wages and beat his price with the same product. "There is always someone out there to give it to them," he says. "And if we're not going to give it to them, then our competitors will. And God Bless our competitors, but no, we would rather do the business."

His comments are a perfect demonstration of structural power. The power is not held by the CEO. The CEO is simply in a position of relative power and wealth within a structure of power. The power is in the structure itself.

A 2007 study of the production of the iPod demonstrates just how complex the global economy has become and how the profits and resources still flow toward the core, even while products are increasingly made all over the world. The 2007 iPod was made up of 451 parts, none of which were made by Apple. The hard drive was made by Toshiba, a Japanese company, but Toshiba also outsources its production to companies in the Philippines and China, and those manufacturers may outsource the production of some of their components to still other manufacturers. Ultimately all of these parts come to China for assembly. The assembly itself costs $4. Everybody along the chain makes money from the final $299 retail sale, but who makes the most of the profits? Despite most of the labor throughout this long process being done in China, the Chinese will only receive about $3 in profit. Toshiba, a Japanese company that designed the hard drive, will receive about $19. In all, Japanese companies receive about $26 in profit. The big winner is the United States, which captures about $163 of the $299 of value – $80 of which goes to Apple. Most of the value is created through design and knowledge rather than raw physical labor or raw materials.

The story of the iPod demonstrates that knowledge and creativity have now emerged as one of the primary means of creating value in today's global economy, while raw labor and raw materials remain cheap. Unfortunately for the world's working poor, it is difficult to get a good education in their impoverished communities while trying to live on $2/day. In this way, the structure perpetuates itself and Wallerstein's original world systems model still holds in demonstrating how core countries can continue to gain wealth and power over poor countries in a world system. Cheap labor, cheap raw materials, and cheap manufacturing of periphery countries continue to provide a large source of wealth for companies in core countries, which now hold a distinct advantage in complex knowledge that allows them to design cutting edge products.

STRUCTURAL POWER & STRUCTURAL VIOLENCE

Life on $2 per day is difficult to imagine. Some people immediately counter that life on $2 per day in a poor country is different than $2 per day in the United States, because you can buy so much more with $2 in a poor country. But this is to misunderstand the statistic. When the World Bank reports that over 700 million people are living on less than $2 per day, they are using an approach called "purchasing power parity" to adjust the numbers so that $2 per day in a poor country is exactly what you would imagine it to be like to live on $2 per day in the United States.

Imagine what this would be like. You would not be able to afford rent, so you would be homeless. You would probably do your best to make yourself a little shack out of whatever scrap materials you could find. You would not have electricity, running water, or a toilet. You may find yourself walking several miles to find clean water and carrying it back to your small shack every day. You would spend some of your money on coal or wood to burn for heat and cooking. The bulk of your money would go toward food – mostly cheap staple foods like rice and potatoes. This is what life is like for about 1 billion people on the planet who live in the world's slums.

Over 700 million people do not have access to clean drinking water. Nearly a third of all humans do not have access to a toilet. As a result, nearly 80% of all illnesses in developing countries come from unclean water. As Dean Kamen has noted, we could clear half of the hospital beds in the world just by providing clean water to everybody on the planet.

The structure of power that binds us together in a world system makes us all complicit in these problems at some level. Each one of us might only be one person, but collectively we make the world what it is. The idea of structural power can make it feel like there is nothing to be done. Like the CEO of my suit, we might just say, "if not me, then somebody else" and let the structure roll on. But there is also a hopeful message within the idea of structural power. It can be a constant reminder of four very important ideas:

1. We are the structure.
2. It is what we make of it.
3. Participation is not a choice. Even the choice to not participate is a form of participation.
4. How we participate is our most important choice.

As we face up to this very important challenge to decide how we will participate in the structure, and what sort of structure we will help to create, it can be useful to examine the damage – the structural violence - that our current structure is doing to the world and the disadvantaged.

In the past three decades we have used about one-third of the natural resources currently available to us. It is possible that new technologies will reveal new resources that we cannot yet imagine, but there can be no doubt that our collective consumption patterns as humans is dramatically reshaping the world. The U.S. population makes up 5% of the global population, yet uses one-third of all the resources consumed each year. Botanist Peter Raven has estimated that if everybody in the world lived like Americans, we would need three planets to support everybody.

The high consumption rates of Americans is a relatively recent phenomenon. If you have ever spent time with someone who grew up in the Depression of the 1930s, you know that there was a time in American history when people valued low consumption levels and sought to save money and energy however they could. But after WWII, businesses and economists worried that we might slip into another depression if spending levels did not rise. They started pursuing ways to increase consumption through two strategies: planned and perceived obsolescence.

Planned obsolescence is the creation of products that break, wear out, or become unusable so that people have to buy new ones.

Smartphones with inaccessible batteries that wear out and operating systems that are not upgradeable or supported after a few years are a prominent modern example that leads most people to have a box or drawer full of old phones. Planned obsolescence is the art of creating products that people "use up" rather than use. For example, you can purchase a good mop that you will use for the rest of your life, or you can purchase a cheap "Swiffer" duster with a disposable head that you "use up" and have to continuously replace. You can purchase a high-quality jacket that you will use for 30 years, or you can purchase a cheap jacket that you will "use up" this year.

Perceived obsolescence uses marketing to create a fast-paced fashion trend so that shoes you purchased last year are no longer in style this year. A fashionista can often identify precisely when a pair of shoes was created, just by examining the color, the shape of the toe box, the width of the heel, the style of its straps, or even just the style of the stitching.

As communications and manufacturing technologies have improved, companies are able to create a dazzling diversity of constantly changing fashions and provide the clothing at a very low cost. This has created the world of "Fast Fashion." In the world of Fast Fashion, there are not just four seasons a year. There are 52.

But as we now know, there is a cost to low-cost clothing, and much of that cost is paid by the developing world who stand on the other end of the world system. While American teens rush to purchase the latest fashion at Gap or H&M, their teenage counterparts in Bangladesh leave their home villages to work in harsh, often toxic, conditions – wearing masks as protection – for less than $2 per day.

Their working conditions are not just uncomfortable. They are often dangerous. A factory collapse at Rana Plaza killed 1,129 workers in 2013, and that was just one of several major disasters that year that killed thousands. Such appalling conditions are driven by a constant need to seek lower and lower prices to serve the demands of fast fashion. The same year as these disasters was also the best ever for the garment industry, as it brought in over $3 trillion.

The situation in Bangladesh is not unlike it was in the United States 100 years ago. In 1911, garment workers in New York City sweatshops were making 14 cents/hour under difficult working conditions. A fire broke out on the eighth floor of the Triangle Shirtwaist Factory. The workers moved for the exits, but the exits were blocked to prevent workers from taking breaks or stealing cloth. As the flames drew closer and the smoke became unbearable, workers started leaping from the eighth floor so that their families could give them a proper burial. People watching thought they were bales of clothing being thrown to the ground. One hundred and forty-six died.

Nearly one hundred years later, on December 14, 2010, a fire broke out on the 11th floor of a garment factory in Bangladesh. The workers moved for the exits, but the exits were blocked to prevent workers from taking breaks or stealing cloth. As the flames drew closer and the smoke became unbearable, workers started leaping from the 11th floor so that their families could give them a proper burial. People watching thought they were bales of clothing being thrown to the ground. At least 27 died.

Knowing that the situation in Bangladesh is so similar to what occurred in the U.S. 100 years ago should not make us complacent, or think that the problems will right themselves with time. As Martin Luther King noted in the height of the civil rights struggle, "such an attitude stems from a tragic misconception of time and a strangely irrational notion that there is something in the flow of time that will inevitably cure all ills."

After the 1911 fire in New York City, 100,000 people marched in the funeral procession and 400,000 lined the streets. The tragedy of that fire fueled a labor movement that continued to build momentum until the Fair Labor Standards Act of 1938 ensured that sweatshop conditions would no longer be tolerated. As Charles Kernaghan, director of the Institute for Global Labour and Human Rights says,

"The middle class was built in this struggle coming out of the Triangle. Now we're seeing everything that the American people had won and struggled for is being destroyed."

As this is written, workers throughout the developing world are rising up just as the workers of New York City did, demanding a higher wage. The workers who died in the Bangladesh fire were making Gap jeans. The jeans sell for $27. The workers were paid 28 cents/hour. They took to the streets demanding a raise. They wanted 35 cents/hour. The police were sent out to stop the protest, attacking them with clubs, rubber bullets, and water cannons. They put dye in the water so they could identify protestors and arrest them later.

And it's not just Bangladesh. All over the developing world, state military and police forces are called out to help keep wages low. In Cambodia, four protestors were killed in 2013 for demanding that the minimum wage be raised to $160/month (just over $3/day). Like other developing countries, Cambodia is desperate for foreign business, and they fear that raising wages will chase away foreign investment. So they keep wages low and fail to enforce labor and safety laws.

What would it cost us to provide a living wage to these struggling garment workers around the world? About 25 to 50 cents per T-shirt. Shima, a Bangladesh garment worker featured in Andrew Morgan's 2015 documentary, *The True Cost*, sums up the structural violence of structural power when she says, "People have no idea how hard it is to produce these clothes. I believe these clothes were produced by our blood." She starts to tear up as she considers those who died at Rana Plaza and concludes, "It's very painful for us. I don't want anyone wearing anything that is produced by our blood."

LIVING ON TRASH

Eventually, this global dance that produces so much ends up producing mountains of trash. The average American produces about 4.5 pounds of trash every day. Just one percent of what we take from the earth is still in use six months later. About 2.4 million pounds of this trash enters the Pacific Ocean every hour. It gets picked up by the currents and gathers in the Great Pacific garbage patch, an island of plastic waste in the Pacific. Photographer Chris Jordan went to an island in this region where humans have never lived and found baby albatrosses dead on the beach. Some of them had decomposed enough to show that they were full of plastic. The rest of our trash is burned and piled into landfills. Sometimes it is sent overseas, where informal trash sorters try to eke out a living looking for whatever they can find of value.

We do not send trash to Haiti, but we do send our used clothing. Americans throw out 80 pounds of used clothing every year. Only 10% of the clothes we donate to charity get sold in the United States. The rest are shipped abroad to place like Haiti, where they undermine the local garment industries by selling used clothing much cheaper than it can be made locally. In Haiti the local clothing industry has all but disappeared, leaving thousands unemployed.

So we end this chapter right where we started. An unemployed woman of African descent who speaks French is living off of trash on an island in the Caribbean. How did it happen? Her ancestors were brought to the island on French slave ships, in quarters so tight that they slept in their own excrement. Her ancestors worked in chains at the hands of whips in brutal conditions to produce luxury goods for the French. Her ancestors eventually said enough is enough. They rose up and fought back. They won. Their victory forced the French to abandon their American lands. The French sold the Louisiana Purchase to the United States, so that my own home states of Nebraska and Kansas became part of the emerging world power.

The French, the United States, and other European powers resented Haiti for their uprising. In those days most people did not believe that blacks were full citizens, let alone capable of running their own country. Thomas Jefferson, the president at the time, was a slave owner. The U.S. and others refused to recognize the Haitian's sovereignty. They refused to trade with them. The French threatened to attack and forced them to pay $21 billion to compensate French slave owners for their "lost property" (their own bodies were "the property.") It took them over one hundred years to pay off the debt.

So they entered the 20th Century billions of dollars in debt, with no money to fund schools, hospitals, roads and other essential needs of a prosperous nation. As a result, over 70 percent are uneducated; 59% live on less than $2/day; 30% are food insecure. Almost 1 in 10 babies will not live to their fifth birthday. They are strong and work hard to find a way, even if it means living off of a mountain of trash.

HOW MUCH DOES IT COST TO BE YOU?

Look at me, look at me, I'm a cool kid
I'm an individual, yea, but I'm part of a movement
My movement told me be a consumer and I consumed it
They told me to just do it, I listened to what that swoosh said
Look at what that swoosh did. See, it consumed my thoughts
Are you stupid, don't crease 'em, just leave 'em in that box
Strangled by these laces, laces I can barely talk
That's my air bubble and I'm lost, if it pops
We are what we wear, we wear what we are
But see I look inside the mirror and
think Phil Knight tricked us all
Will I stand for change, or stay in my box?
These Nikes help me define me, but I'm trying to take mine, off

Mackelmore and Ryan Lewis, WING$

In one of my favorite pictures, I am riding my bike with my kids, hauling a canoe, and wearing a T-shirt that I purchased from Target for $8. It represents so much of who I am, but as I look at it I am also aware that my identity is propped up on things. I am who I am because I consume in a certain way. The products I purchase have a history, most of it hidden from me, that ties me into relationships all over the world.

The origins of something as simple as a T-shirt are hard to determine. It connects me to people all over the world, but who specifically? The shirt says "Made in Bangladesh," but I wonder whose hands actually sewed my shirt. I wonder who manufactured the cloth. I wonder where the cotton came from. I wonder what it really costs to be me. Here is an analysis of my true cost:

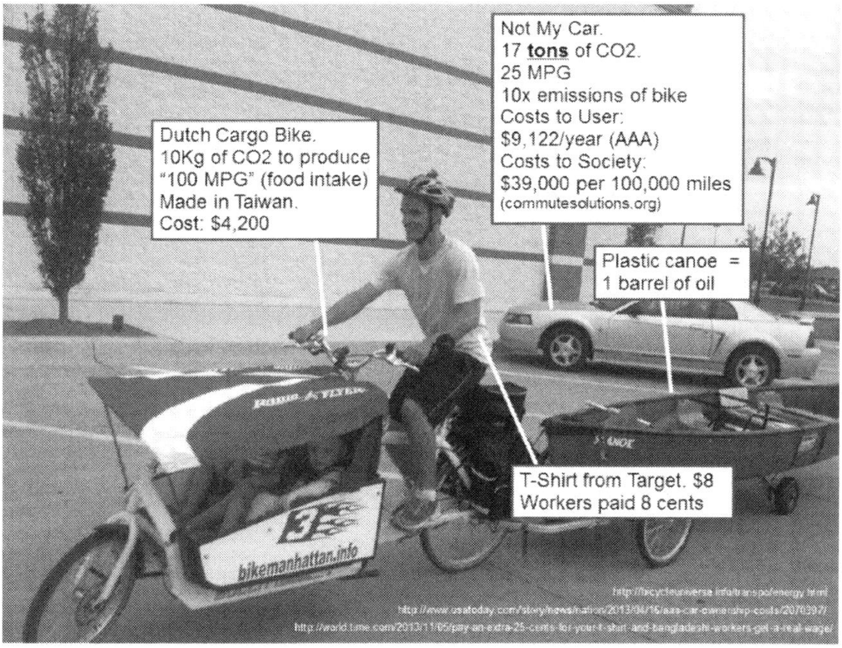

My choice to give up my car and ride a bike is an obvious indicator that I make choices in life to limit the violence I do to the world and to others. I try to limit my consumption and purchase products that support a fair wage and good living conditions for others. But there is still a cost to my purchases and activities that I do not bear.

The first step toward re-shaping the structure and creating a better world is to see how our own actions are already shaping the structure. In this chapter's challenge, you will be analyzing your true cost by considering all the things that you own and consider what they truly cost the world – not just what they cost you to purchase, but what they cost the world to produce. Consider the materials and where they came from. Consider the hands that touched, it that shaped those materials into the product. Consider how those materials and final product were shipped around the world to come to you.

LEARN MORE

- Gandhi the man, by Eknath Easwaran
- World-Systems Analysis: An Introduction by Immanuel Wallerstein
- Guns, Germs, and Steel by Jared Diamond
- Why Can't People Feed Themselves by Frances Moore Lappe' and Joseph Collins
- The Story of Stuff. Video Short by Annie Leonard
- The True Cost. Documentary by Andrew Morgan
- Stealing Africa: Why Poverty? Documentary by Christoffer Guldbrandsen

Challenge Eight: Global Connections

Your challenge is to connect with someone from a foreign country, preferably somebody with a very different cultural and socio-economic background from yourself.

Objective: Expand the mindset, method, and goals of anthropology to a global level, broadening your understanding of cultural differences, global connections, and how the world works to bring about prosperity and well as poverty and inequality.

Option 1: Find someone from a foreign country who actually helped create something that you own. Go to anth101.com/challenge8 for tips on how to find somebody.

Option 2: Connect with an international student using the questions from Challenge 7. Contact your local international student office to find somebody

Option 3: Connect with anyone from a foreign country using the questions from Challenge 7.

Take a picture that represents your experience and share #anth101challenge8

Lesson Nine
The Good Life

Memorizing these ideas is easy. Living them takes a lifetime of practice. Fortunately, the heroes of all time have walked before us. They show us the path.

CREATING "THE GOOD LIFE"

This book started with an invitation to see your own seeing by stepping out of your culture, biases, and assumptions to see that much of what you take for granted as reality is very different in other cultures. In doing this, we discovered a tremendous wealth of possibility in the human condition – physical capacities we did not know we had, unique and insightful ways of seeing and talking about the world, and different ways of surviving and thriving in many different environments. We also encountered different ways of thinking about love, identity, gender, race, morality, and religion. All of this can seem remarkably liberating, giving us a broader vision of what is possible. As anthropologist and psychologist Ernest Becker once wrote:

"The most astonishing thing of all, about man's fictions, is not that they have from prehistoric times hung like a flimsy canopy over his social world, but that he should have come to discover them at all. It is one of the most remarkable achievements of thought, of self-scrutiny, that the most anxiety-prone animal of all could come to see through himself and

discover the fictional nature of his action world. Future historians will probably record it as one of the great, liberating breakthroughs of all time, and it happened in ours."

But the discovery of our "fictions" is not because of anthropology. Rather, anthropology is itself a product of larger social and intellectual trends that moved our society away from the shackles of tradition toward the more intentional creation of modern society. In this sense, the ideas, ideals, values, beliefs, and institutions of modern society are constantly under scrutiny for ways in which they might be changed or improved to maximize human flourishing.

Most people would not question the value of these modern projects, and few would want to return to the more rigid traditional hierarchies and moral horizons of older social orders. However, the modern revisions come with a cost. The old orders provided exactly that: *order*. In order, there is meaning. In a clearly defined social role, there is purpose. In stable institutions, there is a promise for the future. With meaning, purpose, and the future now in question, we cannot help but constantly ask those three big questions: Who am I? What am I going to do? Am I going to make it?

In his landmark book, "Man's Search for Meaning," Victor Frankl claims that it is our Will to Meaning that is the dominant human drive, stronger than the Will to Pleasure or any other drive. But he worries that we now live in an "existential vacuum" due to two losses – first, the loss of instincts guiding all of our behavior, forcing us to make choices, and second, the loss of tradition. "No instinct tells him what he has to do, and no tradition tells him what he ought to do; sometimes he does not even know what he wishes to do."

Compounding the crisis, the last chapter makes it evident that we now live in a time in which it is entirely possible to imagine cataclysmic change so dramatic that it would effectively constitute "the end of the world as we know it." Nuclear war, climate catastrophes, global economic collapse, and the possibility of totalitarian super-states are ever-present threats, with constant reminders bombarding us throughout the 24-hour news cycle. And so we also must constantly ask those other three big questions: Who are we? What are we going to do? Are we going to make it?

These two sets of questions are interconnected. In order to find a personal sense of purpose in the world, one must have some vision of where the world is going and what would constitute a good and virtuous life. As Anthony Giddens has suggested, personal meaninglessness can become a persistent threat within the contexts of modernity that provide no clear framework for meaning.

Modernity leaves us with two unavoidable projects. First, as Giddens puts it, "the self, like the broader institutional contexts in which it exists, has to be reflexively made. Yet this task has to be accomplished amid a puzzling diversity of options and possibilities." This "consists in the sustaining of coherent, yet continuously revised, biographical narratives." Second, we have to choose or create values, virtues, and meanings in a world that does not offer a shared, definitive, unquestioned moral order that could define these things for us. In other words, we are freer than ever to be, do, and think whatever ... but when we all make different choices about who we will be, what we will do, and how we will think, we lose a shared system of meanings and values upon which we can find meaning, construct viable identities, and feel a sense of purpose and recognition.

Until recently, anthropology has been mostly silent on questions of "the good life." While documenting a wide range of different cultures, each of which may define "the good life" in different ways, anthropologists have been hesitant to offer any prescriptions for how one should live. But recent studies are changing that. In this lesson, we will see what anthropology has to tell us that might help us on our own projects of building meaning, setting the stage for your next challenge – to do what you have spent your whole life doing, revising your story and defining your core values.

ARE THERE UNIVERSAL VALUES?

In the late 1990s, psychologists Martin Seligman and Chris Peterson set out to explore the brighter side of human nature. They had grown concerned that psychology was focused only on problems and pathology. They turned instead to the ideas of happiness and human flourishing, and founded the field of positive psychology. One of their first projects was to construct a list of widely shared human values, characteristics, and virtues that would be more or less universally valid and recognized among all cultures. Given the tremendous diversity of cultures in the world, they knew they could not attain true universality, so they settled instead on finding "ubiquitous virtues and values ... so widely recognized that an anthropological veto ('The tribe I study does not have that one!') would be more interesting than damning."

They proceeded by brainstorming characteristics they thought might be universal, and then compared them against key texts from Asian and Western religions, world philosophies, and wisdom traditions. An obvious shortcoming of their study is that they did not include any representation from the Americas or Africa other than Islam. Nonetheless, their lists of virtues and positive character traits are an interesting start toward finding some universally agreed upon human virtues and values. The list of 24 character strengths is broken up into six core virtues:

- Wisdom (curiosity, love of learning, judgment, ingenuity, emotional intelligence, perspective)
- Courage (valor, perseverance, integrity)
- Humanity (kindness, loving)
- Justice (citizenship, fairness, leadership)
- Temperance (self-control, prudence, humility)
- Transcendence (appreciation of beauty, gratitude, hope, spirituality, forgiveness, humor, zest)

These six virtues mirror the six foundations of morality established by Jonathan Haidt, and we can see how each virtue might provide evolutionary advantages that ensured our survival. We need wisdom and courage to survive. We need humanity, justice, and temperance to care for one another and work through inevitable social problems. A sense of transcendence (even of the secular sort) can provide us with a sense of meaning, purpose, and joy that motivates us through life.

The virtues are abstract enough to allow for significant cultural difference while still capturing some sense of what all humans value. Jonathan Haidt points out that we cannot even imagine a culture that would value their opposites. "Can we even imagine a culture in which parents hope that their children will grow up to be foolish, cowardly, and cruel?"

Probably not. But there are cultures where someone who is foolish, cowardly, and cruel will be greeted with kindness rather than scorn. Jon Christopher tells a story from his fieldwork in Bali, where a local drunk was constantly causing problems and failing to provide for his family. Instead of people judging him harshly, he was greeted with "pity, compassion and gentleness." The only way to understand this response is to understand the broader cultural frameworks of the Balinese. They see reality as broken up into two realms; the *sekala* or ordinary realm of everyday life, and the *niskala*, a deeper level of reality where the larger dramas of souls, karma, and reincarnation ultimately shape and determine what happens in the ordinary realm. This man deserved pity and compassion because his behavior in *sekala* was a reflection of the turmoil his soul was facing in *niskala.*

In fact, most cultures, including Western culture up until the Renaissance and Enlightenment, see the world as broken up into two tiers. One is an all-encompassing cosmological framework that provides meaning and value to the other tier of ordinary day-to-day life. According to philosopher-historian Charles Taylor, the West's cultural drive to flatten traditional hierarchies and inequalities through the Protestant Reformation, Enlightenment, democracy, and the scientific revolution called these ultimate cosmological frameworks of the top tier into question, and ultimately rendered them arbitrary at best, and at worst, a threat to human freedom and flourishing.

As a result, hierarchies were flattened and the two-tiered world collapsed. We were left with a worldview that places the individual self at the center as the sole arbiter of meaning and value. Our moral system came to champion the individual's right to choose their own meanings and to pursue happiness however we choose to define it, just as long as we do not impinge on the ability of others to pursue happiness, however they might define it.

Seligman's list of virtues is in many ways an attempt to use reason and science to discover meanings and values that, by virtue of being universal, might not feel so arbitrary. "I also hunger for meaning in my life that will transcend the arbitrary purposes I have chosen for my life," Seligman wrote in 2002 as he was working on the inventory of virtues.

Jon Christopher argues that while Seligman's list is an admirable effort and one worthy of continued discussion and exploration, it is ultimately limited by the Western cultural framework. Remember that Seligman and his colleagues started with a list of virtues, and then tried to find them in other traditions. This had the effect of flattening complex ideas like "wisdom" and "justice" so much that the real wisdom of other traditions was lost in translation.

THE VALUE AND VIRTUE OF OTHER VALUES AND VIRTUES

Christopher points to the example of Chinese philosophy that places five core values at the center of their moral world:

- Role fulfilment.
- Ties of sympathy and concern based on metaphysical commonalities.
- Harmony.

- Culmination of the learning process.
- Co-creativity with heaven and earth.

The contrast with Seligman's list is profound. In fact, "role fulfilment," which is a common value throughout much of the world, is not highlighted in any of Seligman's character strengths. But at an even deeper level, values that are based on "metaphysical commonalities" and "co-creativity of heaven and earth" signal a very different cosmological framework and, in fact, a different theory of being itself. Specifically, the Chinese virtues depend on a two-tiered model that places value on serving and maintaining the upper tier that provides meaning and significance, while Seligman's list depends on a cultural framework centered on individualism and the self.

Other research indicates that cultures live in a different emotional landscape. For example, in Japan the emotion of *amae* is often translated as a desire for indulgence or dependence. It is the feeling a twelve year-old child might have in asking a parent to "baby" them by tying their shoes. According to Takeo Doi, who first introduced the concept of amae to the Western world, the full experience of the emotion depends upon a larger cultural context that values interdependence and harmony, so there can be no adequate translation into the Western context.

Many traditions suggest that the self is in itself the problem. Hinduism suggests that enlightenment can only occur when one recognizes that the self (Atman) is one and the same as the Absolute all or Godhead (Brahman). Buddhism goes a step further by suggesting the concept of anatman or "non-self," which denies the existence of any unchanging permanent self, soul, or essence. Taoism suggests that one must put one's self in accord with the "tao" or way of all things. This "way" is beyond words and cannot be spoken about. It can only be known through living in accord with the "way" of life, nature, and the universe. In all of these traditions, the "self" as it is normally celebrated in the West is a hindrance to the good life.

Western psychology tends to judge "the good life" with measures of subjective well-being (often referred to in the literature as SWB).

Research participants are asked to rate items such as "In most ways my life is close to my ideal" or "I am satisfied with my life." But in many other cultures, what is "ideal" cannot and should not be determined by the individual, and subjective well-being is not necessarily "good." For example, in many non-Western cultures, negative emotions are valued as a sign of virtue when they alert the person to how they are not living in alignment with their role or social expectations. Measurements of subjective well-being often fail in cross-cultural contexts, because subjects refuse to consult their own subjective feelings to assess whether or not something is good. They tend to evaluate the good based on larger cosmological and social frameworks rather than their own personal experience.

But the modern West is not the first worldview to do away with the "second tier" and leave it to individuals to try to construct values and meaning. When Siddhartha Gautama Buddha laid out the original principles of Buddhism he did so in part as a critique of wheat he saw as a corrupt Hinduism in which authority was abused, ritual had become empty and exploitative, explanations were outdated, traditions were irrelevant to the times, and people had become superstitious and obsessed with miracles. Cutting through the superstition and corruption, the Buddha offered a philosophy that required no supernatural beliefs, rituals, or theology. Instead, he offered a set of practices and a practical philosophy (which together make up the eightfold path) that can lead to one living virtuously.

Of utmost importance to virtue in the original Buddhism was the idea that it is not enough simply to know what is virtuous or to "hold" good values. It is easy to know the path. It is much more difficult to walk the path. Therefor Buddha offered practices of mindfulness and meditation to quiet selfish desire, center the mind, and help people live up to their values.

The Buddha saw the source of human suffering in misplaced values. People want wealth, status, praise, and pleasure. But all of these are impermanent and out of one's control. In desiring them, we set ourselves up for disappointment, sadness and suffering. As

Buddha teaches in the teaching of the eight worldly winds, "gain and loss, status and disgrace, blame and praise, pleasure and pain: these conditions amount human beings are ephemeral, impermanent, subject to change. Knowing this, the wise person, mindful, ponders these changing conditions. Desirable things don't charm the mind, and undesirable ones bring no resistance."

The goal of Buddhist practice is to only desire the narrow path of mindful growth and development and to shrink selfish egotistical desires. As such, the practitioner comes to desire what is best for the world, not what is best for the self, and then feels a sense of enlightened joy and purpose.

The ancient Western world also offers an example of a tradition that did away with the "second tier" in Stoicism, which flourished in Greece and Rome from the 3rd century BC to the 3rd century AD. While the Stoics did believe in God, they saw God not as a personified entity but as the natural universe itself imminent in all things. In order to understand God, they had to understand nature, making the study of nature and natural law essential to living a good and virtuous life.

Despite notable differences with Buddhism, the Stoics developed a similar method for arriving at good values and virtues. In short, we should not value those things that are out of our control. As Stoic philosopher Epictetus summed it up, "Some things are up to us, and some things are not up to us. Our opinions are up to us, and our impulses, desires, aversions – in short, whatever is our own doing. Our bodies are not up to us, nor are our possessions, our reputations, or our public offices, or that is, whatever is not our own doing."

Such words and the foundational philosophy of stoicism were essential to Victor Frankl as he endured the horrors of concentration camps in WWII. In the midst of unimaginable suffering, starvation, humiliation, and death he found a place to practice his "Will to Meaning" by recognizing the Stoic truth of detaching from what is out of his control, and instead working to control what he could – his thoughts. He and his fellow prisoners "experienced the beauty of art and nature as never before," he writes. "If someone had seen our faces on the journey from Auschwitz to a Bavarian camp as we beheld the mountains of Salzburg with their summits glowing in the sunset, through the little barred windows of the prison carriage, he would never have believed that those were the faces of men who had given up all hope of life and liberty."

Stoicism has had a big impact on modern psychology, forming the philosophical foundations of Frankl's Logotherapy and Cognitive Behavioral Therapy, the most common form of therapy now used in clinical psychology.

At the center of both Buddhist and Stoic practice is recognizing that emotions are simply signals that can be observed and acted upon, but are not "good" or "bad" in themselves. Such emotions can be observed, which disempowers them, allowing an inner calm to develop. Freed from emotional reasoning, a person is more capable of living virtuously even in the face of complexity, conflict, and turmoil.

In colloquial terms, Mark Manson calls it (in the title of his best-selling book) "The Subtle Art of Not Giving a F*ck." Influenced by Buddhist and Stoic philosophy, Manson notes that the idea is not that one should be indifferent, but that we have to be careful about what we choose to "give a f*ck about" – or in other words, we have to choose our values – "what you're choosing to find important in life and what you're choosing to find unimportant." Manson does not shy away from the fact most people in the West will deny all-encompassing cosmological frameworks as questionable and arbitrary, which means we cannot help but choose our values. However, we can use the basic tenets from different wisdom traditions such as Stoicism and Buddhism to help us evaluate our values.

Manson arrives at three principles for evaluating values. They should be:

1. Based in reality.
2. Socially constructive.
3. Within our immediate control.

Many of the most common values held by people, such as pleasure, success, popularity, and wealth, are not good values, because they are either socially destructive or not in our immediate control. Studies show that people who pursue pleasure end up more anxious and prone to depression. Short-term pleasure just for the sake of pleasure can also lead to dangerous addictions or impulsive behaviors that can lead to long-term trouble.

Good values include character traits that are socially constructive and within our control. These would include honesty, self-respect, charity, and humility as well as many of the items on Seligman's original list, such as curiosity and creativity. But importantly, Manson suggests that these values should not be judged on whether or not they "feel good." One should be honest even when it hurts, humble even if it means forgoing praise and pleasure.

Ironically, it may be our individualistic focus on positive emotions and the pursuit of happiness that make it so difficult to achieve positivity and happiness. As Manson observes, "Our society today ... has bred a whole generation of people who believe that having these negative experiences – anxiety, fear, guilt, etc. – is totally not okay." As he poignantly observes, "the desire for more positive experience is itself a negative experience. And paradoxically, the acceptance of one's negative experience is itself a positive experience."

This reflects a more profound vision of life in which avoiding problems and pain is not necessarily good. Instead, problems and pain become tools and opportunities for change. But studies show that in order to get the most out of our problems and pain, we have to find ways to make sense of them. We have to make meaning.

ANTHROPOLOGY OF THE GOOD LIFE

In a recent study sure to become a landmark in anthropology, Edward Fischer sets out to study ideas of "the good life" in the supermarkets of Hannover, Germany and the coffee farms of Huehuetenango, Guatemala. The two could hardly be further apart, geographically, culturally, and economically. The Guatemalans live with just 1/8 of the income of the Germans, but even worse, must suffer the violence of drug trafficking, creating one of the highest murder rates in the world.

Though the cultural context varies tremendously, Fischer still finds common concerns and themes where visions of the good life overlap. He suggests that these may form the foundation for a "positive anthropology" similar to positive psychology. But while positive psychologists like Seligman and Peterson list internal individualistic character traits or virtues that we should cultivate, Fischer instead finds five elements that a culture or society should aspire toward to ensure that everyone has adequate opportunity to pursue virtue however they might define it. Every society should provide:

1. Aspiration (hope)
2. Opportunity: power to act on that aspiration
3. Dignity
4. Fairness
5. Commitment to Larger Purposes

The list provides an interesting alternative to the current mode of judging cultures and countries based primarily on their Gross Domestic Product (GDP). As anthropologist Arjun Appadurai notes, the "avalanche of numbers – about population, poverty, profit, and predation" provides a limited view of the world that denies local perspectives. Instead, he advocates more nuanced ideas of the "good life" based on local ideals.

Fischer hopes that a turn in this direction could allow anthropologists to investigate and make suggestions about which cultural norms, social structures, and institutional arrangements foster wellbeing in different contexts. It is an inspiring idea. What if, instead of just trying to maximize wealth, we tried to maximize hope, opportunity, dignity, fairness, and purpose?

"It takes more than income to produce wellbeing," Fischer concludes, "and policy makers would do well to consider the positive findings of anthropology and on-the-ground visions of the good life in working toward the ends for which we all labor."

LEARN MORE

- The Good Life: Aspiration, Dignity, and the Anthropology of Wellbeing, by Edward Fischer
- Flourish: A Visionary New Understanding of Happiness and Well-Being, by Martin Seligman
- "Positive Psychology, Ethnocentrism, and the Disguised Ideology of Individualism" by John Chambers Christopher and Sarah Hickinbottom.
- The Subtle Art of Not Giving a F*ck by Mark Manson
- The Dhammapada. Translated by Eknath Easwaran
- Man's Search for Meaning by Victor Frankl
- How to be a Stoic by Massimo Pigliucci

THE POWER OF STORYTELLING

On my first day of graduate school, I watched my new advisor, Roy Wagner, walk onto the stage in front of 200 undergraduates in his Anthropology of Science Fiction class and drop-kick the podium. The podium slid across the stage and crashed to the floor. But Roy was not yet satisfied. He picked up the podium and hurled it off the stage and launched into a tirade. He said he had heard a story that dozens of students had decided to take the class because they thought it would be an "easy A." He wanted to assure them that this wasn't the case, and invited anyone who was not fully committed to leave the room immediately. A couple dozen people walked out. Then he calmly picked up the podium, set it back up, warmly welcomed us to the class, and then proceeded to share with us "the secret" of anthropology: "Anthropology is storytelling."

He proceeded to reveal the importance of anthropology in crafting the storyworlds of classic Science Fiction texts like *Dune* and

The Left Hand of Darkness (written by Ursula Le Guin, the daughter of Alfred Kroeber, one of the most famous anthropologists of all time). But more importantly, he showed us the importance of storytelling in understanding and presenting the cultural worlds and life stories of others. As anthropologist Ed Bruner noted, "Our anthropological productions are our stories about their stories; we are interpreting the people as they are interpreting themselves."

Of course, the real insight here is that we are all always "anthropologists," in the sense that all of us are interpreting the stories of people around us, and the stories people tell about themselves are also simplified interpretations of a very complex history and web of deeply entangled experiences. But we are not just interpreting the stories of others, we are also constantly telling and retelling the story of our own selves. *"Yumi stori nau!"* is the most common greeting you will hear as you walk around Papua New Guinea. The direct English transliteration: "You Me Story Now!" perfectly captures the spirit of the request. It is an expression of the joy felt when two people sit down and share stories together. In Nimakot, where there are no televisions or other media forms, storytelling is king, just as it has been for most humans throughout all time.

Among the Agta, hunter-gatherers in the Philippines, anthropologist Andrea Migliano found that when the Agta were asked to name the five people they would most like to live with in a band, the most sought-after companions were the great storytellers. Being a great storyteller was twice as important as being a great hunter. And this wasn't just for the high-quality entertainment. Storytellers had a profound influence on the well-being of the group. Stories among the Agta often emphasize core cultural values such as egalitarianism and cooperation. So when Migliano's team asked different Agta groups to play a game that involved sharing rice, the groups with the best storytellers also turned out to be the most generous and egalitarian in their sharing practices.

The storytellers were also highly valued for the cultural knowledge that they possess and pass on to others. Societies use stories to encode complex information and pass it on generation after generation.

As an example, consider an apparently bizarre and confusing story among the Andaman Islanders about a lizard that got stuck in a tree while trying to hunt pigs in the forest. The lizard receives help from a lanky cat-like creature called a civet, and they get married. What could this possibly mean? Why is a lanky cat marrying a pig-hunting lizard? Such stories can provide a treasure of material for symbolic interpretation, but the details of such stories also pass along key information across generations about how these animals behave and where they can be found. As anthropologist Scalise Sugiyama has pointed out, this is essential knowledge for locating and tracking game.

One especially provocative and interesting anthropological theory about storytelling comes from Polly Wiessner's study of the Ju/'hoansi hunter-gatherers of southern Africa. While living with them, it was impossible not to notice the dramatic difference between night and day. The day was dominated by practical subsistence activities. But at night, there was little to be done except huddle by the fire.

The firelight creates a radically different context from the daytime. The cool of the evening relaxes people, and if the temperatures drop further they cuddle together. People of all ages, men and women, are gathered together. Imaginations are on high alert under the moon and stars, with every snap and distant bark, grumble or howl receiving their full attention. The light offers a small speck of human control in an otherwise vast unknown. They feel more drawn to one another, and the sense of a gap between the self and the other diminishes.

It is in this little world around the fire where the stories flow. During the day just 6% of all conversations involve storytelling. Practical matters rule the day. But at night, 85% of all conversation involves storytelling or myth-telling. As she notes, storytelling by firelight helps "keep cultural instructions alive, explicate relations between people, create imaginary communities beyond the village, and trace networks for great distances."

Though more research still needs to be done, her preliminary work suggests that fire did much more for us than cook our food in the past. It gave us time to tell stories to each other about who we were, where we came from, and the vast networks of relations that connect us to others. The stories told at night were essential for keeping distant others in mind, facilitating vast networks of cooperation, and building bigger and stronger cultural institutions, especially religion and ritual. Fire sparked our imaginations and laid the foundation for the cultural explosion we have seen over the past 400,000 years.

STORIES ARE EVERYWHERE

Stories are everywhere, operating on us at every moment of our lives, but we rarely notice them. Stories provide pervasive implicit explanations for why things are the way they are. If we stop to think deeply, we are often able to identify several stories that tell us about how the world works, the story of our country, and even the story of ourselves. Such stories provide frameworks for how we assess and understand new information, provide a storehouse of values and virtues, and provide a guide for what we might, could, or should become. Most importantly, they do not just convey information, they convey meaning. They bring a sense of significance to our knowledge.

Stories are powerful because they mimic our experience of moving through the world – how we think, plan, act, and find meaning in our thoughts, plans, and actions.

We are in a constant process of creating stories. When we wake up, we construct a narrative for our day. If we get sick, we construct a narrative for how it happened and what we might be able to do about it. Through a wider lens, we might look at the story of our lives and construct a narrative for how we became who we are today, and where we are going. Through an even broader lens, we construct stories about our families, communities, our country, and our world.

Cultures provide master narratives or scripts that tell us how our lives should go. A common one for many in the West is go to school, graduate, get a job, get married, have kids, and then send them to college and hope they can repeat the story. But what happens when our lives go off track from this story? What happens when this story just doesn't work for us? We find a new story, or we feel a little lost until we find one. We can't help but seek meaning and coherence for our lives.

What is the story of the world? Most people have a story, often unconscious, that organizes their understanding of the world. It frames their understanding of events, gives those events meaning, and provides a framework for what to expect in the future.

Jonathan Haidt proposes that most Westerners have one of two dominant stories of the world that are in constant conflict. One is a story that frames Capitalism in a negative light. It goes like this:

> *"Once upon a time, work was real and authentic. Farmers raised crops and craftsmen made goods. People traded those goods locally, and that trade strengthened local communities. But then, Capitalism was invented, and darkness spread across the land. The capitalists developed ingenious techniques for squeezing wealth out of workers, and then sucking up all of society's resources for themselves. The capitalist class uses its wealth to buy political influence, and now the 1% is above the law. The rest of us are its pawns, forever. The end."*

In the other story, capitalism is viewed positively, as the key innovation that drives progress and lifts us out of poverty and human suffering. It goes like this:

> *"Once upon a time, and for thousands of years, almost everyone was poor, and many were slaves or serfs. Then one day, some good institutions were invented in England and Holland. These democratic institutions put checks on the exploitative power of the elites, which in turn allowed for the creation of economic institutions that rewarded hard work, risk-taking, and innovation. Free Market Capitalism was born. It spread rapidly across Europe and to some of the British colonies. In just a few centuries, poverty disappeared in these fortunate countries, and people got rights and dignity, safety and longevity. Free market capitalism is our savior, and Marxism is the devil. In the last 30 years, dozens of countries have seen the light, cast aside the devil, and embraced our savior. If we can spread the gospel to all countries, then we will vanquish poverty and enter a golden age. The end."*

You probably recognize both of these stories. They operate just beneath the surface of news articles, academic disciplines, and political movements. If we pause, think deeply, and take the time to research, we would probably all recognize that both stories offer some insights and truth, but both are incomplete and inaccurate in some respects.

Haidt proposes that we co-create a third story that recognizes the truths of both stories while setting the stage for a future that is better for everybody. His proposal is a reminder that once we recognize the power of stories in our lives, we also gain the power to recreate those stories, and thereby recreate our understanding of ourselves and our world.

THE WISDOM OF STORIES

During the Great Depression, Joseph Campbell spent five years in a small shack in the woods of New York reading texts and stories from religious traditions all over the world. As he did so, he started to see common underlying patterns to many of the stories, and a common body of wisdom. One pattern he found was that of the hero's journey. All over the world, he found stories of heroes who are called to adventure, step over a threshold to adventure, face a series of trials to achieve their ultimate boon, and then return to the ordinary world to help others.

He mapped out the hero's journey in a book appropriately titled *The Hero with a Thousand Faces* in 1949. The book would ultimately transform the way many people think about religion, and have a strong influence on popular culture, providing a framework that can be found in popular movies like *Star Wars*, *The Matrix*, *Harry Potter*, and *The Lion King*. The book was listed by *Time* magazine as one of the 100 best and most influential books of the 20th century.

In an interview with Bill Moyers, Campbell refers listeners to the similarities in the heroic journeys of Jesus and Buddha as examples:

Jesus receives his call to adventure while being baptized. The heavens opened up and he heard a voice calling him the son of God. He sets off on a journey and crosses the threshold into another world, the desert, where he will find his road of trials, the three temptations. First Satan asks him to turn stones into bread. Jesus, who has been fasting and must be very hungry, replies, "One does not live by bread alone, but by every word that comes from the mouth of God." Satan takes him to the top of the temple and asks him to jump so that the angels may catch him, and Jesus says, "You shall not put the lord, your God, to the test." Then Satan takes Jesus to a high mountain from which all the kingdoms of the world can be seen. He promised Jesus he could have all of it "if you will fall down and worship me." Jesus says, "Away, Satan! For it is written; "Worship the Lord your God and serve him only." The devil left him, and angels appeared to minister to him.

He had conquered fear and selfish desire and received his ultimate boon: wisdom and knowledge that he would spread to others.

Born a prince, Siddhartha lived a luxurious life behind palace walls, protected from the pain and suffering of the world. But at age

29 he made his way past the place walls and encountered old age, sickness, and death. Seeing this he set out to find peace and understand how one is to live with this ever-present reality of human suffering. He found many teachers and patiently learned their beliefs, practices and meditations but he still felt unsatisfied. He set off alone and came to rest under a tree. There it was that Mara, the evil demon, gave him three trials. First, he sent his three daughters to seduce him. But Siddhartha was still and without desire. Then Mara sent armies of monsters to attack Siddhartha. But Siddhartha was still and without fear. Then Mara claimed that Siddhartha had no right to sit in the seat of enlightenment. Siddhartha was still and calmly touched the earth with his hand and the earth itself bore witness to his right.

He had conquered fear and selfish desire and received his ultimate boon: wisdom and knowledge that he would spread to others.

Both stories tell the tale of a hero who is unmoved by the selfish and socially destructive values of wealth, pleasure, and power to serve a higher purpose. Campbell was struck by ubiquitous themes he found across cultures in which people overcome basic human fears and selfish desires to become cultural heroes. In his book, he identified 17 themes that are common throughout hero stories around the world. They're not all always present, but they are common. Seven of them are especially prominent and essential:

1. **The Call to Adventure.** The hero often lives a quintessentially mundane life, but longs for something more. Something happens that calls the hero forth into the adventure. The hero often hesitates but eventually accepts the call.
2. **The Mentor.** There is usually someone who helps the hero as he crosses the threshold into the land of adventure.
3. **The Trials.** The hero must face many tests and trials, each one offers a lesson and helps the hero overcome fear.
4. **"The Dragon."** The hero's biggest fear is often represented by a dragon or some kind of ultimate threat.

5. **The Temptations.** There are usually some temptations trying to pull the hero away from the path. These test the hero's resolve and ability to quell their selfish desires.
6. **The Ultimate Temptation:** The ultimate temptation is usually the demand of social life, a "duty" we feel to be and act in a certain way that is not in alignment with who we really are.
7. **Ultimate Boon.** If the hero can move past fear and desire, he is granted a revelation and transforms into a new being that can complete the adventure.

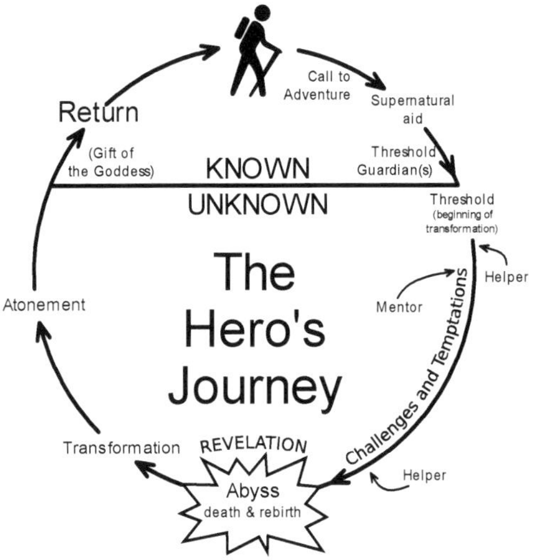

That the same basic structure can be found all over the world in both story and ritual illuminates profound universals of the human condition. Specifically, all humans are born unfinished and in a state of dependency, and must make a series of major changes in identity and role throughout life. Hero stories highlight the key dilemmas we all must face.

But as Campbell studied the stories and traditions of the world, he became more and more concerned that modern society had lost its connection to the key wisdom and guidance that hero stories could provide. He worried that literal readings of the heroic stories in the Bible were not appealing to many people, because the core stories are based in a society of the Middle East 2,000 years ago when slavery was commonplace and women were not equals. Back then it was common to assume, as described in Genesis, that the world is relatively young, perhaps just a few thousand years old, and is shaped like a flat disc with a dome above it – the firmament of heaven – that holds the stars.

Such stories are hard to square with our current knowledge that the earth is over 4 billion years old and sits on the outer edge of a vast galaxy which is itself just a small piece of a larger universe that is about 14 billion years old.

As a result, Campbell lamented, both Christians and atheists do not receive the potential wisdom of religious stories because they are overly focused on whether or not the stories are true rather than trying to learn something from them.

Campbell called on artists to develop new stories that could speak to the challenges of our times and serve the four functions of religion outlined earlier – stories that could teach us how to live a good life in today's world (the pedagogical function), stories that could help us get along and feel connected to one another (the sociological function), stories that could give us a better picture and understanding of how things work today (the cosmological function), and stories that could allow us to feel hopeful and stand in awe of the universe (the mystical function).

George Lucas was one of the first to hear the call.

REBIRTH OF THE HERO

Lucas came across Campbell's work while he was working on *Star Wars*. "It was a great gift," Lucas said, "a very important moment. It's possible that if I had not come across that I would still be writing *Star Wars* today." Thanks to Campbell's work, the stories of Jesus, Buddha, and other religious hero stories from all over the world came to influence characters like Luke Skywalker. George Lucas would refer to Campbell as "my Yoda," and the influence of the great teacher is evident in the work.

Star Wars was just the first of many Hollywood movies that would use the hero cycle as a formula. In the mid-1980s Christopher Vogler, then a story consultant for Disney, wrote up a seven-page memo summarizing Campbell's work. "Copies of the memo were like little robots, moving out from the studio and into the jetsream of Hollywood thinking," Vogler notes. "Fax machines had just been invented ... copies of The Memo [were] flying all over town."

Movies have become the new modern myths, taking the elements of hero stories in the world's wisdom traditions and placing them in modern day situations that allow us to think through and contemplate contemporary problems and challenges. In this way, elements of the great stories of Jesus and Buddha find their way into our consciousness in new ways.

Movies like *The Matrix* provide a new story that allows us to reflect on our troubled love-hate codependency-burdened relationship to technology. The hero, Neo, starts off as Mr. Anderson, a very ordinary name for a very ordinary guy working in a completely nondescript and mundane cubicle farm. His call to adventure comes from his soon-to-be mentor, Morpheus, who offers him the red pill. Mr. Anderson suddenly "wakes up," literally and figuratively, and recognizes that he has been living in a dream world, feeding machines with his life energy. Morpheus trains him and prepares him for battle. Morpheus reveals the prophecy to Neo, who, Morpheus calls "The One" – the savior who is to free people from the Matrix and save humankind. (The name "Neo" is "One" with the O moved to the end of the word.) In this way, Neo's story is very much like the story of Jesus. At the end of the movie, he dies and is resurrected, just like Jesus; but here the story takes a turn toward the East, as upon re-awakening Neo is enlightened and sees through the illusion of the Matrix, just as Hindus or Buddhist attempt to see through the illusion of Maya.

The religious themes continue in the second movie, as Neo meets "the architect" who created the Matrix. The architect looks like a bearded white man, invoking common images of God in the West. But invoking Eastern traditions, the architect informs Neo that he is the sixth incarnation of "The One" and is nothing more than a necessary and planned anomaly designed to reboot the system and keep it under control. Neo is trapped in *Samsara*, the ongoing cycles of death, rebirth, and reincarnation.

In order to break the cycle, Neo ultimately has to give up everything and give entirely of himself – the ultimate symbol of having transcended desire. In a finale that seems to tie multiple religious traditions together, Neo lies down in front of Deus Ex Machina (God of the Machines) with his arms spread like Jesus on the cross, ready to sacrifice himself and die for all our sins. But this is not just a Christian ending. Invoking Eastern traditions, he ends the war by merging the many dualities that were causing so much suffering in the world. Man and machine are united as he is plugged into the machines' mainframe. And even good and evil are united as he allows the evil Smith to enter into him and *become* him. In merging the dualities, all becomes one, and the light of enlightenment shines out through the Matrix, destroying everything, and a new world is born.

The Matrix is an especially explicit example of bringing the themes of religious stories into the modern myths of movies, but even seemingly mundane movies build from the hero cycle and bring the wisdom of the ages to bare on contemporary problems. *The Secret Life of Walter Mitty* explores how to find meaning in the mundane world of corporate cubicles, and how to thrive in a cold and crass corporate system that doesn't seem to care about you. *The Hunger Games* explores how to fight back against a seemingly immense and unstoppable system of structural power where the core exploits the periphery, and how to live an authentic life in a Reality TV world that favors superficiality over the complexities of real feelings and real life. And *Rango*, which appears to be a children's movie about a pet lizard who suddenly finds himself alone in the desert, is a deep exploration of how to find one's true self.

All these stories provide models for how we might make sense of our own lives, and as we will see in the concluding section to this lesson, incorporating what we learn from fictional heroes can have very real effects on our health and well-being.

MAKING MEANING

We all have a story in mind for how our life should go, and when it doesn't go that way, we have to scramble to pick up the pieces and find meaning. Gay Becker, Arthur Kleinman, and other anthropologists have explored how people reconstruct life narratives after a major disruption like an illness or major cultural crisis. This need for our lives to "make sense" is a fundamental trait of being human, and so we find ourselves constantly re-authoring our biographies in an attempt to give our lives meaning and direction.

Psychologist Dan McAdams has studied thousands of life stories and finds recurring themes and genres. Some people have a master story of upward mobility in which they are progressively getting better day by day. Others have a theme of "commitment" in which they feel called to do something and give themselves over to a cause to serve others. Some have sad tales of "contamination" as their best intentions and life prospects are constantly spoiled by outside influences, while others are stories of triumph and redemption in the face of adversity.

These studies have shown that "making sense" is not just important for the mind; "making sense" and crafting a positive life story have real health benefits. When Jamie Pennebaker looked at severe trauma and its effects on long-term health, he found that people who talked to friends, family, or a support group afterward did not face severe long-term health effects. He suspected that this was because they were able to make sense of the trauma and incorporate it into a positive life story. In a follow up study, he asked one group to journal about the most traumatic experience of their lives for fifteen minutes per day for four days. In the control group, he asked them to write about another topic. A year later, he looked at medical records and found that those who had written about their trauma were less likely to get sick.

This was a phenomenal result, so Pennebaker looked deeper into what people had written during that time. There he found that the people who received the greatest health benefit were those who had made significant progress in making sense of their past trauma and experiences. They had re-written the story of their lives in ways that accommodated their past trauma.

McAdams and his colleagues have found that when people face the troubles and trials of their lives and take the time to make sense of them, they construct more complex, enduring, and productive life stories. As a result, they are also more productive and generative throughout their lives, and have a stronger sense of well-being.

But how do we craft positive stories in the face of adversity and find meaning and sense in tragedy and trauma? There are no secret formulas. People often find their stories of redemption by listening with compassion to the stories of others. In other words, they simply adopt the core anthropological tools of communication, empathy, and thoughtfulness to open themselves up to the stories of others. This is what makes our own life stories, as well as the legends and hero stories written into our religions and scripted on to the big screen so powerful and important. It's why we sat up by flickering fires for hour after hour for hundreds of thousands of years, and why we still find wisdom in the flickering images of movies and television shows.

LEARN MORE

- "Embers of Society: Firelight talk among the Ju/'hoansi Bushmen" by Paul Wiessner. PNAS 111(39):14027-14035.
- The Storytelling Animal: How Stories Make Us Human by Jonathan Gottschall
- The Power of Myth, by Joseph Campbell and Bill Moyers. Book and Video.
- The Happiness Hypothesis: Finding Modern Truth in Ancient Wisdom, by Jonathan Haidt
- What Really Matters: Living a Moral Life amidst Uncertainty and Danger, by Arthur Kleinman

Challenge Nine: Meaning-Making

Your challenge is to leverage what you learned in this lesson to make meaning by defining your values or re-writing your story of yourself or the world.

Objective: Reflect on your values, your past, or the world and take responsibility for the type of meaning you will make in your life and in the world.

Option 1: Define Your Values

Assess your current values and ideals and use the wisdom outlined in lesson nine to intentionally create and defend a set of core values.

Option 2: Rewrite Your Story

Use the hero story structure to rethink the obstacles, problems, or pains of your life in a way that makes sense of meaning.

Option 3: Rewrite the World

Take Jonathan Haidt up on his challenge to write a "third story" that explains the history, problems, and paradoxes of the world in such a way that provides a meaningful way for you to live in it.

Go to anth101.com/challenge9 to download a worksheet to get you started.

Lesson Ten

The Art of Being Human

They show us that collectively, we make the world. Understanding how we make the world – how it could be made or understood differently – is the road toward realizing our full human potential. It is the road to true freedom.

THERE ARE NO ACCIDENTS

In 1983, a young anthropology graduate from Duke University named Paul Farmer set off for Haiti. He had done research on Haitian migrant workers at Duke and become deeply interested in their home country. He wanted to become a doctor and an anthropologist and thought he might sample a bit of both by going to Haiti and volunteering in health clinics.

While there, he boarded a bus with a new friend, Ophelia Dahl. Ophelia, the daughter of movie star Patricia Neal and author Roald Dahl, was just 18 at the time, and looking for a calling in life. As they navigated the rough, unkempt roads of Haiti, Paul leaned out the window and waved happily to all who greeted them, which Ophelia found nerdy but beautifully innocent and charming. Then they came upon an overturned bus on the road. Mangos destined for the market were scattered everywhere as people meandered about making sense of what had just happened. A woman lay lifeless, with a strip of cardboard covering her body.

Paul went stone silent. Ophelia tried to comfort him by saying, "It's just an accident." But Farmer was "seeing big" like an anthropologist. He saw that the neglected road was no accident. The worn shocks of the bus were no accident. The overloading of the bus with peasants going to market with their mangoes was no accident. These were all a result of poverty, and Farmer could see through this poverty the past 400 years of history in Haiti. He saw the 17th century slave colony of France, the brutal and bloody fight for independence, the French demand that Haiti pay back $21 billion for their "lost property" (the slaves who were now the citizens of Haiti being asked to pay for themselves), and the environmental collapse that came from trying to pay those debts. So when he saw the woman who was riding in a worn-out bus over a torn-up road to sell mangos in a Third World market, lying dead on the side of the road, he turned to Ophelia and responded, "It is never 'just an accident'."

This peculiar view of the world, that there are no pure accidents, is also an empowering one. Paul Farmer and Ophelia Dahl would soon recruit the young anthropologist Jim Kim to their cause and set out to provide the best healthcare possible to the world's poor. Thirty years later, their efforts would be celebrated as "the friendship that changed the world." And it all started by applying the anthropological perspective of seeing your own seeing, seeing small, seeing big, and seeing it all to realize that there are no pure accidents. If the message building from the preceding chapters was "We make the world," the message of this trio has been, "We can do better."

"TOUT MOUN SE MOUN"

During one of his first trips to Haiti, Farmer shadowed an American doctor. He was enamored with his competence, talent, and care, and saw him as a great role model. But he was soon disenchanted to find out that this American doctor had no intention of staying in Haiti. "I'm an American, and I'm going home," the doctor said. Farmer kept pondering the conversation and hanging on those words, "I'm an American," wondering how it is that we come to classify ourselves into these exclusive categories, thus limiting our responsibilities and allegiances to others.

That night, a pregnant woman suffering from severe malaria came in and crashed into a coma. She needed a blood transfusion, but the only place to get blood was far away in the capital city, and the blood would cost money. Farmer ran around the hospital gathering money and came up with fifteen dollars. The woman's sister took the money and set off for the city, but returned empty handed. She did not have enough money for the bus and the blood. The pregnant woman, a mother of five, died.

The sister was distraught, sobbing and crying. Through her tears Farmer heard her say, "You can't even get a blood transfusion if you're poor." And then she kept repeating, "*Tout moun se moun. Tout moun se moun.*" We are all human beings.

Tout moun se moun. Driven by such words, Farmer dedicated himself to serving all humans as humans. He turned his attention to those who had been most neglected by the world. He set off for Cange in the central highlands of Haiti, the poorest of the poor in the poorest country in the Western hemisphere.

STRUCTURAL VIOLENCE

Cange was the perfect place for Paul Farmer. From the mountain road entering Cange, there is a beautiful vista of an expansive blue lake framed by the steep mountainsides. But Farmer, who could see that same scene through the eyes of local Haitians, with the benefit of an anthropological lens to see the bigger picture, saw that this was no simple beautiful mountain lake. It was, despite the deceptive calm and tranquility of the mountain lake, one of the many reasons for the extensive poverty of Cange, and it was no accident.

The lake was artificially created by a dam project led by the U.S. Army Corps of Engineers to provide irrigation and power to Haiti. However, the recipients of the water and power were not the poor of Haiti, but American-owned agribusinesses and the Haitian elite living downstream.

The lake swallowed up the best farm land of Cange and destroyed people's homes. Farmer called the people who had to evacuate the valley "the water refugees," and they were some of the most poor and destitute in a country full of the poor and destitute. Instead of farming in the once-fertile valley the river ran through, the people were forced onto the steep mountainsides where water would not hold. They tried to farm anyway, which led to devastating erosion. Pushed beyond malnutrition toward famine, virtually everything green was consumed and used up, so that today Cange is a shocking glimpse into a world that has suffered true environmental devastation.

Paul Farmer frequently writes and speaks about the dam near Cange as an example of structural power and the structural violence that can result.

"THE ANTHROPOLOGIST WITHIN"

Farmer enrolled in a program at Harvard that allowed him to pursue a degree in anthropology while simultaneously earning his doctorate in medicine. He knew that if he was going to serve the world's poor, he would need the anthropological perspective to understand the broader cultural environment and issues impacting their health outcomes.

Throughout his training, he continued to spend most of his time in Haiti. His professors were not against it, as he was providing important medical care to people who needed it, and it proved to be a fruitful place to apply what he was learning in graduate school.

His work had a profound influence on anthropology. In one of his first essays, "The Anthropologist Within," he argued that the traditional manner of practicing anthropology as an impartial observer made him feel restricted in his ability to help solve the many problems surrounding him in Haiti. Since that article was written in the early 1980s, anthropologist have become much more active in their work, and are more likely to actively participate in providing solutions to local problems rather than standing idly by as impartial observers.

But Farmer was struggling to make a big impact in Cange. He needed money to complete his vision of building a free hospital providing outstanding medical care to the poor. His essay caught the eye of Tom White, the owner of a construction company in Boston who was interested in donating money to feed the poor in Haiti. In fact, he planned to give away every last dollar of his substantial fortune before he died. In Paul Farmer, he thought he had found someone who could make sure his money was well spent.

With the first $1 million donated by White, Paul Farmer established Partners in Health/Zanmi Lasante. The plan was not to simply support Paul Farmer in Haiti, but instead to create "partners in health" by training community health workers throughout rural areas of Haiti.

"O FOR THE P"

As the three friends – Farmer, Kim, and Dahl – set about crafting the core goals for Partners in Health, they continually came back to the idea of "O for the P," short for "preferred option for the poor." The "preferred option" refers to the idea that poor people should not just get the bare essentials of healthcare, but they should receive the same top-quality "preferred options" that the wealthy receive. *Tout moun se moun* – we are all human beings – drove every aspect of their operating philosophy.

While this might seem like an obvious and uncontroversial goal, it ran against the operating consensus of other development professionals, as well as the top global aid organizations such as the World Health Organization. The standard consensus at the time was organized around the idea of "cost effectiveness." Instead of providing the "preferred option" the scarce resources available to development projects should be used to maximize benefits to the most people.

"O for the P" opened up a serious controversy. Imagine a fairly common scenario that one might face in rural Haiti or any other impoverished area. A patient has a complicated case of TB that will cost $5,000 or more to cure. Ordinary cases of TB cost just $200 to cure. Do you cure the one for $5,000 or do you cure 25 ordinary cases for the same amount? The principle of cost effectiveness would suggest that you cure the 25, not the one.

But Farmer, Kim and Dahl were taking a longer view. They so strongly believed that the highest quality healthcare should be available to all that they decided to go down that long, hard, unexplored path of providing the best for everyone, in hopes that they might be able to attract more money, lower costs, and ultimately save even more lives than they could by following the traditional model of "cost effectiveness."

THE STRUCTURAL POWER OF MEDICINE

The key barrier to O for the P was the cost of medicine. When they first decided to try to treat the most complicated cases of TB, the treatment drugs could cost as much as $60,000 for just one patient. With such high prices, the World Health Organization (WHO) would not recommend the drugs, since it goes against the logic of cost effectiveness. And since the WHO would not recommend the drugs, generic manufacturers would not produce them. These three factors create an interlocking triad in which prices are high, so the WHO will not recommend it, so generics will not produce it, so prices stay high – a vicious cycle that continues as people all over the world continue to die while drugs are readily available that could save their lives.

Jim Kim took the lead on trying to break through this vicious cycle that kept prices so high. As he did, he kept encountering a prevailing supporting myth for why the drugs were not being made more available: 'Poor people are poor because they are stupid and lazy.' They are lazy, so they do not deserve the drugs. Their lives are not as highly valued as those of the wealthy. And they are stupid and will likely misuse the drugs, build resistance to the drugs, and cause further harm.

The WHO and development professionals who held these views were not as prejudiced as you might think. They formed their opinions based on experience. They came into their careers idealistic and full of hope, but constantly found their carefully crafted plans fell apart in practice, and treating TB was especially difficult. To properly treat TB, the patient must take the proper drugs and keep taking them after the symptoms have cleared in order to ensure that the TB does not recur or get passed on to others. Unfortunately, when people do not complete the drug sequence, the TB can develop resistance to the cheap drugs, and an outbreak of multi-drug resistant TB can take hold.

Paul Farmer saw the same patterns, but he refused to blame the patients. Instead, he studied them anthropologically and developed a new prescription for TB. His new prescription was not just for drugs, but also for regular visits from community health workers who would travel throughout rural areas to check up on the patients and make sure they were taking all of their drugs. And as a third element, he even prescribed money – a cash stipend so that they could pay for good food and childcare while they were sick. His studies had shown that the poor were not stupid, they were simply constrained and forced to make bad decisions while they were sick in order to make ends meet. A small cash stipend of just $5 was enough to let them rest properly and pay for help until they were fully recovered.

The success rates before Farmer's intervention were dismal. Afterward, the success rate soared to nearly 100 percent. When he published the results, it became a model for others all over the world.

With their success, they decided to push harder against the structural power that was keeping the drugs for more complicated forms of TB so high, and launched a project in the shanty towns outside of Lima, Peru where there was an outbreak of Multidrug Resistant TB (MDR). Farmer held to his same prescription: drugs, regular visits, and a cash stipend. The problem was that the drugs were $15,000 per patient.

The World Health Organization and other development professionals pushed back. It was not cost effective to treat people for $15,000 each. It was not sustainable. *Tout moun se moun*, Farmer thought, and they set off to find a way.

With their background in anthropology, Farmer and Kim know that price is a social construction. There is no inherent quality of the drugs themselves that make them worth $15,000. So they set about changing the structure to lower the cost. Jim Kim, with his passion for policy and transforming bureaucratic structures, threw himself into the problem. He had to find a way to convince generic manufacturers to produce the drugs, which would create competition and drive down the cost. But the WHO would not recommend the drugs due to their high cost, and because of their concerns about poor people and poor regions not having the knowledge and resources to properly administer the drugs.

To convince the WHO, Kim promised them that Partners in Health would set up a "Green Light Committee" to create standards and require training to ensure that the drugs would be administered responsibly. With the WHO on board, Kim went to the generic manufacturers, who agreed to make the drugs. Prices fell 97%. 750,000 lives were saved.

It was an amazing feat. Jim Kim was trained as a medical doctor and hoped that one day he would save lives—and here he had just saved 750,000 lives without even touching a human body. He simply recognized a configuration of structural power that was causing great structural violence, and changed the structure.

AIDS IN AFRICA

By 2001, their money was running out. Tom White was determined to die without a dollar to his name, and he was nearing his end. They had created an effective treatment for TB that was spreading throughout the world, and they were having great success treating AIDS in Haiti at a time when much of the world thought that treating AIDS among poor people would not be "cost effective" or "sustainable."

At that time, thirty million people in Africa had AIDS, and only 50,000 of them were receiving treatment. The Partners in Health model was working in Haiti, in circumstances similar to those in many African countries. This made people hopeful, and The Global Fund to fight AIDS was launched, raising millions of dollars to combat AIDS. The Gates Foundation followed soon after this with a $45 million initiative.

Paul Farmer joined Dr. Agnes Binagwaho in Kenya to set up a system that followed the same prescription Farmer had always preferred: the proper drugs, follow-ups by health workers, and a cash stipend to cover expenses while sick. While many still saw the treatment (and especially the stipend) as radical, the results were proven time and time again. The program in Kenya worked, and it showed people throughout the entire system that we could go after AIDS in Africa.

The WHO was brought on board, the generic manufacturers started producing the drugs, and the cost of treatment plummeted. "Anti-viral drugs can extend life for many years," President of the United States George Bush announced in his State of the Union address later that year, "And the cost of those drugs has dropped from $12,000/year to under $300/year, which places a tremendous possibility within our grasp ... Ladies and Gentlemen, seldom has history given an opportunity to do so much for so many." He proceeded to ask Congress to dedicate $15 billion over the next five years "to turn the tide against AIDS in the most afflicted nations of Africa and the Caribbean." His request was greeted by a jubilant standing ovation, delivered from both sides of the political aisle.

Jim Kim, Paul Farmer, and Ophelia Dahl were astonished. In just twenty years of deeply dedicated service to their calling, they moved from working and struggling outside the system to being insiders. A few years later, Jim Kim was appointed by Barack Obama as the new President of the World Bank, an opportunity to use tremendous wealth and power to bring better health and well-being to the world.

LEARN MORE

- Mountains Beyond Mountains: The Quest of Dr. Paul Farmer, by Tracy Kidder

- Bending the Arc: A Friendship that Changed the World. Documentary Film.

IF PAUL FARMER IS THE MODEL, WE'RE ~~SCREWED~~ GOLDEN

At Partners in Health headquarters there is a sign that says, "If Paul Farmer is the model, we are golden." But "golden" is on a piece of paper taped over another word, "screwed" (or rather, a synonym of screwed starting with "F"). It is a favorite saying of Jim Kim. What he meant was that nobody can hope to be just like Paul Farmer. He is incredibly intelligent and selfless with natural gifts for medicine and anthropology. It would do us no good to hold ourselves up to that high of a standard. Instead, we can learn from Paul Farmer (and Jim Kim and Ophelia Dahl) that seemingly impossible problems can be solved. We can discover that "we make the world" and that "we can do better."

In a recent commencement address at the Maharishi University of Management, comedian Jim Carrey reminded us that the dynamics of fear and love operate in every moment of our life. "Fear is going to be a major player in your life," he said, "but you get to decide how much. ... You can spend your whole life imagining ghosts, worrying about your pathway to the future, but all there will ever be is what's happening here, and the decisions we make in this moment, which are based in either love or fear."

Perhaps we have all caught a little glimpse of what lies down the road of the hero's path. We have had moments of hope where fear fades away. For a brief moment, we have that sense of connection, clarity, and conviction that allowed Martin Luther King to say in his final speech, "We got some difficult days ahead, but it really doesn't matter to me now, because I've been to the mountaintop. I've seen the Promised Land." He was, by that time, living beyond fear and beyond even the most basic desire to preserve his own life. He was living for something much greater than himself. "I may not get there with you," he told the overflowing crowd. "But I want you to know tonight, that we, as a people, will get to the Promised Land." For that moment, we feel that sense of connection that the heroes who have come before us talk about.

Most of us will not lead a movement like Martin Luther King. We will not lead a revolution like Gandhi, or end apartheid like Nelson Mandela. But we will all have to face millions of decisions, some mundane and others momentous, and each time we will do so out of fear or love.

To find out how these decisions play out in everyday life, and how the lessons of this class might help in those decisions, I reached out to alumni of this class and asked them to share with me their own heroic journeys through life. I received letters back from all over the world.

They were now engaged in every kind of career you could imagine all over the world, applying the mindset, methods, and goals of anthropology to a wide range of problems. One had been paid by Virgin Records to travel across the United States in an RV studying how young people listen to music. Another was working with Facebook on what to do with social media profiles after people die. Many were living abroad in places like Dubai, Cambodia, South Africa, Iraq, Afghanistan, and Vietnam. Some were working on global health care while others held military leadership positions in combat zones. Others had settled into jobs in the United States in a wide range of careers including game design, clinical psychology, advertising, and business.

All of them had stories to tell about how the "art of seeing" or how communication, empathy, and thoughtfulness had been essential to their careers, but I was especially struck by how many of them had found these ideas so essential in helping them in their everyday lives. Indeed, it was their letters that inspired me to write this book.

One shared her journey out of fear toward true love and how anthropology helped her understand her journey. She realized that she had fallen into an abusive relationship because she feared being alone. "It was my default to love myself through the eyes of men," she recalled. "I treated relationships as a safety net, holding me high above a pool of insecurity." It was like a spider's web, she said, and she was like a fly, "stuck there on my own accord ... smack in the middle while a spider consumed me."

She ended up in an extremely abusive relationship. "I lost hold of myself and ended up where I had been leading myself all along, existing as an object for him." She realized that the core of her fear that led to these poor decisions was the fear of being alone and unloved. She went to a very rural area for several months where she was forced to live with her loneliness. There she found that she was not afraid. She felt free to love herself, which freed her to love others rather than to simply be consumed by them.

Another former student shared how he had battled against the dynamics of fear and hate, and how he came to discover these dynamics through the anthropological perspective. He fell in love with a girl who had been in an abusive relationship. One night he had a dream, and in the dream he could see ships burning on a lake.

"I watched a burning ship that represented her old boyfriend, who had abused her, sailing past other ships, catching them each on fire. Those ships would sail on and set fire to more ships, and so on. I watched as his ship pull alongside her and lit her on fire. They pulled up to me on my island and began shooting fire at me, and it seemed to me like it was the most important thing in the world that I not catch on fire, that I don't topple.

"Do people who are hurting spread the pain to others in an attempt to elicit empathy?" he wondered. "And does this create a cycle of hurting that spreads like a fire, like burning ships bumping into one another on a lake?"

He resolved to not allow himself to get burned, but she burned him. He tried to withstand the pain and let it dissipate so he would not spread the fire, but it only smoldered inside of him, ready to ignite into a raging inferno at any moment. She could see it inside of him. "She didn't think we could stay together," he said, and so, "I told her that I wouldn't see her that evening. I was going to fight my demon."

He rode his bike out to the lake where they had camped together for the first time, and laid down on top of a hill. A massive thunderstorm moved in. "I was scared," he recalled. "That thing could really kill me ... 'You're nothing,' God seemed to whisper." But then the winds calmed and the sky opened up as he gazed up at the stars. "It really was the balance of infinity staring me in the face," he remembers. "The moon seemed so close. The stars became joined by strands of light, forming a beautiful web. The sky fell then rose, zooming towards me and retreating like the lungs of an animal." And this is when he had his revelation:

> I somehow ended up kneeling back on my blanket, and the world collapsed inside of me. I saw myself. I knew myself. It was terrifying. I held myself before me, suspended in the air above me. Every piece of my identity was evident. Every fabric of construction, every pride, stubborn impulse, and conceited motivation. Each piece of my ego swirled together and formed me, suspended in the air beside the full moon.
>
> I was hugging myself in a child's pose and I remember crying out, almost screaming as I saw myself like never before. In horror. In awe. I saw me. I saw the pieces of me

that were destroying me. I knew and understood. I also saw her. I saw hurt and love.

I took these things, these destructive aspects of myself which I had been too proud to recognize before, which was producing the pain within myself, and let them float into that yawning abyss above me. They were not bound by gravity, but by my ego.

I spent the entire night on that moon-bathed hill.
I learned that that my conflict was not coming from without, but from within myself, due to pride and stubbornness. I was able to let them go. It was painful and terrifying to look so deeply into myself, but I found that the source of my pain was within myself, not within her.

That night on the hill wrestling with myself was one of the most intense experiences of my life, but it worked. I'm currently in the healthiest, most fulfilling relationship that I can imagine. If I had placed the blame on the world around me and bolstered myself on my own ego, I would have collapsed, our relationship would have collapsed ... we would have set fire to more ships.

As it is, we are able to pass our joy and loving relationship to others every day.

He ended his letter by recounting the lessons of anthropology that have become a part of his everyday life, his way of being the best human he can be. His ability to see big and see small allow him to empathize with others, and also to reflexively understand himself, the inner forces that drive him, and where they come from. "I would not be with her today if I had not made the basics of anthropology an integral part of my life, my identity, and my way of thinking about the world."

A HERO'S GUIDE TO EVERYDAY LIFE

by Dean Eckhoff
Class of 2012
FedEx Courier

I began college with lofty, idealistic hopes and dreams about who I wanted to be, and how I wanted to change the world. I think at one point, I convinced myself I wanted to be President of the United States. I do not regret those ambitions, but a little over halfway through college I began to realize (literally, make real) two things:

1. The depth, breadth, and diversity of the tedious mess the world is in.
2. How I, personally, am a blatant, contributing part of the problem.

I want to be certain that this is not seen as hopelessness, so I will clarify that these were very positive, grounding, and educational realizations…even if they felt kind of crappy at the time.

Sure, at the time, it was not fun to see how I not only had no real power to change the world in all the idealistic ways I thought I did, but was actually participating in reinforcing all the corrupt, irresponsible ways people and our planet are being treated. That "downer," however, was very brief.

Through lessons learned in cultural anthropology and in life, and through my own desire, I began to discover a deeper, heart-level awareness: I may not have the power to change the world, but I have all the power to change and be responsible for myself and my own life.

Gandhi said it best, in regard to being the change we wish to see in the world, when he stated, "If we could change ourselves, the tendencies in the world would also change. As a man changes his own nature, so does the attitude of the world change towards him. ... We need not wait to see what others do."

I began to learn through my experience in cultural anthropology that my willingness to change myself might be simultaneously the ONLY and BEST thing I can offer the world; that challenging myself to be a healthy, responsible human might not only be incredibly beneficial to me, but also to those around me; that the world is just a reflection of its people, of me; that healthy, responsible individuals can create a healthy, responsible world.

The power part of this realization was that it applies to me, at all times, where I am at, and as I am! I didn't (and don't) need to have a lot of money, or incredible amounts of soft power, or an amazing ability to move millions with my words, or be the President of the United States. I can work on myself at any time, and choose to learn and grow and live and give responsibly in every aspect of my life, and in any given circumstance. In fact, I am the ONLY one who has the power to do that in my life.

From this realization came decisions, some rather hard and personal ones, which were (and continue to be) met with considerable criticism, even from those I was close to. However, the gifts I have gained from these decisions have been deep and personal and profoundly meaningful.

Through working on growing in relationships, finances, physical health, and other areas of my own life, I have met people and discovered opportunities and done things I never would have dreamed I'd be able to in the past.

I was able to pay off my student loans, which turned out to be one of the most difficult, empowering, and educational endeavors I've ever faced (even more than, dare I say, getting my degree).

I have chosen to embark on a program that has helped me heal myself and outgrow cluster migraines, stomach ulcers, depression, and other debilitating illness, which was even more difficult and profound than student loans.

I have chosen to travel and challenge myself and place myself in uncomfortable territory to learn and grow and experience myself and the world.

I have been able to share my music at venues around Denver, and challenge myself to be vulnerable with music in front of people in new ways.

This only scratches the surface for me, but these and many other decisions gifts can be attributed to that realization I gained through my experience at K-State, and most of all with lessons in cultural anthropology.

These decisions are not monumental. They are not going to upset any corrupt establishments, or end hunger, or create peace among the nations, or abolish modern forms of slavery, or create economic equality, or reverse the degradation of our beautiful planet and its resources. At least, I have a very hard time finding any correlation between these things and the decisions I have made. Singing cover songs in a Denver brewery doesn't exactly exude heroism.

I'm just a normal guy. I live a normal (pretty mundane, from a surface view) life. I am merely a human, learning how I can be the best (however flawed) human I can be, and make the most out of my life.

However, if I can help anyone around me, or anyone who allows me to share this with them, to discover within themselves the courage, freedom, creativity, empowerment, and love I have discovered by choosing to take back my life and take responsibility for who I am, I would like to.

I would like to, because it is the most meaningful (yet somewhat terrifying) experience I have had.

I would like to, because I my life means more to me than I ever thought possible, thanks to the decisions I've made and the people from whom I've learned.

I would like to, because these decisions continue to shape me into a healthier, more open person whose effect on the world will be at least a little more positive.

I would like to, because there is something redemptive about the raw, unfiltered, falling-down-getting-back-up beauty of everyday human life.

Challenge Ten: Your Manifesto

Your challenge is to reflect on what you have learned in this class and write a manifesto for your life. This document should outline a vision for your highest goals for yourself, your future, and for how you will contribute to life on earth. In addition to the manifesto, post a collage of the work you have done in this class on Instragram, or post a photo or work of original art that captures your vision for who you want to be or how you want to contribute to the world. #anth101challenge10

Your manifesto should include:

1. Your life goals (What problems do you want to address in your life and/or the world?)

2. Your ideas, ideals, beliefs, and values (Why do these problems matter to you and to the world?)

3. Your view of the world, past, present, and future.

4. Why your goals and vision for the future matter. (What are the consequences of failure?)

5. Key lessons learned from this class (How will these lessons and insights help you in your quest?)

6. How your goals, ideas, values, and vision have been changed, strengthened, or questioned in this class.

Go to anth101.com/challenge10 for more inspiration, and a helpful worksheet to get you started.

ABOUT THE AUTHOR

Dubbed "the prophet of an education revolution" by the *Kansas City Star*, Michael Wesch is internationally recognized as a leader in teaching innovation. The *New York Times* listed him as one of 10 professors in the nation whose courses "mess with old models" and added that "they give students an experience that might change how they think, what they care about or even how they live their lives." Wesch is well-known for his digital work. His videos have been viewed over 20 million times, translated in over 20 languages, and are frequently featured at international film festivals and major academic conferences worldwide. Wesch has won several major awards for his work, including the U.S. Professor of the Year Award from the Carnegie Foundation, the *Wired Magazine* Rave Award, and he was named an Emerging Explorer by *National Geographic*.

Made in the USA
Las Vegas, NV
07 January 2022

40776195R00203